WOMEN
of
DORSET

WOMEN
of
DORSET

Diana Trenchard

DORSET BOOKS

First Published in Great Britain by Dorset Books

British Library Cataloguing in Publication Data
A catalogue record for this book is available
from the British Library.

ISBN 1 871164 19 2

DORSET BOOKS

Halsgrove House
Lower Moor Way
Tiverton, Devon EX16 6SS
Tel: 0884 243242
Fax: 0884 243325

The cover illustration shows a portrait of Mary Anning, pioneer fossil collector of Lyme Regis, Dorset, painted c.1840 by an unknown artist. Reproduced by kind permission of the Natural History Museum, London.

Printed and bound in Great Britain by the Longdunn Press, Bristol.

To Richard

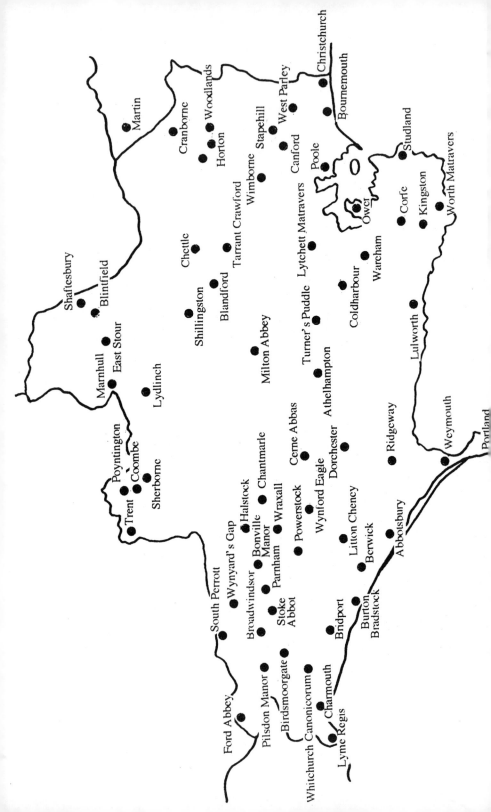

CONTENTS

ACKNOWLEDGEMENTS

The material in this book could not have appeared without somebody, usually anonymous, having taken the trouble to record it, and other equally anonymous persons carefully preserving the documents, through many centuries in some cases. My gratitude extends to all these unkown people, and also to those of the present day in whose charge the documents are now safely preserved, particularly the staff of the Dorset County Museum, Dorchester, and the Dorset County Records Office. I have made use of both previously published and unpublished source material, and their inclusion in the References and Notes carries also my grateful acknowledgements to their respective authors. At a more personal level I would like to thank Mary Brown for her continual encouragement, Brian and Pam Hoyle for their friendship and more, and Ken Venton-Prentice LRPS for his photographic help. Finally, this book would never have appeared without the interest, discussions, belief, encouragement and reassurance of my son Richard, to whom I will always be indebted.

The author and publishers also gratefully acknowledge the help of the following organisations and individuals in providing illustrations for use in this work: The National Trust, Lacock Abbey; Mrs Hayward, Blynfield Farm, Stour Provost; Hon. John Best; Rev. Mother Abbess, Holy Cross Abbey, Whitland, Dyfed; Mary Brown; Mary Evans Picture Library; Public Records Office; The Governor, The Verne YOI, Portland; David Arnold; Dorset County Museum, Dorchester; His Grace the Duke of Bedford; Lyme Regis (Philpot) Museum; K.A. Venton-Prentice.

INTRODUCTION

"But there aren't any famous women in Dorset!" was the usual response from friends when they heard that I was writing a book on the women of Dorset. Some had heard of Mary Anning the fossilist of Lyme Regis, and Lady Bankes the defender of Corfe Castle in the Civil War, and there was a vague memory of a queen who had murdered a king at the same castle many centuries earlier. But that was all. "There aren't any others are there? How on earth will you write a book on those few?" By that time I already knew that there were a lot more stories about Dorset women waiting to be told.

My interest in the subject developed from my researches into the history of my family, much of which is centred in Dorset. When people talk of their family history, they usually mean ancestors bearing the same surname as themselves. In other words, the history of the male line only. Female members of the family are usually only noted in passing - and then ignored. When I tried to find out more about some of these females, it was brought home to me how seldom women are featured in the history of this county - and in history in general. Frequently their names are not given, being referred to merely as "the daughter of" or "the wife of". This "invisibility" of nearly half the population was all the stimulus I needed.

How does one define a woman as "of Dorset"? It would be easy if she had lived all her life in the county. But should someone be excluded, for example, if she had been born over the county boundary, but spent the rest of her life in Dorset? The same problem was confronted by J.J. Foster in the Introduction to his book "Worthies of Wessex" (which in spite of its title was restricted to Dorset "Worthies").ᵉ He answered it by saying that "...it is not so much having been born in a county or district, as having taken part in its life in some definite way, perhaps to the extent of modifying its history: or of having so identified oneself with its people as to have a just claim to be remembered by them.....". In general I have followed the same criteria.

In many cases I have included a pedigree of the woman in question in order to give her a family background, and to counterbalance the fact that she is usually only known by her husband's surname. I have also given several royal pedigrees, including information on females that is usually omitted in general history books.

The civil administration of this country has often made changes to county boundaries: events described in this book occurred within the Dorset county boundary pertaining to that time. The village of Trent is one example. When Charles II stayed there during the Civil War, it was in Somerset, but it had become Dorset by Jessie Brook's time: the former is excluded, the latter included. Similarly, Lillie Langtry's connection with Bournemouth occurred when it was part of Hampshire, and her story has also been excluded.

I make no apology for the absence of *Tess of the D'Urbervilles* and other characters from the works of Thomas Hardy - they are purely fictional characters in spite of the almost human reverence in which they are held by many. There are more than enough true-life stories available in Dorset without resorting to fiction. Riotous living, kidnapped heiresses, murderesses, child-brides, running the largest iron-works in the country, leading armies into battle, bargaining with a king for a better marriage settlement, becoming a female U.S. ambassador to France, are just some of the stories of real "Women of Dorset".

There is no systematic presentation of the different stories, merely a grouping of material on a particular subject into chapters - marriage, land-owning or crimes for example. Some subjects such as royalty or the religious chapter can easily be given in chronological order, while others do not lend themselves to this form of presentation. Most stories relate to members of the upper classes: this is purely a reflection of the fact that information connected with them was more likely to be written down, and preserved. One cannot begin to estimate how many stories of "ordinary" women have been lost because no-one recorded them. The sad little story of Molly Paddock née Giles is a good example of this, for had she not related it to someone who was compiling a scrapbook of her village, the story would have been lost for ever.

Finally, once I started unearthing stories about Dorset women, more and more kept appearing. I had to stop somewhere. If, therefore, you do not find someone you think ought to be here, or you have further information on any of those included, I should welcome hearing from you.

Walter de la Mare wrote the following short poem entitled *An Epitaph,* dedicated to an anonymous West Country lady. I trust that the contents of this book have contributed something towards answering the question in the last two lines, at least in relation to the more than two hundred Dorset women mentioned in these pages.

Here lies a most beautiful lady,
Light of step and heart was she:
I think she was the most beautiful lady
That ever was in the West Country.
But beauty vanishes; beauty passes,
However rare, rare it be;
And when I crumble who shall remember
This lady of the West Country?

Diana Trenchard
Beaminster
April 1994

1
LAND-OWNING
WOMEN OF DORSET

INTRODUCTION

Until recent years, married women were not allowed to administer their own lands and property. Like the rest of their possessions - and including themselves - everything became part of their husbands' chattels. One would not therefore expect to find many women being land-owners in their own right, but as shown elsewhere in this book (see Chapter 9) when it came to taxation of land in the 14th Century, a surprising one in 13 of those listed was a female.

How could a woman come to be owning land in her own right? Land could, in theory at least, be given to a female as a gift from the King (or Queen), although it was unlikely that many women would acquire land in this way. But in Dorset we do have a 13th Century example, Nichola de Morteshore, being given land directly by the King, and there is a strong suspicion that another, Joan Gorges, may also have been so rewarded, but initially in her husband's name.

The majority of female land-owners acquired their possessions in one of two ways, either from her husband after his death, or by inheritance from a member of her family - father, mother, brother and even a sister. As the following will show, Dorset contains many examples of women acquiring land in each of these ways, and perhaps of more interest are the problems that almost inevitably arose as a consequence of the land being in female hands - including examples of child-brides, kidnapping, prolonged court actions and armed attacks, among others.

At the time of a marriage, or usually just before, a marriage settlement was laid out legally to establish exactly what provision was to be made for the bride in the event of her future widowhood - her *dower*. It specified exactly what land, etc. the bride was bringing to the marriage as her *dowry*. Although administered by her husband during his lifetime, her dowry remained her property - in name only - and she could dispose of part or the whole of her dowry during the marriage, but only with her husband's permission (see Hadwidia Fitzgrip). A woman's dowry also came to her intact when widowed, or divorced - but not when the ex-husband was King John (see Adelicia of Gloucester, Chapter 8). Under normal circumstances, a widow could dispose of her dowry as she wished, frequently giving or willing it to her daughters as part of their dowries in turn.

A widow was also entitled to one-third of her deceased husband's lands for the remainder of her life, but after her death they reverted to the heir, who had enjoyed the remaining two-thirds of the estate: this frequently led to great disputes within a family - see Lady Tregonwell. The widow was not able to dispose of these dower lands, except with the consent and agreement of the eventual heir.

It was also possible to acquire lands by purchase or exchange, but this does not appear to have been much indulged in by females. One example was Lady Elizabeth Hatton (see Chapter 8) who sold Corfe Castle; she owned this as a gift from her first husband, but found it too costly to maintain after the death of her second husband.

There is one very unusual case of acquiring land in Dorset at the end of the 17th Century, when a female, Ann Michel, won an estate in a lottery - or at least she would have acquired it if things had gone smoothly (see later).

OWNING LANDS BY THE KING'S FAVOUR

One very frequently reads in history of how a King rewarded someone who had given him good service with a knighthood, and also lands to furnish him with an income to keep him in his new station in life. These rewards were usually granted for valour in battle, diplomatic or political missions, and occasionally for favouritism. In return the grantee was expected to pay a rent to the King, not usually in money, but something in lieu - providing a certain number of days' service as a knight; providing a certain amount of meat for the King's table; paying a rent of a "peppercorn" or a "red rose at Midsummer". When a King wished to reward someone for personal service, he frequently made them a member of his retinue with a specific job to perform - for example, holding the King's stirrup every time he mounted his horse.

NICHOLA DE MORTESHORE

If the King wished to reward a female, then she was usually appointed to the Queen's retinue. It is therefore surprising to find a female rewarded with lands in return for giving personal service to the King, but this is exactly what happened when Edward I (1272-1307) gave the manor of Kingston (Russell) to Nichola de Morteshore. What is more intriguing is that the service she was to render to the King was "by service of counting the King's chessmen, and putting them in the box when the King has done playing with them". What had she done to deserve such a reward? In his usual romantic way, Treves[n] has lyricised on the reason

> "The service was strangely small for so great a recompense. Possibly the fair Nichola played chess with the Prince before he became King, and it may be that the game was a cover for some love-making, and the Plantagenet saw

more of the lady's blue eyes and smiling lips than of the knights and pawns. Possibly also there was some tender wrangling as to who should put the chessmen away in the box, and that Nichola did it so prettily that the Prince vowed that no-one should ever do it but she. He was a man of his word, whose favourite motto was *Pactum serva*, "Keep your promise", so the lady, or the memory of her, was present "whenever the King had done playing", and in token of many rosy hours he granted her this King's Town among the Dorset hills."

It would appear that Nichola was not only the owner of Kingston (Russell), but also owned at least the Manor of Allington, near Bridport.[1] As soon as King Edward died in 1307, Nichola disposed of both of these manors to William Russell and his heirs, with no strings attached. It would appear that Nichola was not as grateful a recipient of King Edward's gift as he had thought!

JOAN GORGES

Although strictly speaking Joan Gorges acquired her land on the death of her husband, there seems to be something of a mystery tied up with her occupancy of Powerstock Castle in the 13th Century. It is therefore included as part of the acquisition of land by the King's favour. But before we come to her story, it is necessary to give a little of the background.

Nestling under the bare slopes of Eggardon was a hunting lodge, called Powerstock Castle, surrounded by Powerstock Forest spreading for many miles in all directions. [Only a trace of this primeval woodland remains today, close to Powerstock.] No doubt it was the hunting that had attracted King John to the area, and he obtained it - probably by force - from Robert Newburgh in about 1205.[f] The Castle must have been of a substantial size, for when it was restored by King John, it required the provision of thousands of roof tiles. It was often visited by King John, but his son, Henry III, used it less frequently, and in about 1231 he gave the tenancy of it to his Sergeant-at-Arms, Thomas Gorges. [The Gorges family were previously "of Litton Cheney and Shipton Gorge", having originally come from Normandy.[2]] There was nothing unusual in this gift. What made it strange is what happened when it passed to Joan Gorges, the wife of Thomas, after his death in 1234.

Thomas Gorges had not been a particularly good tenant. As part of his lease he was permitted to take a large allowance of brushwood from the Royal Forest of Powerstock for his fires. But he frequently exceeded his powers, being often reported for taking more wood than his entitlement, and he was frequently behind with his rent. Nevertheless, when he died his widow Joan was in turn granted a tenancy of Powerstock Castle "for life", plus a pension of £12 *per annum*. But King Henry III did more than this, for he gave one of her sons (Ralph) a handsome allowance and maintained the other son (Thomas) at University. The King also increased Joan's allowance of brushwood from the Forest, and gave her "husbote and heybote" - the right to take wood to make or repair fences and houses respectively. In addition to all these increases, the King also remitted her rent and, quite surprisingly, often ordered dresses to be made for her by his own tailor, Roger.

All this might sound a little suspicious, but it becomes increasingly so when it is realised that this was King Henry III, who was always short of money, mainly due to the extravagances of his wife, her family, and his own extended family. For a King who was always trying to borrow money, it seems rather strange that he showed these financial kindnesses to Joan Gorges, remitting her rent, supporting her two sons, etc., and even going so far as to have dresses made for her at his expense. Methinks there is a story hidden away in all this. One clue, although extremely speculative, to the identity of Joan Gorges is to be found in her Christian name, which is the feminine version of John. We know that King John had a daughter called Joan by his second wife; this was the Joan who married the King of Scotland and was subsequently buried at Tarrant Crawford in Dorset (see Chapter 6). We also know that at the same nunnery at Tarrant was buried a natural daughter of King John, also called Joan after her father (see Chapter 6). Was Joan Gorges perhaps a third (natural) daughter of King John, who had been married off to one of the sovereign's retinue? Was Joan Gorges possibly born in the Powerstock area? Her "suggested" father, King John, had been visiting there since at least 1205, and it was not until 1231 that Thomas Gorges was given his tenancy - about the right time interval for a daughter to have grown up and married.

If Joan Gorges was indeed a natural daughter of King John, it would explain why his son, Henry III, treated her so favourably, even in his financially-straightened circumstances, for she would be none other than his half-sister, and it is known that he was very generous to all members of his extended family. This is pure speculation, but it would certainly provide an explanation for Joan Gorges being a land-owner!

In 1969 a 13th Century coffin lid was uncovered in the churchyard at Powerstock, and is now displayed inside the church. It was obviously from the coffin of a person of some importance, and it has been suggested that it might have belonged to a member of the Gorges family, perhaps Joan herself.[2] She is believed to have died in about 1266, for on 14 November in that year the King granted the tenancy of Powerstock to her son Ralph: by this time Joan would have reached a good age for she already had a son of University age in 1234.

TOLA

Very little is known about Tola (or Thola), and even less about how she acquired her lands, but as will be shown below, there is a strong likelihood that they came to her by the influence of the Queen of the time.

14

Most books on Dorset refer to the Benedictine Abbey at Abbotsbury being founded by Orc and his wife Tola in approximately 1030, during the reign of King Canute.[d] They also usually refer to Tola's name living on in Tolpuddle where she owned lands. Nobody pays any attention to this wife, who was a Norman lady, and yet she appears to have owned considerable lands in Tolpuddle and *together* with her husband founded the Abbey - most Abbeys were founded by men only.

Who was Tola? How did she, a Norman, come to be owning lands in Dorset half a century before the Norman invasion of 1066? As might be expected, virtually nothing is recorded of her, except that she came from Normandy. But then that adds to her mystery. What was a lady from Normandy doing in England owning lands and married to a Scandinavian in the time of King Canute?[3]

Answers to such questions must of course remain purely speculative, but one clue may be found in the wife of Canute. It may be noted from elsewhere (see Chapter 5), that the wife of Canute was Emma, daughter of Richard the Fearless, Duke of Normandy, and widow of the Anglo-Saxon King Ethelred the Unready, who had been killed by Canute. The dates of her respective weddings were approximately 998 for Ethelred and 1017 for Canute.

Putting two and two together, it is very suggestive that Tola was in the retinue of Emma when she came from Normandy for the second time, to marry Canute. Orc, Tola's husband, was one of Canute's favourite henchmen, and it can therefore easily be seen how under these circumstances a Norman lady could meet and marry a Scandinavian man. It would also explain the large areas of land owned by Orc, the favourite of Canute. But it wouldn't explain Tola's grants of lands, unless she was highly favoured by the other partner of the royal marriage, Queen Emma. Although there is no direct evidence, this would provide a possible explanation.

Tola and Orc lived on into the reign of Edward the Confessor when, dying without children, they bequeathed all their lands and wealth to the Abbey they had founded at Abbotsbury.[dn]

LANDS OWNED BY THE CHURCH

In common with other counties prior to the Dissolution, Dorset possessed female land-owners in the form of Abbesses. Although these females can be considered land-owners in their own right, they only held them by virtue of their position as Abbess; thus they were able to administer their lands freely, but were not able to dispose of them as they wished. The Abbess of Shaftesbury ultimately became one of the richest landowners in the country; so much so that it was jokingly said that if the Abbess of Shaftesbury was to marry the Abbot of Glastonbury, then their children would own more land than the King himself.

When a female entered a nunnery to give herself to the religious life, she was expected to bring a "dowry" with her as a gift to the foundation. When added to the other gifts and bequests, it can be seen how quickly the amount of land "owned" by an Abbess would rapidly multiply. Further details of the role of Abbesses in owning and administering their lands are mentioned elsewhere (see Chapter 2).

LANDS OWNED THROUGH INHERITANCE

ELA OF CANFORD

Although Ela's story begins just over eight hundred years ago, we have a surprising amount of detail of several incidents in her life; a life that was dramatically influenced by the inheritance she received from her father. The story begins when she was quite young, and is told thus by Treves.[n]

> "The Manor of Canford[Magna] belonged at one time to a little girl of eight, named Ela, who was the sole heiress of Walter de Eureux. The child being regarded as especially precious was hidden away privily in Normandy. At an auspicious moment she was brought over to England and presented to Richard I, who promptly gave her in marriage to William de Longespée, whereby he became Lord of the Manor of Canford. This William of the Longsword was a son of Henry II by the fair Rosamund. He was a fighter of no mean parts....."

Poor little Ela, and so many other young girls who were treated in the same way in those times. She had lost her father when very young and by becoming the heiress to a Manor that was held of the King, he had the right to give her in marriage to whomsoever he wished. William Longespée is known to have been born in the reign of his grandfather, King Stephen (died 1154),[x] so that he must have been at least in his mid-forties when he was presented by King Richard I (1189-1199) to the eleven-year-old Ela as her husband-to-be. But then William *was* the half-brother of the King, and a great favourite of his. By marrying Ela, as well as becoming Lord of the Manor of Canford, he also inherited the title of Earl of Salisbury from her deceased father, plus all the wealth that went with the estates - it also included the shrievalty (sheriff) of Wiltshire. Not a bad present to give to your favourite half-brother!

As well as making one minor error in telling the story of Ela, Treves has completely missed out the most romantic part of this story of Ela's early life, a story that is certainly worth telling. But to deal with the minor error first. Richard I - the Lionheart - only spent a very short time in England; a few months in 1189 at the time of his coronation, and then a few weeks in 1194 after the ransom had been paid for his release from imprisonment on his way back from the Crusade (where William Longespée had saved his life). On Richard's second visit, Ela was only seven years of age and it was to be another two years before her father died and she became the rich heiress of Canford. The betrothal between Ela and William Longespée must therefore have taken place in Normandy and not England.

All our history books tell of the mainly legendary story of the troubadour, Blondel, wandering about Europe singing beneath the walls of every castle, until in 1194 he recognised the voice of his master, the imprisoned Richard the Lionheart. The history books - and Treves - don't tell us that an almost identical story was enacted only a couple of years later when a young knight went in search of the imprisoned Ela of Canford! When young Ela succeeded to her father's titles and estates in 1196, we are told that she was "hidden away privily" in Normandy[n] but we are not told who did this hiding, or where. There was no wicked uncle, for her father's only brother, Patrick, had died without heirs. There was no wicked stepmother, for there is no record of her father having been married more than once. It must therefore be concluded that it was Ela's own mother, Eleanor de Vitri - or her mother's family if she had already died - who did the hiding away.

Into the picture now steps Sir William Talbot, "an eminent soldier",[4] who spent the next two years searching for Ela. He remains a mystery figure. Was he a friend of Ela's dead father? It is extremely unlikely that he was in love with Ela, who was only nine years old, but it might be that her father had planned to betroth Ela to William Talbot, against the wishes of her mother - hence her being hidden away. It is also possible that William Talbot was related to Ela through the family of her father's mother. This lady's maiden name was Talvas (see accompanying pedigree, 1.1). Bearing in mind that the last consonant of the names would not have been pronounced in Norman-French, there is a strong similarity between Talbot and Talvas.

Whatever the reason, William Talbot certainly set out to search for Ela in Normandy and spent two years doing so. He disguised himself in a pilgrim's habit and wandered up and down the length and breadth of the country for the next two years looking for Ela. At length he located her: he then did a quick-change from being a pilgrim to appear as a harpist. In this role he gained admission to the castle - or house - where he was well received. At last he was able to make contact with Ela. She evidently knew and trusted him, for the next thing we hear is that Ela and William Talbot are together at the Court of King Richard, where she is presented to the King.

17

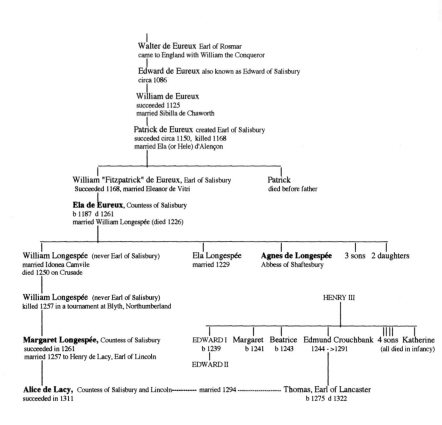

Walter de Eureux Earl of Rosmar
came to England with William the Conqueror

Edward de Eureux also known as Edward of Salisbury
circa 1086

William de Eureux
succeeded 1125
married Sibilla de Chaworth

Patrick de Eureux created Earl of Salisbury
succeded circa 1150, killed 1168
married Ela (or Hele) d'Alençon

William "Fitzpatrick" de Eureux, Earl of Salisbury
Succeeded 1168, married Eleanor de Vitri

Ela de Eureux, Countess of Salisbury
b 1187 d 1261
married William Longespée (died 1226)

Patrick
died before father

William Longespée (never Earl of Salisbury)
married Idonea Camvile
died 1250 on Crusade

William Longespée (never Earl of Salisbury)
killed 1257 in a tournament at Blyth, Northumberland

Margaret Longespée, Countess of Salisbury
succeeded in 1261
married 1257 to Henry de Lacy, Earl of Lincoln

Ela Longespée
married 1229

Agnes de Longespée
Abbess of Shaftesbury

3 sons   2 daughters

HENRY III

EDWARD I   Margaret   Beatrice   Edmund Crouchbank   4 sons   Katherine
b 1239   b 1241   b 1243   1244 - >1291   (all died in infancy)

EDWARD II

Alice de Lacy, Countess of Salisbury and Lincoln---------- married 1294 ------------------- Thomas, Earl of Lancaster
succeeded in 1311   b 1275 d 1322

Pedigree 1.1   Families of Ela of Canford and of her descendants, the Longespées and Alice de Lacy

Did William Talbot hope to marry Ela himself? Or was he merely a knight riding - or rather walking - to the rescue of a damsel in distress in those chivalrous times. I hope it was the latter, for otherwise his hopes were certainly dashed when the King gave Ela's hand in marriage to William Longespée. Sir William Talbot now fades out of the picture, his chivalrous duty done, or his suit rejected. There is no record of his having been rewarded for rescuing Ela, again suggesting that he might well have been a relative.

Before moving on to the next stage of Ela's life - her marriage to William Longespée - it is interesting to fill in her background and show how, as well as being a rich heiress, she also came to have the title of Countess of Salisbury.[7] She was the sixth generation of the Eureux family in England since her ancestor, Walter, came with the Conqueror (see accompanying pedigree 1.1). Her grandfather Patrick was created Earl of Salisbury in 1153 by Matilda, claimant to the English throne (see Chapter 6). He was married to Ela (or Hele) d'Alençon, daughter of William Talvas, Count of Alençon and Ponthieu, and

18

widow of William de Warenne, Earl of Surrey. It was obviously after this lady, her grandmother, that the heiress Ela was given her name by her father William, the second Earl of Salisbury. This is an interesting indication of how the name of Ela was introduced into Dorset; an uncommon name judging by there being no others in the list of 14th Century names of Dorset females (see Chapter 9).

Ela's father succeeded to his estates and titles in 1168 and died in 1196, leaving Ela as his sole heiress: she also assumed his titles in her own right. As was the rule of the day, immediately upon the marriage of Ela and William, her husband assumed the titles she had inherited from her father. William Longespée was therefore subsequently known as the Earl of Salisbury and Lord of Canford *jure uxoris* or by right of his wife. As mentioned earlier, Ela had also inherited the office of Sheriff of Wiltshire, and again this was transferred to her husband. By virtue of this office, Ela or her husband were entitled to receive annually both a considerable sum of money, and also payment in kind, consisting of 150 hogs, 2 bushels and 16 gallons of wheat, the same quantity of barley, 480 hens, 1,600 eggs, 100 cheeses, 52 lambs and 140 fleeces of wool.[4]

A year after Ela's marriage saw the death of Richard Lionheart (1199) and the accession of William Longespée's other half-brother, John. William had shown great allegiance to his father, Henry II, to his half-brother, Richard I, and now he was to do the same for his other half-brother, John, although relations became very strained in the later years of John's reign. Ela and William must have frequently entertained King John at their home at Canford during the latter's many visits to Dorset for hunting.

Presumably Ela spent most of these years at Canford. She is said to have had eight children, four boys and four girls.[4] Two of them are known by name, confusingly called Ela and William after their parents. Her husband appears to have spent most of John's reign on royal business until, in 1213, he was given command of the fleet defending Flanders against Philip of France. He was taken prisoner at the Battle of Bouvines in 1214 and held to ransom. Ela must have paid this - perhaps helped by the King - for the following year William was at John's side at Runneymede for the signing of the Magna Carta. Although the King's brother, William Longespée was respected by both sides, the rebellious barons as well.

The following year, 1216, saw the death of John and the accession of his young son, Henry III. As soon as Ela's husband had given his allegiance to the new King, he was off to the Holy Land on a Crusade that was to last for four years from 1216 to 1220 - he must have been into his mid-sixties by now. According to the story told by Treves,[n] Ela was left behind at Canford, now approaching thirty years of age. Treves tells us of the next incident in her life:

> ".....He [William Longespée] was a fighter of no
> mean parts, whose love of adventure carried him away to the
> Holy Land. During his long absence a certain Hubert de
> Burgh set afloat the rumours that William de Longespée was
> drowned. He whispered this to the gentle Ela, and, after

fumbling expressions of sympathy, solicited her in marriage for a relation of his. The lady of the manor would hear him not; her lord was not drowned, she said, and one day a ship would sail into Poole harbour on whose deck her husband would be standing, looking for her welcome; moreover, even if he were dead, she would never be faithless to his memory.

In the fullness of time he of the long sword came home to find the loyal Ela awaiting him at Canford and to hear of the false accusation of Hubert de Burgh. The chronicles say that "he resented" the doings of this Herbert, and in those days resentment meant much and took strong form. However, at an entertainment at the Castle of Sarum Hubert contrived to poison the lord of Canford so that he died. This was in 1226. Ela, the widow, became a nun, and in the course of years an abbess. She died at Lacock in 1261, at the ripe age of seventy-four, and in the choir at Lacock she was buried."

One might take exception to the way Treves has presented this tale to make it a romantic story. Although what he says is essentially true, reading his version of the story makes it appear that William went off on Crusade soon after they were married, leaving his young wife to sit and pine for him. As already stated, they had already been married for nearly twenty years when he went off on Crusade, and he was well into his sixties and Ela about thirty!

Then again, Treves tries to give the impression that as soon as William returned from the Holy Land and found out what Hubert de Burgh had been saying to Ela, he challenged him to a duel, but William was poisoned before it took place. The facts show that William returned to Ela after the Crusade in 1220: he was poisoned in 1226. Hardly the interval of time one would expect for a vengeful husband to take his revenge!

The explanation for this delayed action on the part of Ela's husband is that Treves - and others - have confused two events. William returned from the Crusade in 1220, and then went overseas again several years later. It was during this latter journey that Hubert de Burgh spread the rumours about his death. In April 1225 William Longespée took his nephew Richard (born 1209, the brother of King Henry III) to Gascony in order to initiate him into warfare.[X] On their return, they were delayed for over three months at sea in a succession of violent storms, and it was due to this that Hubert told Ela that her husband was drowned.[4] It is quite probable that Hubert believed this to be the truth, for a three month delay in the journey across the Bay of Biscay in the middle of winter was unlikely to have any other explanation.

William and his nephew finally arrived safely at Canford in January 1226. At that time the King plus his favourite, Hubert de Burgh, were at Salisbury, having gone there for the first service in the newly opened Cathedral.[4] (Six years earlier, in 1220, both Ela and her husband had been among the first to lay foundation stones of the new Cathedral.) Ela together with her husband and his nephew went quickly to Salisbury to join the King and Court there for the first service which included a great procession. Whether it was actually in the procession or soon after is not certain, but it appears that William and Hubert had a great quarrel. By the 7th March Hubert de Burgh had pretended to be reconciled to William and invited him to a banquet at Old Sarum. William was taken violently ill and died the next day - before Ela could reach him, says one source.[4]

The seventy-year-old William was buried the following day without any inquest into the cause of his death. He was buried in the Trinity Chapel, the only part of Salisbury Cathedral that had been completed; and there his tomb can still be seen today. In one record of his funeral service it states that in spite of a great storm of wind raging at the time, the candles borne in the funeral procession were not extinguished.[5]

But this is not the end of Ela's story, for she was just about to start on the third stage of her life, the religious part. She had already founded the Monastery of St Clement's at Poole.[n] (The Church belonging to that monastery still stands on the Quay at Poole, a permanent reminder of Ela, having been put to a variety of uses in the centuries since the Dissolution.) In 1232 Ela also founded the Priory at Hinton and the Abbey at Lacock in Wiltshire, which she was subsequently to enter.

After the death of her husband in 1226, Ela was still Countess of Salisbury and Lady of the Manor of Canford, plus the Sheriff of Wiltshire, all in her own right. She carried on her duties of administering these lands, etc., until she was assured that her eldest son, William, was suitable to succeed her. It was only then that she became a nun at Lacock Abbey - which she had founded - taking her vows on Christmas Day, 1238, at the age of fifty-one.[4] Two years later she became its Abbess, and lived there for over twenty years in relative peace, until she died in 1261. (Her husband William would have been at least 115 years old by then!) Shortly before her death she resigned her position of Abbess and lived in strictest seclusion until the end.

During all those years at Lacock what a lifetime she had to look back on: hidden away in Normandy until rescued by a chivalrous knight; presented to the legendary Richard Lionheart; marrying into the Royal Family; a frequent entertainer of Kings at her Canford home; an absent husband for most of her married life, either on Crusade or at war; a husband that she never gave up for lost in spite of being told that he was dead; helping to found Salisbury Cathedral and other monasteries; and then having her husband murdered. Quite a life to look back on!

And what of Ela's family? We learn[7] that Ela must have been short of money in 1229, three years after William's death, for she received a licence from the King to raise a mortgage on Canford for five years "to receive money to marry Ela, her daughter, to the Earl of Warwick". [A mortgage then was not the same as today: before 1571 it was not possible to receive interest on a loan - called "usury". Instead, the lender would take possession of the lands for the specified period, and received all the income from them during that time. At the end of the period the lender would take permanent possession if the loan was not repaid on time[13]. Ela obviously managed to repay it!]

Ela's son, the second William Longespée, took over the running of Canford when his mother retired to Lacock in 1238.[7] Ela also wished for her son to assume the title of Earl of Salisbury, as his father had done before him. But there was a problem to this. The title was Ela's, and not her husband's who had only held it by right of his wife. When she petitioned the King on her son's behalf, he refused stating that it was against feudal law for her son to assume the title while she, the Countess of Salisbury, was still alive. William therefore had to remain a mere esquire. This still applied even after his mother had entered the nunnery, and here was a big problem for the family. With the title went all the revenues of the estates. But now that Ela was a nun she was not able to receive them: neither could her son, for he was not in possession of the titles. While this situation lasted, the revenues went to the one person who had it in his power to alter the situation - King Henry III. It is not surprising that he would not make an exception while he enjoyed an extra income!

In 1247 Ela's son went to Rome to try to get the Pope to intercede on his behalf to gain the title, but to no avail. The following year, 1248, he determined to go on Crusade but lacked the necessary funds. He leased Canford for four years, and also granted Poole its first charter (for 70 marks) in order to raise money to go to the Holy Land. He in fact led the Sixth Crusade, but owing to lack of French support, he was overwhelmed by the Saracens, and died there in 1250. At the exact time that her son was killed, it is recorded that Ela had a vision of her son being received into Heaven. She was therefore prepared when the actual news of his death finally reached her.

Ela's grandson, a third William Longespée, was killed in a tournament at Blyth in Northumberland in 1257. Ela had therefore outlived her husband, her son, and her grandson. When she died in 1261, Ela was succeeded at Canford by her great-grand-daughter, Margaret Longespée, who had already been married for four years to Henry de Lacy, Earl of Lincoln. At last, in 1261, the revenues from the Earldom of Salisbury and Lordship of Canford were "unfrozen", for Margaret (Longespée) Lacy inherited the titles directly from her great-grandmother, and her husband was able to assume them by right of his wife. We may be sure that he obtained every penny of what was due to the estates after the lapse of twenty-three years! It is with Alice Lacy, daughter and heiress of the new Earl and Countess, that a new chapter of the history of Canford unfolds, but that is told elsewhere in this book (see Chapter 8).

There is one further little postscript about Ela. When she died, her possessions at Lacock included a copy of the Exemplification of Henry III's Re-issue of Magna Carta of 1225.[15] Ela would have received a copy of this 1225 Revision in her role as Sheriff of Wiltshire,[6] while her husband was abroad. William Longespée died the following year. It is therefore of interest that Ela guarded this document with great care, eventually taking it with her to Lacock Abbey. [It remained there even after the Dissolution; in 1945 it was presented to the British Museum - another permanent reminder of Ela in the present day.]

The interest lies in the way that Ela kept it safe in her custody, rather than handing it over to the Civil authorities - presumably she was fully aware of what might happen to it if she did so, from her knowledge and experience of affairs of State.

The tale of Ela started over 800 years ago, and although we only have detailed pieces of her life-story, there are still quite a few permanent reminders of her today: her tomb at Lacock Abbey (now moved from its original position); her husband's tomb at Salisbury Cathedral; a building at Poole; and a carefully guarded copy of the Re-issued Magna Carta. Nothing remains of the original Manor House at Canford in which she was born, married, and lived a large part of her life, raising a family and worrying about her husband in those troublous times.

ADELICIA DE BRIONIS

As people wander around the beautifully preserved buildings and gardens of Forde Abbey in West Dorset, it is doubtful if anyone gives a thought to the fact that if it hadn't been for a woman, none of these surroundings would exist. The woman in question was Adelicia (or Adela) de Brionis, who died in 1142.[d 8]

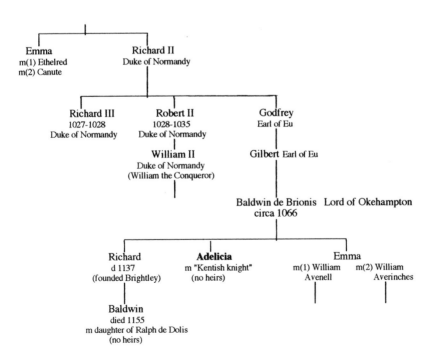

Pedigree 1.2   Family of Adelicia de Brionis, foundress of Ford Abbey

Adelicia came from a line of distinguished ancestors (see accompanying pedigree). Her great-grandfather, Godfrey, Earl of Eu, was a natural son of Richard II, Duke of Normandy: her grandfather Gilbert, Earl of Eu, was therefore a first cousin of William the Conqueror. It was his son - Adelicia's father, Baldwin de Brionis - who first came to England at the time of the Conquest. For this he was rewarded with the Honour (Lordship) of Okehampton and the Sheriffdom of Devon. Adelicia had a younger sister, Emma, and an elder brother, Richard, who inherited on his father's death. Although Richard had a son, Baldwin, the latter died without issue before his father, and Adelicia therefore became the heiress of her brother. All that is known of Adelicia is that she was married to a Kentish knight - name unknown - and was widowed, childless, at some time prior to the death of her brother in 1137. At the time of this story she was living on the Manor of Thorncombe on the Dorset-Devon border, one of the possessions inherited from her brother.

While Adelicia was involved with the founding of Forde Abbey at Thorncombe, its story began eight years earlier when her brother made the original foundation on his lands at Brightley in Devon. He had persuaded thirteen monks to leave Waverley Abbey in Surrey and make the long journey to Devon to found this daughter Cistercian Monastery in 1132.

It was only three years later that the Civil War between Matilda and Stephen broke out in England, as described elsewhere (see Chapter 6). During all this fighting, the monks at Brightley had been quietly carrying on with their efforts to establish themselves. But the poor soil defeated them, and they were not able to support themselves. After persisting for eight years they decided it was impossible to continue, and in 1141 the decision was made to return to their parent Abbey at Waverley. Their route took them close to Thorncombe, and they decided to pay their respects to the sister of their benefactor and offer an explanation for their return to Waverley.

The story of how Adelicia greeted them and, after hearing their story, offered to exchange her Manor of Thorncombe for Brightley, has come down to us through the centuries.[b] But even more surprising is that the actual words she used have been preserved.[d]

> "Far be it from me, my lords and most holy fathers, to deserve so dire a reproach and to incur so ignoble a risk as this. What my lord and brother Richard, out of a heart full of pure devotion for the honour of God and the salvation of us all, began so solemnly, shall not I, his sister and heir, into whose hands, before his death, he delivered all his possessions, be willing or able to accomplish? Behold my manor on which I now reside! It is sufficiently fertile - it is sheltered and shaded with woods - it is productive of grain and other fruits of the earth; behold we give it to you in exchange for the barren land of Brightley, together with our manor house for ever! Remain here till somewhere else on

this estate you can have a more fitting monastery. We shall not fail you in this; nay we shall help you to build it."

And so the former Abbey of Brightley was re-founded as Forde Abbey, at a place called Hartesbath, near West Ford in the Manor of Thorncombe. Whether Adelicia remained at her home, sharing it with the monks while the new Abbey was built, is not known. She must have been quite elderly by this time, for her father came with the Conqueror nearly eighty years earlier. It was only a short time after the arrival of the monks that Adelicia died (in 1142), and there she was buried. When Forde Abbey was completed six years later, the first service performed by the monks was to erect a tomb to Adelicia de Brionis, their foundress. Her tomb sadly disappeared at the Dissolution when the Church was demolished, but we are left with the magnificent buildings we see today, part of which may date to the original foundation - thanks to Adelicia.

ALICE RUSSELL

Nowadays, if you were called upon to prove that you owned the house you lived in, or one you owned elsewhere, it would simply be a matter of showing the Deeds, involving minimum cost and energy. How different it was in earlier times, and how costly. In the 15th Century Alice Russell of Dorset must have rued the cost of going to Court to prove her entitlement to various properties, but at least it ended up to the great advantage of her family.[9] They were of especial value to her great-grandson, John Russell who, in 1506, left Dorset for Windsor and the eventual founding of the House of Bedford (see Chapter 6). At that crucial time when he was starting out on his career at Court, he was able to sell some of these properties to raise the money very necessary to him at that time. If it hadn't been for Alice Russell and her Court cases, he would never have inherited them, and hence been in a position to sell them.

At some time before 1419, Alice (of the family of de la Tour) had married Stephen Russell, a merchant of Weymouth. Her husband was a man of some standing in the community, his name appearing in various deeds there between 1393 and 1433, and he was returned as their MP in 1394. But he doesn't seem to have been much of a land-owner. Alice was, but she had to go to law to prove it.

Being female and married, Alice was not able to bring a legal action in her own right, so it was her husband Stephen who had to make the claim on her behalf. Alice appears to have been the sole heiress - or at least the only surviving one - of both her parents, and it was in connection with claiming her right to these inheritances from both her parents' families that she had to go to law.

Alice's mother, Isabella, came from the family of de Blynchesfield, who took their name from the property of that name in the lowlands immediately to the south east of Shaftesbury. A farm still bears the name, which by the following century had become converted to Blintfield and subsequently Blynfield. It is possible that Isabella had died just prior to 1419, for it was in that year that the legal action commenced in the Manorial Court of Stour Provost, whereby Alice was laying claim to Blynchesfield as her inheritance, but of which she had become dispossessed. It was to be another three years before the case reached the Assize Court in Dorchester. Again Stephen, Alice's husband, was the claimant on Alice's behalf, and the defendants were a John Dyer and his wife. Who these latter were, whether any relation to Alice, is not stated; nor is it obvious how they came to be in possession of Blynchesfield.

So how did Alice set about trying to prove that the property was hers by inheritance? Quite simply by having her pedigree recited in open Court. Each generation, their dates of marriage and birth of their children had to be given. Then came decision time. Did both sides accept that the pedigree was as given, and in particular, was the jury satisfied? If not, then appropriate corroborating documents had to be produced; copies of wills, marriage settlements, etc., anything that could prove the truth of what had been said in the pedigree - this was two centuries before Parish Registers of baptisms, marriages and burials were kept. If the appropriate documents couldn't be produced, then witnesses had to be called to testify to a particular fact in the pedigree, even to swear on oath that "they had heard it said".

Fortunately for Alice Russell the defendants agreed to accept that she was indeed the heir-general of her maternal grandmother. The attorney on behalf of Alice had just begun to state her case for having been dispossessed of this property by John Dyer and his wife, when there came a technical hitch. The defendants, the Dyers, now complained that the jury before whom the case was being heard, although chosen by the Under-Sheriff, Edward Coleford, had in fact all been nominated by the plaintiffs. The judge considered the matter and then ordered a re-trial, severely reprimanding the Under-Sheriff.

At the new trial the pedigree had to be recited all over again before the new jury, and the rest of the evidence given, and argued about. Alice finally won her case; the Dyers were evicted and Alice was awarded £20 damages against them - a substantial sum in those days. Alice was now the legal owner of the Blynchesfield property, and although it had to be administered by her husband, it remained hers to dispose of in her will as she wished. In fact the property remained with the Russell family, but Alice could, had she wished, have bequeathed it to anyone outside the family.

Four years later the Russells were back in the Assize Court at Dorchester, and again it was Stephen making a claim on behalf of his wife. On the previous occasion the claim had concerned Alice's inheritance through her mother: this time it was her inheritance through her father's side of the family - the de la Tours. The property in question was Berwick, in the Parish of Swyre.

Again Alice's pedigree had to be recited in Court, this time showing that Berwick had been in the possession of the de la Tour family from the time of King John (1199-1216), and that through her father she was the heir-general to the property.

The jury again accepted the pedigree and agreed that Alice was the true and only heiress to the property of Berwick. That was not the problem however, for there were two other claimants to Berwick, and the jury also found in both their favours against Alice. The explanation of this conundrum is that while Alice was the true heir, the property had been tied up by various settlements in previous generations during the descent to her. The one claimant, Margaret Gogh, was Lady of the Manor of Swyre in which Berwick stood. The other claimant was Edith Deverell, whose case was pleaded by her husband Hugh.

The case dragged on into the following year, 1428, and finally a settlement was reached. Margaret Gogh obtained a "release" of Berwick from both Alice Russell and Edith Deverell, on the condition that on her death it would pass to Edith and Hugh Deverell and their heirs, and ultimately, after failure of the Deverell heirs, it would pass back to Alice Russell and her heirs. Thus although Alice didn't get immediate possession of Berwick, she now had the legally-documented decision that it was hers by right of inheritance, and would eventually come back to herself or her descendants.

Margaret Gogh lived there and always styled herself as "of Berwick" until her death in 1441, thirteen years after the end of the Court action. Then Edith and Hugh Deverell resided there, but both Alice and her husband had died before the property was free of any Deverell descendants who had a right to live there. It is not known for certain when it came back to the Russell family: possibilities are to their son Henry (died 1463), their grandson John (died 1505), and their great-grandson James (died 1506). It was certainly in the hands of the next generation, John Russell, when he came to sell it to help fund his new life-style at the Court of King Henry VII (died 1509), thanks to the money expended four generations earlier by Alice Russell.

HADWIDIA FITZGRIP

The female who owned the largest area of land in Dorset (apart from a Queen or the wife of a King) appears in the Domesday Book of 1086. Her name was Hadwidia Fitzgrip, and she owned 47 manors of which 10 were in Purbeck.[d] She also held other manors as tenant. Her total holdings amounted to over 30,000 acres:[10] by comparison, the King held 100,000 acres, and his wife, Matilda, held 38,000.

The explanation as to how Hadwidia came to have so much land is also given in Domesday Book, for it is stated that she was the wife of Hugh Fitzgrip[16] and had recently inherited the lands upon his death.

The allocation of land to Hadwidia's husband - and ultimately to her - had not gone smoothly, for in Domesday Book we also read such things as:

"...to this manor [Abbotsbury] belongs one virgate of land which

Hugh, son of Grip, *unjustly took; and his wife still holds it by force.* This, in King Edward's time was for the sustenance of monks ...

...Hugh held this land of the Abbot of Abbotsbury, *as his vassals say, but the Abbot denies it...*

...With this manor [Winterbourne] the same Hugh *holds one virgate of land unjustly,* which belongs to William de Moione...

...Hugh *gave this hide* [at Orchard] *to the Church* of Cranborne for his soul; it is worth twenty shillings. But *the wife* [widow] of Hugh *holds the half hide.* "

It would therefore appear that in the years after the Norman invasion, Hugh took more lands than those to which he was entitled, and after his death his widow, Hadwidia, held on to them "by force" if necessary.

Is there anything more that we can learn about this avaricious Hadwidia, apart from the name of the person she married? Until a hundred years ago the answer to that question would have been "no", but then a document came to light concerning a nunnery in Normandy that literally put Hadwidia in her place. It gave her a father, and it showed her place of origin. In this charter Hadwidia was giving the Manor of Waldune [Waddon] in Dorset to this nunnery "for the health of her soul and those of her husband and of her friends". As was required by the law of the time, the Charter also states that it "was with the commendation and by the advice and consent of her husband". (Of interest is the fact that in Domesday Book it states that it was her husband who had given this Manor - omitting the female participation!) The same Charter mentions that she was Hadwidia, daughter of Nicholas de Baschelville, wife of Hugh de Varham [Wareham] son of Grippon (see pedigree).

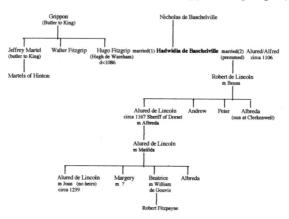

Pedigree 1.3   Family of Hadwidia de Fitzgrip née Baschelville

Nothing more is known of Hadwidia's father: whether, for instance, he had inherited Baschelville, or whether it was a reward for aiding William the Conqueror in 1066. He is not listed as owning any land in England in Domesday Book, but there are two explanations for this: either that he preferred to remain in Normandy and therefore handed over his English possessions to his daughter and her husband; or that he had already died and Hadwidia had inherited: in both cases they would have "belonged" to her husband Hugh Fitzgrip. We have the evidence of the Normandy Charter that she owned Waddon in her own right: other possessions listed in Domesday as her husband's may therefore have belonged to her too. It would certainly go some way towards explaining the large Fitzgrip possessions, if they were the joint estates of husband and wife separately acquired when William the Conqueror was allocating lands.

The same Charter also gives Hadwidia another relative, a brother-in-law. One of the witnesses to the Charter is listed as "Jeffery Martel, brother to Hugh Fitzgrip". He is believed to be the ancestor of the Martels of Hinton Martel in Dorset. Hadwidia already had one known brother-in-law, Walter Fitzgrip, who held considerable possessions in Suffolk according to the Domesday Book.

So now Hadwidia has a name of her own, a father, a husband and two brothers-in-law. It is also possible that she can be given a second husband, a son and several generations of descendants. A very rich widow in those times was not likely to remain so for very long, especially when there was money to be gained by the King for "selling" the widow to a new husband. We know that Hugh Fitzgrip had died by 1086. There is no direct evidence that Hadwidia remarried, but circumstantial evidence points to her having married Alured (Alfred) de Lincoln, a member of a rich land-owning family in Lincolnshire. At some time prior to 1106, this Alured came into possession of all the Fitzgrip property in Dorset, as he would have done if he had married Hadwidia. If he had merely acquired the possessions from the King after Hadwidia's death without heirs, then it is unlikely he would have received the whole estate intact; the King would have been more likely to split it among several people.

A little detective work has therefore given Hadwidia a family background, but it still doesn't answer the question of why she so voraciously defended those Fitzgrip lands, some apparently acquired illegally. Or, more interestingly, how she *did* defend them in those Norman times when males dominated and "might was right".

LADY ELIZABETH TREGONWELL

For the latter part of her long life, Elizabeth Tregonwell lived at the post-Dissolution Milton Abbey, in its lovely setting surrounded by gentle hills. Her second husband was Sir John Tregonwell, best known in Dorset as being one of the Commissioners for the surrender of the Monasteries at the Dissolution. In March 1539 he had dissolved the six principal religious establishments of Tarrant, Bindon, Cerne, Sherborne, Shaftesbury and Milton. He obviously had his eyes on the latter, for a short while later he purchased Milton from the King for £1,000. The Abbey Church was given to the village of Milton to be its Parish Church, while the rest of the monastery buildings became a magnificent house for the Tregonwell family. (It was totally rebuilt in the 18th Century.) Sir John Tregonwell died in 1565, almost twenty years before his wife. Although his heir was his grandson, the house formed a major part of the widow's dower of Elizabeth; that is, she could live in it during her lifetime, receiving the income from the estate, and after her death it would go to the heir in its entirety.

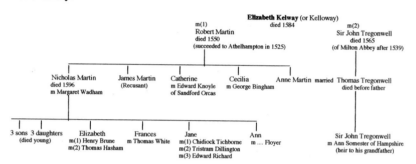

Pedigree 1.4   The Tregonwell and Martin Families

When Elizabeth married Sir John Tregonwell they were both widowed, each with a family by a former spouse (see accompanying pedigree, 1.4). Sir John had a son, Thomas, who was to die before his father, leaving a son, also Sir John Tregonwell, as heir to his grandfather. Elizabeth Tregonwell had been Elizabeth Kelway (or Kelloway) when she first married Robert Martin of Athelhampton. They had several sons including the eldest, Nicholas, heir to his father's estate of Athelhampton, and James, later to become a well-known Catholic recusant. There were also several Martin daughters; Catherine, Cecilia who married George Bingham, and Jane who subsequently married Thomas Tregonwell, Sir John's son by his first marriage. Elizabeth remained on very good terms with her eldest son by this first marriage, Nicholas Martin of Athelhampton, and her younger sons lived with her at Milton.

It would be expected that after Sir John's death, Elizabeth would be especially close to his heir, her grandson John, since he was the son of both her daughter Jane and her step-son Thomas. Not a bit of it! The avaricious John Tregonwell Junior couldn't wait to get his hands on the rest of his inheritance, including the former Milton Abbey, but was prevented from doing so because of its occupation by his elderly grandmother, as devised by his grandfather's will.[j]

She was to live for another twenty years, and relations between them became worse and worse during that time.

The principal bone of contention became the old Tithe Barn and 600 acres of land. Tregonwell was living in the neighbouring village of Milton, [not the newer Milton Abbas, but the old, now-disappeared village that was on the doorstep of Milton Abbey,] and believed that this part of his inheritance was being usurped by the Martins in such a way that he would not eventually be able to claim it.[17] Lady Elizabeth would not give him a lease on it either. After litigation on his part had failed, matters came to a head when John Tregonwell came with a group of men to take it by force. He failed. Mediation by two neighbours plus John's father-in-law finally came to an agreement whereby they would form a Trust to administer the disputed land and Tithe Barn, and then rent it back to Lady Elizabeth. Whether she was too trusting or whether a lot of bribery went on, is not known, but when she sent her servants to the Barn to receive the keys from the Trustees, they found it occupied by armed guards of her grandson.

The old lady rallied her forces at dead of night; apart from her own steward and servants, she assembled her Martin sons, her son-in-law Bingham, and a party from Athelhampton.. They set off to make an armed assault on the guards. The ensuing melée was sufficient to bring out the Constable from the nearby village of Milton plus a lot of the villagers. Lady Elizabeth's party withdrew without gaining possession.

Undeterred, she next appears six weeks later at the Blandford Quarter Sessions, where she obtained a Writ of Restitution in her favour, directed to the Sheriff. By coincidence the Sheriff was one of the Trustees who had deceived Lady Elizabeth a few weeks earlier: now he had to march to the Barn and evict the very men to whom he had given the keys shortly before. Lady Elizabeth was back in possession. The feud between the Martin sons and her Tregonwell grandson continued right up to the bitter end, for while Lady Elizabeth lay dying in the house, a bare-fisted fight was going on below her windows between her now elderly son, Nicholas Martin, and her grandson, John Tregonwell.

There is a strong suspicion that it was the hatred of John Tregonwell for his grandmother that led him to inform on her to the authorities in 1580 for being a recusant. [Originally the word recusant was used to describe anyone who refused to attend his or her Parish Church: after 1570 the word was usually only applied to Roman Catholics - as in the case of Elizabeth Tregonwell.]

Whether or not it was John Tregonwell, somebody laid the charge against her, and the Justices were ordered to submit Elizabeth Tregonwell to an examination. Five Justices conducted the examination, all local gentry, including one who had been one of those deceitful Trustees seven years earlier. There is no doubt that she was a practising Roman Catholic, but she seems to have been let off very lightly, being merely required to enter into a bond for 1,000 marks in respect of repairing the Parish Church - the former Church of Milton Abbey, sitting almost literally on her door-step.

31

That year after her examination two notable things occurred: her eldest son, Nicholas Martin of Athelhampton, was made Sheriff of Dorset, and he and his wife Margaret, née Wadham, moved in to live with Lady Elizabeth at Milton. This latter was almost certainly principally to provide both moral and physical support against her warring grandson, but it probably had quite a lot to do with the practice of Roman Catholicism there!

Now matters became a lot worse in the relationship between Lady Elizabeth and her grandson. The latter was staunchly Protestant and he now kept his eagle eyes open for the slightest suspicion that his Uncle Nicholas had any dealings with Catholicism. Exactly what evidence he collected was to be revealed after Lady Tregonwell's death in 1584, when almost immediately he informed on Nicholas Martin, who found himself having to answer charges in the Star Chamber in London . But that was after the death of his mother, and it is at this point we end the story of the old fighting spirit of Lady Elizabeth Tregonwell.

THE MARTIN SISTERS

Nicholas Martin of Athelhampton - the eldest son of Lady Elizabeth Tregonwell - died in 1596, leaving no male heirs but four daughters.[1] What happened to his property is typical of the rigid inheritance laws of those times. An estate normally passed to the eldest son or, if he had predeceased his father, then to the next eldest son, and so on. If there were no sons, then the daughters were the beneficiaries in equal shares, not in order of precedence as with the sons. As can be seen from the Martin pedigree, this was the situation when Nicholas Martin died. Of his ten children, only four daughters - Elizabeth, Frances, Jane and Ann - survived him, all married. In these circumstances some settlement was usually reached between the daughters: for example, one daughter might take the house with a proportional cash compensation to her sisters; alternatively, the property might be sold and the money divided equally.

Not so the Martin daughters. They all apparently wanted Athelhampton and wished to live there. Obviously none would give way, for they eventually reached an unusual agreement. All of them *would* live at Athelhampton by the simple expedient of dividing the house into four equal parts. And this is exactly what they did; the four sisters had an exact quarter of the lands, and an exact quarter of the house. Over the next fifty years the Brunes - the family of the eldest sister - acquired two of the other quarter shares, but the remaining share remained with the Floyers - the family of the youngest sister - until 1848, when George Wood, the then purchaser of the three quarters of Athelhampton was also able to exchange the remaining quarter share. After an interval of two and a half centuries, Athelhampton became a home for one family again, instead of being divided into four parts owing to the peculiar nature of the female inheritance laws.

THE BAIEUX SISTERS

In the time of King Henry III (1216-1272) the Manor of Upwey near Weymouth was inherited by the two Baieux sisters on the death of their father.[n] The same inheritance laws applied then as for the Martin sisters just described, namely that the estate was inherited in equal parts by all the daughters. The lands were held of the King, and since both girls were under age, it was the King's right to decide whom they should marry. He granted the elder sister, Maud Baieux, in marriage to one of his most trusted followers, Elias Rabayne, in the mid 1250's.

Since by law a married woman could not administer property in her own right, Elias automatically gained his wife Maud's half-share of her father's estates. This was not enough for Elias Rabayne, and he cast covetous eyes on his sister-in-law's half-share as well. He soon arranged for his wife's sister to be taken to Normandy and kept there more or less a prisoner. Now Elias Rabayne had "inherited" the whole of the Upwey Manor with its rich revenues.

Before long the news of Elias' behaviour towards his sister-in-law reached the ears of the King, who immediately ordered the forfeiture of the entire Manor and also the loss of his other lands and titles, including the Governorship of Corfe Castle. Ten years later, in 1267, they were granted back to him, and they were also confirmed by the new King, Edward I, immediately after his accession in 1271. There is no further information as to what happened to the younger Baieux sister: presumably she regained her inheritance.

LANDS ACQUIRED IN OTHER WAYS

ANN MICHEL OF WYNFORD EAGLE

The 17th Century story of how Ann Michel acquired the property of Wynford Eagle by chicanery was related by Hutchins, and his version has been followed by subsequent authors.[iln] In 1980 more light was thrown on the subject as a consequence of documents deposited at the County Records Office,[12] and a different version of the story emerged. While researching the subject, the author has come across a piece of information that changes the picture yet again, but still leaves a mystery over what part Ann Michel actually played in the whole affair - whether she was completely innocent or one of the conspirators.

The basis of the story as first presented was that impecunious William Sydenham of Wynford Eagle planned to put his estate up as the prize in a lottery in 1699, but (fraudulently) arranged that the winning ticket should go to a friend of the family, Ann. She would then sell the estate back to William for a small recompense - paid out of the proceeds of the lottery. The lottery was duly "won" by Ann, but she failed to keep her part of the bargain, for she used the estate as a dowry to lure a neighbouring squire, Doyly Michel, into marriage on the day after the prize was won. Sydenham refused to hand over the estate to the Michels and ended his days in prison together with his two middle-aged daughters.

The documents that came to the County Records Office concerned the legal battle by the Michels to gain possession of the property. (As a married woman Ann could not take the action herself, and it was therefore conducted on her behalf by her husband.) In addition to the legal action, these documents also contain a detailed account of the lottery itself, how it was drawn up and conducted, and how Ann Michel came to have the winning ticket. The manner in which the lottery took place throws great doubt on the possibility of there being any fraud involved, and suggests that the prize may genuinely have come to Ann Michel without any prior "arrangement".[12]

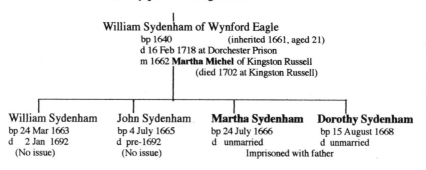

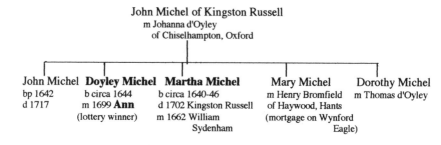

Pedigree 1.5   Families of Sydenhams of Wynford Eagle and Michels of Kingston
Russell, showing inter-relationships of people involved in Lottery of 1699.
('bp' = date of baptism)

34

Ann Michel's maiden name is not given in any of the reports, and it was while investigating this that the previously unreported information emerged. Ann's new husband, Doyly Michel, was in fact William Sydenham's brother-in-law, being the brother of his wife Dorothy Sydenham, née Michel (see accompanying pedigrees 1.5). And even more intriguing, the holder of a large mortgage on the Wynford Eagle estate was none other than the brother-in-law of a second Michel sister - see Michel pedigree, 1.5. It begins to look as if the Michel family played more of an underhand role in the whole proceedings than has previously been appreciated, and while not clearing William Sydenham of complicity, it suggests that his part was not as black as painted by Hutchins.

But to begin at the beginning. In 1661 William Sydenham (baptised 1640) had inherited Wynford Eagle at the age of twenty-one upon the death of his grandfather, a few months after that of his father. (His grandmother was the Mary Sydenham murdered by Royalists during the Civil War, as mentioned elsewhere in this book: William would have been aged about four at that time.) His grandfather, father and four uncles had been prominent Parliamentarians, and expended much of the family wealth during the Civil War, considerably reducing William's inheritance. The following year, 1662, he married Martha Michel of nearby Kingston Russell and they had a family of two sons and two daughters. By the early 1690's William Sydenham (now into his fifties) was deeply in debt in spite of having achieved high public office - he was Squire of the Body to King William III - and both his sons were dead. As was brought out by the subsequent litigation, Sydenham appears to have started mortgaging the Wynford Eagle estate at least from 1690 onwards and probably as far back as 1684. None of these early mortgages was revealed until several years after the lottery in 1699. From 1696 onwards a Thomas Bromfield of Haywood in Hampshire appears prominent among new mortgagees, even to the extent of obtaining judgements against William Sydenham in 1698 for debts in connection with them. (It is a *Henry* Bromfield of Haywood, Hampshire, who was married to Mary Michel.)

The next act in the story is that in July 1699 a female known only as Ann (later to be Ann Michel) went to live at Wynford Eagle being variously described as a distant relative, a companion, and a servant to Martha Sydenham, wife of William. It has proved impossible to trace either her maiden name or any relationship to the Sydenhams - or Michels (prior to marriage).

It was the same year, 1699, that William Sydenham came up with the idea of a lottery to ease his financial problems.[18] William Sydenham's lottery, although a private one, followed similar principles to the State ones. Thus it was held in public at the Mercer's Hall in London, and supervised by independent Trustees and Cashiers, the actual drawing of the tickets and prizes was carried out by Blue-Coat boys from Christ's Hospital. Two hundred thousand tickets at five shillings each were to be issued for purchase by "adventurers": if all were sold a sum of £50,000 would be raised, from which £4,000 would be deducted for overheads. A total of 13,584 prizes were to be given, to the value of £20,000, leaving William Sydenham a profit of approximately £26,000 with which to end his days, assuming all the tickets were sold.

The lottery was known as a Land Lottery due to the nature of the principal prizes which were parcels of the Wynford Eagle estate of varying values. Winners were able either to take the cash equivalent, or to receive the annual income from the land. First prize was valued at £600 per annum (or £12,000 equivalent) and there were several others at £400 per annum: the remaining prizes were varying amounts of cash.

Prior to the lottery being drawn - which was scheduled to take place from 12-23 December - William Sydenham was required to deposit with the Trustees sufficient Deeds etc. to cover the value of the prizes, in other words the Deeds of entitlement to his property of Wynford Eagle. This is where Sydenham's fraud apparently started - rather than with the draw itself - for there is no evidence that the Trustees received these Deeds either before or for several years after the draw, and Sydenham appears not to have publicly disclosed that there were long-outstanding mortgages at the time of the lottery. William Sydenham had still not conveyed the property to either the prizewinner or the mortgagees in March 1706, over five years after the lottery was drawn, and it was for this reason that he was sent to prison together with his eventual beneficiaries, his two daughters.

So how did Ann Michel get mixed up in the story, which from the foregoing appears to be a purely male affair? As mentioned earlier, Ann had joined the Sydenham household at Wynford Eagle in July 1699. Several months later - it was subsequently claimed by the Michels - Sydenham's daughter Dorothy gave Ann two tickets for the lottery, numbers 146,206 and 146,207, saying that one was a present from her Master and the other from her Mistress. Ann kept these tickets safely in her custody.

In the later litigation a very confused story emerges concerning this event: it was said that Dorothy Sydenham knew nothing or could remember nothing of such a transaction, and that William had not sanctioned his daughter to dispose of any of the tickets except for money. The Sydenham daughter said that the tickets were left in a chest-of-drawers belonging to her mother: William Sydenham deposed that he had told his wife and daughters that they were not to give any of the tickets to the servants (including Ann), but they could if they wished give them money with which they could purchase the tickets directly. A confused story indeed, and difficult to know whose version was the truth.

The lottery draw duly started on 12 December 1699, and as each prize was drawn in the usual manner, it was registered by a sworn notary in the presence of several of the Trustees and numerous members of the public: each day the winning numbers were called out in the streets by a public crier, to encourage more people to purchase tickets. On the last day of the draw, 23 December, ticket number 146,206 was drawn as winning the first prize, the estate worth £12,000 or £600 per annum. This first prize was claimed the following day by Ann Michel. According to the story told by Hutchins, Ann and Doyly Michel were married immediately after she knew she had won the estate, and before she claimed the prize. This "romantic" version states that Ann was a penniless young lady who had long been in love with Doyly Michel but having no dowry she had no hope of achieving her heart's desire. Her sudden elevation to being the owner of the estate won in the lottery dramatically altered the situation, and they were immediately married. (No record of their marriage at this time has so far been found either in London or in Dorset.)

As stated above, William Sydenham refused to convey the estate to the Michels, but interestingly, there is no further mention of what happened to the other major prizewinners: presumably they duly received their entitlements. The legal actions brought by the Michels to gain possession dragged on for year after year with more and more old and previously-undisclosed mortgages on the property coming to light. The Michels appear to have lost all right to its ownership when in 1706 the Trustees of the Lottery were finally able to convey Wynford Eagle to the principal mortgagee, Thomas Bromfield, and it was at this point that William Sydenham and his two daughters were sent to Dorchester Prison for contempt in not completing this transaction. William's wife Martha was not included as she had already died in 1702. Her place of death is given as Kingston Russell, the Michel family home, and although several authors comment on this fact - "did the Michels give her a home after the trouble?" is one[14] - nobody seems to have realised that she had returned to her childhood home.

Reading the details of how the Lottery draw was transacted makes it unlikely that there could have been fraud involved in the actual draw. William Sydenham was not sent to prison as a consequence of fraud, neither was it because he refused to hand over the prize to the Michels: he was imprisoned because he was in contempt for not conveying the property to the mortgagee as ordered by the Court in 1706, seven years after the Lottery had taken place.

Thus the facts concerning Ann Michel are that she was some kind of poor relation or friend who went to live at Wynford Eagle in July 1699. She was definitely in possession of the ticket that won first prize in the Land Lottery of December 1699. On 24 December, the day after she won the first prize, her husband was Doyly Michel - although when and where this marriage actually occurred has not been established. William Sydenham refused to hand over the property to Ann and Doyly Michel. Since it is unlikely that there was any fraud concerning the actual drawing of the lottery tickets, the only bone of contention was how Ann actually came to obtain the ticket that won the first prize.

But what part did her husband Doyly play in the affair? William Sydenham had not disclosed that the property of Wynford Eagle was heavily mortgaged at the time of the Lottery. While William Sydenham's wife Martha might not have known of this and hence not been in a position to tell her brother Doyly, it is extremely unlikely that nothing would have been said to him by the holder of the principal mortgage, his other brother-in-law. It also appears from the papers in the Record Office that two of the smaller mortgagees were called

Charles and Francis Michel, but what their relationship was to Doyly is not stated. A further complication about the whole matter might come from the same Michel family, for one of the Trustees of the Lottery was listed as Robert Michel. Would Doyly therefore have rushed into marriage with Ann, knowing that her dowry-to-be was heavily mortgaged to his brother-in-law? Or were Ann and Doyly already married before the affair of the Lottery even arose, which would explain why no record of their marriage at the time of the Lottery can be traced? Was she already Martha Sydenham's sister-in-law when she went to stay at Wynford Eagle in the July preceding the lottery? Altogether, far too many Michels seem to have been involved in the whole affair! If there was any fraud involved in the matter of the draw, was it pre-planned by the Michel family, rather than by William Sydenham?

Or was it simply that everything concerning the Lottery was above-board - bearing in mind that William Sydenham was never charged with fraud - and it was just that he didn't like the idea of his family estate being won by Ann Michel, a poor relation of his family?

2
RELIGIOUS WOMEN
OF DORSET

INTRODUCTION

Apart from royalty, most of the earliest records of women in Dorset are of those who took up a religious life. Prior to the Norman Conquest, there were at least four major nunneries in the County - Wimborne, Shaftesbury, Tarrant Crawford and Horton - and many minor ones. There were only two left at the time of the Dissolution in the 16th Century, Shaftesbury and Tarrant, but several more came into existence over the next few centuries, primarily for nuns escaping from religious persecution on the Continent: the one at Stapehill has just closed after nearly two centuries of existence, for example.

As well as life in nunneries, we also have information about three Dorset women who became Saints in Anglo-Saxon times. Two of these probably spent all their lives here; the other went to Germany, where she is much better known than here.

Many well-to-do women in their later years - usually after they were widowed - turned to a more devotedly religious life. Two prominent women of Dorset who did this were Ela of Canford, who eventually became Abbess at Laycock (see Chapter 1), and Margaret Beaufort, mother of King Henry VII - see later.

Other women, while not entering a nunnery, led a very religious life and suffered for it. Such were the recusants who continued to practise their Roman Catholic religion after England had become a Protestant country.

NUNS OF DORSET

At first sight it might be thought that women became nuns for the sole reason that they wished to devote themselves to a religious life. But this was only one of the reasons. Young girls from the age of five and upwards were quite frequently - especially in Norman times - dedicated by their parents to the religious life, not for their own sakes, but that they might be in a position to pray for the souls of their parents and hence secure their safe passage to everlasting life. The little girls would have no choice in the matter. (It was very rare for boys to be so dedicated.) There were also various other reasons for entering a nunnery, or rather "being required" to enter a religious life: a daughter who had been "left on the shelf"; parents not able to afford a suitable dowry for her to be married; a convenient way of disposing of an illegitimate daughter; considering a nunnery as a place of safety for women-folk in troubled times; an orphaned girl; and finally, as a place of education.[11]

In Anglo-Saxon times when there were few schools and no higher places of education such as universities, nunneries played an important part as places of learning, as can be seen by the stories of the nuns of Wimborne. Apart from being the only places where books were kept, both nunneries and monasteries played important roles in the actual writing and illuminating of them. When celibacy in religion was enforced in Norman times, what can be termed an academic life became completely closed to women, and nunneries became of even greater importance in the promulgation of learning to women. It is therefore not surprising that many women of average or brighter intellect sought a cloistered life. Here they could pursue their learning in the company of like sort, in comparison with life in a manor house or castle, with the prospect of becoming a wife/chattel of an uncouth and blood-thirsty nobleman.[5] In the peace and tranquillity of a nunnery she would be with companions of similar learning and gentility and, within the rules of her Order, she would still possess more rights than in the outside world.

Apart from receiving instruction in religious studies, nuns would also be taught needlework, tapestry, calligraphy and illumination. Many nunneries also provided education for lay children, both girls and boys, where a nun would be able to use her abilities in teaching others.

NUNS OF WIMBORNE

Wimborne was the earliest of the nunneries to be founded in Dorset, at some time between 704 and 718 A.D., and there is a surprising amount of information about some of its earliest nuns and Abbesses. It was attacked and destroyed by marauding Danes towards the end of the 10th Century, after which it was re-founded for monks prior to 1066.

CUTHBURGA

The *Anglo-Saxon Chronicles* for the year 718 has the following entry:[1]

"This year Ingild the brother of Ina died, and their sisters were Cwenburga and Cuthburga. And Cuthburga built the monastery of Wimburn; and she was given in marriage to Aldfrid King of the Northumbrians; but they separated during his lifetime."

Thus we are told that Cuthburga founded the nunnery at Wimborne and became its first Abbess. But we know considerably more about Cuthburga than this for, being a member of the ruling royal family of Wessex (see pedigree 5.1 on page 113), there is more information about her than is usual for the time.[2] Her cousin Caedwalla had usurped the throne of Wessex, and on his death in 688, Cuthburga's brother Ina (Ine) became King (688-726): he it was who founded the Abbey at Sherborne - the first in Dorset - in 705, and also rebuilt Glastonbury Abbey and founded Wells Cathedral. It is also known from the above reference that Cuthburga and Ina had another brother, Ingild, and a sister, Cwenburga.

No doubt more for political reasons than any other, Cuthburga was married to Ealdfrith (Aldfrid) King of the Northumbrians. But this was to be a marriage with a difference, for it was never consummated. Cuthburga preferred a religious life, and was able to persuade her husband to respect the vow of chastity she had made for herself some years previously. (Why did she agree to the marriage in the first place!). It is of interest that the same thing happened to the preceding King of Northumbria for similar reasons of his wife. Cuthburga left her husband in the North and retired to the nunnery at Barking in Essex, which at that time was part of Wessex.

Cuthburga remained as a nun at Barking until after the death of her husband in 704, when her brother King Ina asked her to return to him in central Wessex, probably for the specific purpose of founding a Benedictine nunnery there, and becoming its first Abbess. The exact date of the foundation remains obscure: it couldn't have been earlier than 704, the date of her husband's death, nor later than 718 when it is mentioned in the *Anglo-Saxon Chronicles.* Cuthburga dedicated her nunnery to The Blessed Virgin.

Approximately one and a half centuries later, the buildings and all within them were destroyed by Danish invaders; what happened to the nuns at the time was not recorded. In the 11th Century it was re-founded as a monastery for monks only. In honour of its original foundress, it was dedicated to St Cuthburga, the name by which the Minster is still known, even though all other traces of the monastery disappeared at the Dissolution .

Whatever the date of its original foundation, Cuthburga remained there until her death in 720. She could therefore not have been Abbess for more than fifteen years at the most, during which time the buildings were constructed and the first nuns chosen and settled in. During that time she made it into a centre for devotion as well as for learning, and it was soon to earn a great reputation for the training of missionaries. At Cuthburga's death it was her sister Cwenburga - also mentioned in the quotation at the beginning - who became

Wimborne's second Abbess. This sister is believed to have been a nun with Cuthburga at Barking, and to have moved to Wimborne to help in founding the Abbey.[1]

TETTA

Tetta was either the third Abbess of Wimborne or possibly the second, for some historians believe Tetta was an alternative name for Cwenburga, the sister of Cuthburga and Wimborne's second Abbess. Whichever she was, she certainly followed soon after Cuthburga, and it was during her tenure of the post that Wimborne reached its greatest eminence.[1]

About the year 750, Lioba (see later) was one of a party of nuns who left Wimborne to go as missionaries to what is now Germany. Lioba had worked, studied and trained under Tetta, and it is from a biography of Lioba that we learn something of life at Wimborne under Tetta.

Wimborne like most if not all of the monasteries built in those early days of Christianity was a double monastery. That is, it was for both women and men. The idea had come to this country from Gaul, and the nunnery at Barking where Cuthburga had spent her time before founding Wimborne was also a double monastery. The two sexes were kept strictly apart, and not even allowed to see each other, let alone converse, each having their own living quarters. Even the Church was divided down the middle by a high screen, with separate entrances for nuns and monks; only the altar end was in communication with both sides of the Church (see Stapehill, later, for description of a double Church in present-day Dorset). It was truly a religious life, dedicated to God, as might be expected from this relatively newly introduced faith of Christianity. How different matters were to become in the not-too-distant future (see later).

One major feature of these double monasteries was that on numerous occasions it was a female Abbess who was in charge of everyone, both nuns and monks. Cuthburga, Cwenburga and Tetta each performed this role. As well as ruling the whole monastery, it was the duty of the Abbess to deal with all communications with the outside world - always conducted through a grated window. The only exception to the rule of segregation of the sexes were the two priests who came into the female part of the monastery to hear confessions and to administer the Sacrament; even in those days it was not considered an appropriate duty for females! Apart from these priests, no other male entered the nunnery, and it is recorded that Abbess Tetta would not even permit a visiting Bishop to set foot within the nunnery.

To assist the Abbess at Wimborne there were several other nuns in various offices: a prioress (the Abbess' deputy); a deacon; a novice mistress in charge of the newly-admitted females in their preparations to become nuns; a portress who, in addition to having a ring containing all the keys (some very large in those days), also had the task of opening and closing the Church for services and ringing the bell at appropriate times.

During Lioba's time at Wimborne under Tetta, she tells of a novice mistress who was intensely disliked by the young nuns because of her severity. They were relieved when she died, and was buried within the Abbey's precincts; but their true feelings towards her were displayed shortly afterwards when the novices returned to the cemetery and literally danced on her grave. So much so that when they had finished, instead of a mound of earth over her grave, there was a sunken hollow six inches below the neighbouring ground. When Tetta heard of the event, she summoned the novices in question to her and reproved them. For penance she imposed a three day fast to be spent in prayer. At the end of that time she led the novices into the church to pray for the soul of the late novice mistress. It is recorded by Lioba that as Tetta finished the prayers, the sunken earth in the grave rose until it was level with the surrounding ground.

But we can still return to the fact that a female was in charge of the whole establishment at Wimborne - and elsewhere - at a time when England was torn apart by almost continual fighting. One suggestion to explain the roles of such as Cuthburga and Tetta is that they were members of a royal family. Kings and other leaders were usually chosen from either a direct or a collateral line of succession, since there was a strong tradition of following members of such families - hence the ability of females to lead armies (see Chapter 5). As these Abbesses were from the same royal families, then it would be natural to accept them as leader, especially as they were also likely to be the best-educated. Most male members of these families were committed Christians by this time, and many had made the long and treacherous pilgrimage to Rome to receive the Pope's blessing. But it was rare for any of these aethelings (princelings) to take up a monastic life: they were usually too ambitious and preferred fighting. Princesses, on the other hand, very often preferred this monastic way of life, and hence became the superior figure in their religious establishments and the automatic choice for their leaders.

ABBESS LIOBA

Lioba is the Anglo-Saxon Abbess about whom we know most since, as already mentioned, her biography was written in later life.[1] She was born in the West Country, exact site unknown, and was originally baptised Truthgeba; she was more usually known by the nicknames of Leobgytha and Leofe. When later she went to Germany, this latter name was changed to Lioba (Liebe = Well-beloved), and it is by this name that she is best known. Her mother's name was Ebba (see accompanying pedigree 2.1), and her father was Dynne (or Tinne); her maternal uncle was christened Winfrith, but is usually known by the name later given to him by the Pope - Boniface; he was to prove a great influence in Lioba's life.

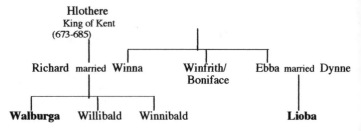

Pedigree 2.1 Family of Lioba and Walburga, nuns of Wimborne.

At a young age she was accepted into the care of Abbess Tetta at Wimborne and spent many happy days there, devoted to her religious life as a nun, but still having time to read all the Classical authors as shown by her later life. There is one black mark against the young Lioba - plagiarism. As a young woman she appears to have developed a hero-worship for her Uncle Boniface, who had already been engaged for some years on missionary work in Germany, together with his nephews Winnibald and Willibald. A letter written from Lioba to her uncle in Germany has survived:

"To the most reverend Boniface, invested with the insignia of the highest order [archbishop] beloved in Christ, his kinswoman Leobgytha, the lowliest of the handmaidens of God, health and eternal salvation. I ask of your clemency that you would deign to remember the friendship that you had in bygone days with my father Tinne, in the western regions. He died eight years ago. Do not refuse to pray for the repose of his soul. I also commend to your remembrance my mother Ebba, related to you by the ties of blood. Though she still lives, she suffers much, and for a long time has been troubled with ill health. I am the only daughter of my parents, and unworthy though I am I would that I might regard you as my brother, for there is no man in whom I can place more confidence than I can in you. I venture to send you this little missive; not that it is worthy of your notice, but that you may have some remembrance of me, and that in spite of our distance from each other the bond of love may unite us for the rest of our days. My dear brother I beg of you that by your prayers you will shield me from the poisoned darts of the enemy. One more thing I beg of you, and that is that you will courteously send me some few words by way of reply. You will find below some verses that I have tried to compose in accordance with the rules of poetic tradition, not audaciously, but to exercise my mind even though it be in a feeble way and to ask your counsel. All that I know I have learnt from Eadburgh my mistress, who was ever studying the Divine Law. Farewell. Live long and happily. Intercede for me.

> May the Almighty Judge, Who made the earth,
> And glorious in His Father's kingdom reigns,
> Preserve your chaste fire warm at its birth,
> Till time for you shall lose its rights and pains."

It is the poetry that lets Lioba down, for it had been plagiarised from a treatise on the construction of Latin verse by Aldhelm of Malmesbury![21]

An intermittent correspondence appears to have continued for quite a few years between the nuns of Wimborne and Boniface, until finally he sent a letter to the Abbess, Tetta, requesting that some nuns might be sent out to Germany to help with the missionary work, particularly among the women: he especially asked Tetta that his niece, Lioba, might be included in their number.

Ten nuns of Wimborne therefore left these shores to begin a new life among the heathens and newly-converted Christians of Germany.[4] As requested, Lioba was one of the number, which also included Walburga, Tecla and Cynehild. Left behind were the Abbess Tetta and the novice mistress Eadburgh, mentioned in Lioba's earlier letter.

Lioba was to spend the remaining thirty years of her life in Germany, dying there on 20 September 780. She trained many nuns to become Abbesses, and was herself in charge of the many convents in her area for all but the last few years of her life. She was renowned for her knowledge of the Holy Scriptures, as well as the Classical writers and philosophers. Her wisdom and knowledge were appreciated by kings and bishops alike, who frequently consulted her. In all, quite a remarkably learned woman. She spent more than half her life in Dorset, and had presumably gained most of her learning here - a great tribute to the nunnery at Wimborne.

Little or nothing is known of what happened to eight of the nine companions of Lioba on her journey to Germany. A relic of St Agatha - her thigh bone - was later recorded as being among the relics in Wimborne Minster, but it is not known for certain whether it was from this Agatha or the better-known Agatha of Catania. Tecla remained with Lioba for many years before becoming head of her own nunnery, where she died in the year 790. Much more is known of her companion Walburga, who is described in detail later.

NUNS OF SHAFTESBURY

The foundation of the Abbey at Shaftesbury by King Alfred in 888 A.D. and its first Abbess, his daughter Ethelgiva, have been described elsewhere (see Chapter 5); also the reburial there of the relics of the murdered King Edward in about the year 980. Virtually nothing is known of the events at Shaftesbury Abbey in the century between these two dates, other than the names of two of its Abbesses, Aelfryth and Herleva. Edward was canonised in the year 1008, and from this date Shaftesbury grew rapidly in importance as more and more pilgrims came to visit the shrine of Edward the Martyr.[fn]

The number of nuns at Shaftesbury was never very large, not many more than a hundred at maximum, and in the last half century prior to the Dissolution, it was probably only half this number. But what it lacked in numbers it certainly made up for in richness. As well as the often very large donations it received from the thousands of pilgrims to the tomb of Edward the Martyr, many people bequeathed money or land to the Abbey in their wills in order for the nuns to pray for their souls. But a considerable part of the Abbey's acquisitions of land came with the "dowries" brought by the novices as they entered the Abbey, and many of these records still survive:

"The daughter of Alured, the King's butler, brings with her five hides.

"Drogo de Montacute gives two hides with his daughter."

"The Church of Torinton, with lands adjacent, tithes and a little weir, is given by Odo, son of Gamelin, with his two daughters"

As part of her duties, the Abbess administered all these lands and many deeds exist to show her involvement. The actual physical visiting of the lands and the collection of tithes, etc., would normally be undertaken by lay male servants of the Abbey, but all would be supervised by the Abbess, who normally only talked to them through a grated window in the usual custom of Abbesses. Apart from benefactions, gifts and "dowries", there are some records of land being bought and sold, and occasionally exchanged, usually to consolidate isolated areas of lands into a more practical area, easier to administer.

With all these rich revenues the nuns were able to live very well, employed servants to do many of the tasks that in smaller nunneries would have been done by the nuns themselves, and could buy in any food not provided by their tithes, such as imported goods and wines. Another source of revenue to the Abbey arose from the nature of its initial foundation by Alfred the Great - the sharing of the Manor of Shaftesbury between the King and the Abbey. (In Domesday Book the Abbey owned one hundred and eleven of the houses in the Town, compared with the King's sixty-six.) Because the Manor was shared, so too was the income from the Manorial Court. Accordingly, the fines, lands and goods of any convicted felon were shared between the Abbess and the King.

The office of Abbess at Shaftesbury was a magnificent one for any woman, and together with the Abbesses of Barking, Winchester and Wilton, she ranked as a Baroness, and was required to perform the services of such a position. Thus she was summoned to attend at Parliament - but was excused by reason of her sex. [What a difference there might have been to the politics and history of centuries if these females had been able to attend!] She was also required to send a quota of knights to serve the King as and when ordered to do so. This obligation was usually fulfilled by the knights in question renting some of the Abbey's lands, not for money, but for the necessary knight's service.

A significant number of the names of the Abbesses of Shaftesbury are known (see Table 1).

Table 1
Abbesses of Shaftesbury from Foundation to Surrender (888-1538)

888 Ethelgiva or Ethelgova, Aethelgeof, Angelina: daughter of King Alfred
948 Aelfryth
966 Herleva
1001 Alfrida
1089 Eularia, also 1088, 1135
? Eustachia
1107 Cecilia, sister of Mabel Fitzhamon
1125 Emma
1135 Cecilia
1190 Mary, also 1189 and 1199   (1216 in King's hands)
1222 Amicia Russell, died 1242
1243 Agnes de Longespée   (1246 in King's hands)
1247 Mary
1266 Agnes Ferrars, or Ferare; also 1246, 1251, 1257 and 1267
1276 Juliana de Bauceyn, or Bauchin; also 1276 and 1280
1280 Laurentia, also 1285 and 1290
1302 Alice de Lavynton/Lavington; also 1312 and 1314
1315 Margery/Margaret Auchier; also 1318 1327   (1327 in King's hands)
1329 Dionysia la Blounde/Blount; also 1340
1350 Joan
1350 Margaret de Leucemore; also 1353, 1355 and 1359
1362 Joan Formage   (1395 in King's hands)
1397 Egelina   (1398 in King's hands)
1398 Cecilia Fovent, also 1399
1423 Margaret Stourton, died 30 October 1441
1441 Edith Bonham, died 1460
1460 Margaret St John, also 1480: nun in 1441, Abbess in 1460, died in 1491
1492 Alice Gibbes, died 1496
1496 Margaret Twyneo/Twyniho
1504 Elizabeth Shelford, also 1524
1528 Elizabeth Souch/Zouch, surrendered Abbey in 1538; nun in 1498

There is a little more information about some, however. Thus Cecilia (1107) was one of the sisters of Mabel Fitzhamon of Cranborne (see Chapter 8) who married Robert of Gloucester, half-brother to Matilda, claimant to the English throne. Cecilia appears to have died in 1135, the same year that the Civil War broke out between Matilda and Stephen (see Chapter 6), and was therefore not tested as to her loyalty to her brother-in-law's involvement in the War.

The next but one Abbess (Mary of France) would also have had her loyalties tested by the same conflict, had she come to the position earlier, for she was also "related" to Matilda. She was the illegitimate daughter of Geoffrey of Anjou, second husband of Matilda, and hence half-sister of King Henry II (1154-1189). Marie had spent a large part of her life at the English Court of her half-brother, and was renowned for her artistic abilities. It may be more than coincidence that the first mention of her at Shaftesbury is the year that Henry died, and she became Abbess the following year. She was famous as a poetess, wrote ballads, and also translated from English to French such works as *Aesop's Fables* and *The Purgatory of St Patrick*. Marie de France was also known as a writer of romances - stories based on folk stories and historical legends of the Celts, Bretons, English and Norse. Her great popularity came from the fact that instead of presenting the whole of the story as a saga, she picked on isolated incidents and made them into little vignettes that could easily be understood by her listeners or readers, and identified with their everyday life. Quite often, and in a manner not used by others of her times, she presented the stories from the woman's point of view. Evidence of her popularity comes from the copies of her writings that still exist in English, French, German, Italian and Norse (Norwegian).[3]

Love played a large part in all her writings, but pure love, the love encouraged by the age of chivalry that was just commencing. Interestingly, we know nothing of her own love-life, but perhaps something is revealed in her *Eliduc*, a story similar to that of *Tristan and Isolde* but where the main characters, unable to find true love, all go to end their days in monasteries. Was she perhaps revealing something of her own life? For that is how she ended her days, first as a nun and then the Abbess at Shaftesbury.

One deed from the time of Marie de France as Abbess records the gift of the Manor of Bradford (afterwards Bradford Abbas) by King John her nephew, or more correctly, her half-nephew.

The next Abbess, Amicia Russell, died in 1242 and apparently there was great dissent among the nuns as to who should be chosen as her successor, for two appear to have been elected simultaneously. The younger nuns chose Sister Constance Saunz Aver, while the more senior nuns chose Sister Agnes de Ferrars. It would be interesting to know the full story of the dispute, for the next thing we hear is that neither nun is promoted to Abbess; instead a nun from another nunnery was appointed. She was Agnes de Longespée, a nun from Whorwell in Hampshire, one of the daughters of Ela of Canford who at that time had become Abbess at Lacock Abbey, Wiltshire (see Chapter 1). [This was a triple achievement for Ela's family, for while she was Abbess at Lacock, and this daughter Agnes was Abbess at Shaftesbury, a second daughter was Abbess at nearby Romsey Abbey in Hampshire.] Four years later Agnes de Longespée had presumably died - or resigned - for Agnes de Ferrars is again the candidate for promotion to Abbess. This time King Henry II intervened to block her election, claiming that she was a "blood relation of William de Mariscis the traitor". Six months passed and the determined Agnes - her name cleared - at last became the Abbess of Shaftesbury and reigned from 1246 to at least 1267.

In 1302 Alice de Lavington was promoted from Prioress to Abbess, following a Shaftesbury Town scandal involving some of the nuns under the previous Abbess.[20] After investigation by an envoy of the Pope, the Abbey was ordered to pay a fine to the Pope; the nuns were restricted to the Abbey precincts and to their religious duties, and they were required to submit to an annual inspection. What *had* they been up to?

Joan Formage became Abbess in 1362, and her will was written on 4 May 1392, when presumably she felt she was nearing her end. The will was however annulled on the 25 October 1393 on the grounds that it was prejudicial to the Abbey: how this was so is not specified.

The next Abbess about whom something extra is known apart from her name is Margaret St John, who became Abbess in 1460 and died in 1491, having first become a nun before 1441. She was therefore Abbess during the troubled times of the Wars of the Roses, and while the country was torn apart, Margaret had a more personal split. She had an uncle who was firmly on the Yorkist side, and an aunt (Margaret Beaufort) who was in the Lancastrian line of succession (see pedigree 6.2 in Chapter 6).[22] As the powers of the Lancastrians and Yorkists waxed and waned in turn, did Margaret St John manage to stay aloof from the politics of the day, or did she favour one side? She apparently kept her thoughts to herself, for there is no record of her ever being reprimanded by one King or another.

Elizabeth Zouch entered Shaftesbury Abbey at the end of the 15th Century, and became its Abbess in 1528; she reigned only a few years before called upon to surrender it at the Dissolution. This end came on the 23 March 1539 when Elizabeth Zouch led her fifty-three nuns out of the Abbey for the last time. (During its life, the number of nuns at Shaftesbury had varied between fifty-five and one hundred and twenty.) The financial gain to King Henry VIII was enormous, for the annual revenues were estimated at about £1,300. In addition there were "the great bakehouse, the pastry house, the breadhouse, the Long Stable, the three great base courts, the laundry house, the wardrobe chamber, the green chamber, the second great stable, the malthouse, the millhouse, the brewhouse, the hay-house, the larder-house, the woodhouse, the gardens, the park, and the dovehouse."[d]

The nuns were by no means left destitute for each was paid an annual pension: the total amount for the fifty-four nuns in the first year amounted to £431, and fourteen years later, in 1553, the Abbess and thirty-eight nuns were still being paid a total of £29-13s-4d. The initial pensions were certainly not meagre: Elizabeth Zouch the Abbess received £133-6s-8d; Katharine Hall the Prioress, £20; Elizabeth Monmouth the sub-Prioress, £7-7s-0d; the other nuns received variously, £6-13s-4d, £5-6s-8d, £5, £4-13s-4d, £4, or 6s-8d per annum according to their ages, infirmities and years of life in the nunnery.

Almost immediately the Abbey buildings totally disappeared, for later the same year Leland noted that it was already demolished.[f] Perhaps it was a sign that the townspeople held the Abbey in low esteem at that time, for there was certainly no reverence in the speed with which they removed its stones - even those of the Church - to build homes for themselves in the Town and surrounding areas. It should be remembered that many of the townspeople had been tenants of the Abbey, and had perhaps suffered great hardships in trying to raise the rents and tithes to keep the occupants of the Abbey in their life-style.

Excavations from just over a hundred years ago have gradually revealed most of the outlines of the Abbey site, which is open to visitors - at least in the summer months. In 1992 a modern version of a tomb was placed over the site before the High Altar to commemmorate the place where the original tomb of St Edward the Martyr probably stood. It is hoped that at some future date the relics of St Edward might be placed within it. It would appear that before Elizabeth Zouch handed the Abbey over at the Dissolution, the nuns buried their most precious possession, the bones of St Edward: in January 1931 what are almost certainly these relics were unearthed during an excavation on the Abbey site, in the form of a small lead casket containing "some bones belonging to a youth not fully grown, about 5 feet 4 inches in height". Unfortunately, owing to a dispute within the family who owned the site, the bones were presented to a branch of the Russian Orthodox Church, and have spent most of this century in a bank vault in Woking, Surrey, until a legal dispute over their ownership is settled.

Other than these relics, there is surprisingly little physical evidence of these women whose lives were concerned with this once magnificent Abbey at Shaftesbury - its Church was said to have been of the same size as Salisbury Cathedral. Six and a half centuries of mainly Dorset women's lives are now little more than dust.

NUNS OF TARRANT CRAWFORD

Most references[hi] say that the Abbey at Tarrant Crawford was founded for Cistercian or White nuns by Ralph de Kahaines who came over with William the Conqueror. If so, then the founder must have been an extremely old man, for the first Cistercian monastery in England was not founded until 1129 (at Waverley, Surrey). Tarrant could therefore not have been founded until a minimum of seventy years after the Conquest, if it was for Cistercian nuns, by which time Ralph de Kahaines would have been approaching a hundred years of age. However, it appears that a grandson of this original Ralph de Kahaines bore the same name as his grandfather,[6] and there has been confusion by authors about these two. Records from this early period of the Abbey's life are virtually non-existent, but it is known that it was re-founded in 1230. It is therefore more likely that its original foundation was for Benedictine (Black) nuns, who had been in England for several centuries prior to the Conquest, and for Cistercian (White nuns) after its re-foundation.

Whatever its original foundation, tradition has it that Tarrant Crawford was founded at the end of the 11th Century by Ralph de Kahaines near to his manor House. (He also gave his name to the nearby Tarrant Keyneston.[23]) His son William further enriched and endowed the Abbey, giving it tithes of all the bread baked in his house, all the pork salted, and all the cattle killed: the nuns could not have been short of food!

In spite of these endowments, the nunnery at Tarrant Crawford fell by the way-side in less than a hundred years, and was re-founded by Bishop Richard Poore in 1230 - definitely for Cistercian nuns this time. He had been born in the village of Tarrant Crawford and had been succesively Bishops of Chichester, Salisbury and Durham. In his older age he remembered this decrepit nunnery close to the village of his birth. After re-founding and endowing it, he presented it to Joan, wife of King Alexander II of Scotland and eldest daughter of King John (see Chapter 6). Bishop Poore was buried in the Church of the Abbey in 1237, and within a year Queen Joan was buried there too.

It was now that the nunnery at Tarrant became well-known and prospered, in contrast to the first part of its life. As described elsewhere (see Chapter 6), Queen Joan had been the favourite sister of King Henry III: he richly endowed it after her burial there and continued his interest in it until his death in 1272. In 1269 Henry III granted half the Manor of Bere Regis to the Abbey, and it was for some unknown reason that many of the later Abbesses of Tarrant were buried there instead of at the Abbey.

The names of a few of the Abbesses are known through deeds and other documents:[fh] Claricia, Emmelina, Matilda de Bryonis (1270); Isolda, Elena (1298); Anne, Clemence de Cernyngton, Joan Kingeston (1389); Joan, Avice, Edith Coker (1506); Margaret Lynde (1534) and Margaret Russell who was Abbess at the time of the Dissolution. Interestingly, the names of four Abbesses given above are all from well-known Dorset families of the time, unlike those at Shaftesbury, suggesting that Tarrant Crawford remained a "local" nunnery.

The last Abbess Margaret Russell was first cousin to John Russell, first Earl of Bedford (see Chapter 6), and like him she was born at Swyre in Dorset. At the Dissolution she received a pension of £49 (cf the Abbess of Shaftesbury who received £133), her Prioress Ann Cheveral (another local name) £5, and the other seventeen nuns decreasing amounts according to their age and service. Margaret Russell's will was dated 20 January 1567, and proved in July 1568.

In it she requested that her body be buried in Bere Church (which it was); she left her cousin John, Lord Bedford, her "piece of plate double gilt" and a great ring, and £4 to be distributed to the poor.[m]

The Abbey buildings at Tarrant - said to be the richest of the Cistercian nunneries in the country[5] - were destroyed soon after the Dissolution; a barn and possibly part of the adjoining farmhouse are all that remain. A small Church that may or may not have been part of the Abbey, stands near the site. It has been suggested that the lack of windows on the south side of this Church indicates that it stood adjacent to the Abbey on that side, meaning that it could have been the public half of a double Church, as at Stapehill (see later). This idea is supported by its age, the chancel being Norman and the nave 12th Century. The tombs of the Abbesses of Tarrant Crawford still remain in the ancient Church of Bere Regis, usually totally ignored by the many visitors who come to see the fictitious site of one of the episodes in the "life" of *Tess of the d'Uurbervilles*.

NUNS OF HORTON

In the year 1122 Roger, Bishop of Sarum, annexed the remains and possessions of the derelict Abbey of Horton and made it into a cell of Sherborne, continuing its life as a Priory for monks until the Dissolution. Before that time it is variously described as a monastery, abbey or convent; but in spite of these numerous references to its earlier existence, none of them states whether it was for nuns or monks.[h7] It would therefore appear that when later writers were unable to determine which it was in earlier writings, they have carefully skated over it! They all mention that it was founded in about the year 970 by Ordgar, Earl of Devonshire, who had extensive possessions in the area (he is better known as the father of Elfrida, stepmother of the murdered King Edward the Martyr, see Chapter 5).

One recent reference[22] (which unfortunately doesn't give the source of its information) states that Wolfrida was the founder, endower, and first Abbess of Horton, built on her estate. (Possibly she was of Ordgar's family, and hence also related to the "wicked" Queen Elfrida.) When Barking Abbey was destroyed by raiding Danes, it was restored by King Edgar and Archbishop Dunstan, and Wolfrida was sent there as its Abbess, while still retaining her post at Horton. After Edgar's death she is said to have been ejected from Barking, but was later restored to that position by King Ethelred, Elfrida's son. After a brief sojourn in London following another Danish attack, she is said to have died in 980 and been buried at Barking.

Two pieces of evidence suggest that Horton was originally for nuns. Both the existing Church at Horton and its predecessor, demolished in 1722, were dedicated to St Wolfrida, the only Church to be so dedicated in the whole of the country. One reference states that it is named after an Abbess of Horton, who later retired to Wilton Abbey. [Slightly different version from above.] The second piece of evidence is pure "tongue-in-cheek" speculation on the author's part! One of the ghosts described elsewhere (see Chapter 9) was of a nun, walking in a lane near Horton - seen even in the 20th Century by a vicar's wife. I should like to think that this is a folk legend carried down the centuries of a nun trying to find her long-lost Abbey at Horton, after it had been converted to a Priory for monks.

It is very sad that nothing is left to tell us of the nuns of Horton - and it is probable that the first foundation was for nuns - apart from the name of one of its Abbesses. Who were they? How many were there? Why did the Abbey at Horton fail to flourish?

NUNS OF CANFORD

Canford has turned up several times in this book as a private home in the hands of females, from Ela in the 12th Century (Chapter 1) to Lady Charlotte Guest in the 19th Century (Chapter 4). At the end of the 18th and into the beginning of the 19th Century it had a short life as a religious establishment for women.[9]

In 1611 the Manor of Canford had been purchased by Sir John Webb: it remained in this staunch Roman Catholic family during the next few centuries when it secretly sheltered resident priests who both administered to local Catholics and ran a school training young men prior to their being ordained on the Continent. In 1794 the property was owned by another Sir John Webb who only had one daughter and heiress, Barbara Ashley married to Anthony Ashley, fifth Earl of Shaftesbury. She offered Canford House to some English Carmelite or Teresian nuns who had left Hoogstraat in Belgium and fled to England. They settled into their new life at Canford, but it was not to last for long.

In 1814, the daughter of Barbara, Countess of Shaftesbury - also named Barbara - married Francis Spenser Ponsonby who was later created Lord de Mauley and was the one who negotiated the sale of Canford to the Guests in 1845-48 (see Chapter 4). The newly-married couple gave the nuns at Canford ten years in which to find a new home. In September 1825 they packed up and left for France, after a sojourn of just thirty years in Dorset. Canford settled back into being a private home again. It was as if these women had never been, for on their departure they left no mark of their thirty years existence in this County.

NUNS OF STAPEHILL

Visit Stapehill on the road between Wimborne and Ringwood and you will see a very rare sight not just in Dorset but in the whole of the country, an intact nunnery that is open to the public. But sadly this one is no longer functioning as a nunnery, having closed in very recent years. It is now both a craft centre and an historical farming exhibition, and also has superbly laid-out gardens. While the latter are well worth seeing, it is the nunnery that draws one's attention in the present context. One can wander around the buildings and gardens where the nuns lived, prayed and worked. Of particular interest is the double Church, divided down the middle except at the altar end, a feature that has already been described in connection with earlier Abbeys - as at Wimborne - for the separation of female and male worshippers. (At Stapehill it was for separation of the nuns from the general public.) Although built in what might be termed a traditional style, the nunnery at Stapehill is not a mediaeval nunnery however; it only began its life at the beginning of the 19th Century.[8,9]

Stapehill in the parish of Hampreston belonged to the Arundels of Wardour from the 16th to the 19th Centuries. As might be expected with this staunch Roman Catholic family, and with the secluded position of Stapehill (at least it was secluded in those times), the house became a hot-bed of recusant activity from the 16th Century onwards. Indeed, its close proximity to Canford gave rise to the legend - still persisting today - that the two houses were connected by a mile-long tunnel so that the Roman Catholic priests could freely communicate with each other.

In 1802 Stapehill - which was little more than a semi-derelict farmhouse - was offered by Lady Arundel to a group of Cistercian nuns who had fled from the French Revolution. They were from the Royal Abbey of St Antoine de Champs in Paris, and had been imprisoned under sentence of death. After the murder of Robespierre in 1794, they had fled to Switzerland under the leadership of twenty-five-year-old Marie-Rosalie de Vergeres de Chabannes (later to be Mother Augustin de Chabannes). She had taken vows seven years earlier under the name of Sister Augustin as a Cistercian, vowed to a life of silence. Under her leadership, and disguised as peasants, the group of nuns escaped on foot to St Valais in Switzerland, but after a few years they were off on their travels again after France conquered and occupied Switzerland. They travelled through Germany, Austria, Poland and Russia before returning again to Hamburg in Germany. It was there that Mother Augustin de Chabanne and three others separated from the rest of the group and sailed to England.

They arrived in London in 1801 and stayed there for ten months, before being offered the farmhouse at Stapehill by Lady Arundel. For nine months they resided at Burton House near Christchurch while necessary alterations were made at Stapehill, by which time their numbers had increased to ten. The nuns had expressed a wish to find a more secluded place away from

London, and close to a similar Cistercian establishment for monks: these latter would be able to supply their needs for male chaplains, confessors and administers of the Sacrament. Stapehill fulfilled this requirement, for only a few years earlier, as a result of the generosity of Thomas Weld, six Cistercian monks had set up a small community at Lulworth. Its proximity to Stapehill (20 miles) met the criteria, and the ten nuns took up their residence at Stapehill on 21 October 1802, still under the leadership of Mother Augustin de Chabannes.

Initially the nuns resided in the farmhouse while the rest of the monastery (later raised to an Abbey) was slowly built. [Some of the original rooms, and particularly the kitchen with its old cooking range, are still to be seen there.] The ten nuns tried to work the barren land to make themselves self-sufficient - as is required of the Cistercians - but in 1804 they hired a farmer, Charles Hock, to live near their farmhouse and help them on their farm. Initially he received annual wages of £10 to be paid "in sickness and in health". Under the guidance of Farmer Hock the nunnery flourished as the garden and fields became more and more productive. They certainly needed to be self-sufficient, for their only other regular income was a small pension paid by the British Government to all French refugees. At first they were also helped with supplies of milk from the monks at Lulworth, who later presented them with their first cow.

May 3rd was the Patronal Festival of Stapehill Abbey, the Feast of the Invention of the Holy Cross, but on that day in 1818 the young community at Stapehill received a serious set-back when a fire broke out in an out-building. It spread quickly and within two hours the Guest Room, wash-house, stable, barns and cow-sheds were totally destroyed, and the farm-house and monastery threatened. The Mother Superior, Madame de Chabanne, seized their fragment of the Holy Cross, threw it into the flames, and prayed for deliverance. What happened next was later described by the nuns as a miracle: the fire stopped and from the ashes the relic was later retrieved, completely unscathed. Every year on the anniversary of this event the nuns always held a special service of Thanksgiving for their deliverance from total destruction, and to commemorate this miracle.

Madame de Chabanne, who had been their leader during their wanderings from Paris at the time of the French Revolution, remained their Abbess until her death on 13 June 1844 at the age of eighty-five: she was buried within the precincts of the Abbey, and her name can still be seen on a stone cross within the walls of the former cemetery, along with those of her fellow-nuns.

From these small beginnings, the Abbey of Our Lady of the Holy Cross of La Trappe flourished at Stapehill throughout the 19th Century until by 1904 there were up to sixty nuns in residence there. But fewer and fewer girls wished to take up the very strict life of this silent Order, and numbers declined in the 20th Century, until by 1989 there were insufficient nuns to maintain Stapehill, and it was sold. The remaining handful of nuns left to start a new life at Whitland in Dyfed, South West Wales.

Whereas all the other Abbeys of Dorset described previously - Wimborne, Shaftesbury, Horton and Tarrant Crawford - were destroyed in the 16th Century, Stapehill still retains something of the atmosphere of what life must have been like for all the women of Dorset who lived there.

NUNS OF MARNHULL

Like the nuns of Stapehill, those at Marnhull also came to Dorset to escape from the French Revolution, but what a very different reception they received![n,9,12] The scattered village of Marnhull lies peacefully between Shaftesbury and Sherborne, and in 1795 it became the home of these seventeen Benedictine nuns who had escaped from the horrors of Paris. During the Reign of Terror following the execution of the French King in 1793 they had been confined as prisoners, but following the creation of the National Assembly the following year they had come to England and settled at Marnhull.

Their monastery in Paris had been in the Rue de Champ d'Alouette, Fauxbourg St Marcel since 1664, following its foundation in 1651 by the Royalist refugee Clementine Cara, whose father Viscount Falkland had been killed serving Charles I. It had been founded by, and remained solely for the benefit of, Englishwomen. This possibly helped in their coming through two years of confinement/imprisonment at various places in Paris during the Revolution, until they were at last liberated in 1795. They were virtually destitute and had to sell their remaining belongings to pay their fares to England.

They reached London on 5 July and as a result of being befriended by its owner Lady Arundel, they were offered a home at Nash Court in Marnhull which, by coincidence, had become available to let on the very day they had arrived in England. Under their Abbess, Abbess Johnson, the eighteen English nuns arrived at Marnhull where they were to remain for twelve years, a time that was not to be as tranquil as they had hoped. The local people were suspicious of these black-veiled strangers right from the time of their arrival. Not only were they Roman Catholic in an area with strong Non-Conformist leanings, but they were from France - a country of which the English had long had a great distrust.

The nuns had also been befriended by a lady (name unknown) who was an heiress of a Cuthbert Tunstall. She was a frequent visitor and benefactress. On her visits to Marnhull she both lived and slept in the nunnery, but kept a separate table from the nuns. Her maidservant, being a Protestant, was not allowed to sleep there and boarded in the village. This gave rise to further speculation among the villagers that "odd things" were going on in the nunnery at night.

In common with other nunneries through the ages, they had male priests visiting them to hear confessions and to administer the Sacrament. On one of these visits a priest (Abbé Charles Leonard Premond) was seen to be accompanied by several large and heavy trunks. This time the idle village gossip turned into greater and greater speculative rumour until it became "a definite fact". The nuns were really French Revolutionaries in disguise, and the trunks were full of weapons and ammunition. These French*men* were going to join up with others, similarly smuggled in as nuns, and start an uprising in England!

Eventually the authorities were roused to action, and a magistrate with appropriate support from the village arrived to search the trunks at the nunnery. It was with something approaching disbelief that the trunks were found to contain .....old books! They were purely a benevolent gift from the priest to the nuns, of a valuable library of old books and manuscripts to replace those they had lost in France.

The distrust of the villagers was not completely vanquished by this simple explanation, and it was not long before the magistrate was back. This time he had an authority to search for Napoleon Bonaparte, whom the nuns were suspected of concealing under their protection. Another fruitless search, needless to say!

But still the villagers remained suspicious of these black-robed and veiled "foreign" residents who kept themselves to themselves. All sorts of rumours spread about the various dubious activities going on behind closed doors, and matters finally came to a head when it was suspected that a body had been buried in the back garden at Nash Court. This time the rumours were correct, for subsequent investigation revealed that one of the seventeen nuns had died - of natural causes claimed the nuns - and following their usual custom, she had been buried within the precincts of the nunnery. The suspicions of the villagers about these strange females were at last vindicated. But surprisingly, what had chiefly aroused the ire of the local inhabitants was not that someone had died, nor that she had been buried by the nuns in secret, but that this had all happened without that ceremony enshrined in the hearts of all English people - a Coroner's Inquest!

The ensuing outcry against the nuns was the last straw as far as they were concerned. They had come to England to escape one kind of persecution, only to face one of a different kind. Before long the "obnoxious" nuns (as the local people called them) departed from Nash Court in 1807 and went to a new home at Cannington, near Bridgwater in Somerset. The parishioners of Marnhull were at peace at last.

ANCHORESSES OF TARRANT

It was at Tarrant Crawford that Joan, daughter of King John, wife of Alexander II of Scotland and later Queen of Scotland, was presented with the nunnery re-founded by Bishop Poore in 1230 (see Chapter 6) and where she was subsequently buried. At about the same time at the nearby hamlet of Tarrant Keynes(ton), three sisters "of gentle birth" decided to retire from the world and become anchoresses. It was to them that Bishop Richard Poore addressed his famous treatise *Ancren Riwles* (Rules for Anchoresses).[d,10,11]

Being anchoresses and leading this hermit-like life had been in existence long before the beginning of Christianity, but since early Norman times it was becoming more and more popular among Christians both here and on the Continent. The number of women wishing to cut themselves off in this way had been steadily increasing in the century previous to these three sisters becoming anchoresses at the beginning of the 13th Century. Anchoresses were not completely cut off from the world; they needed at least one servant to assist them, as they were bricked-up into a small cell against the outside wall of a Church. They would never again leave this cell for the rest of their lives, but were still in communication with the outside world through a grated window, by means of which they could talk and receive their food.

It was to these three anchoresses at Tarrant that the treatise by Bishop Poore was addressed personally, and not to anchoresses in general, as indicated by:

> "There is much talk of you, how gentle women you
> are; for your goodness and nobility of mind beloved of many;
> and sisters to one father and one mother; having, in the bloom
> of your youth, forsaken all the pleasures of the world and
> become anchoresses."

He went on to detail their daily life, religious and secular ; how they were not to be liberal with other people's alms; not to buy and sell ("a buyer and seller selleth her soul to the chapman of hell"); not to possess any animal except a cat; to talk "with maidens and direct yourself together with instructive tales". This last is interesting for it strongly suggests that their hermit-like cells were close enough together so that the sisters could easily speak to each other, or even that they shared one cell.

In the *Ancren Riwles* the three anchoresses were instructed not to wear hair shirts, go barefoot, or scourge themselves; and they were not to have no contact with outsiders as had been the advice to anchoresses in the previous century by Ailred, Abbot of Rievaulx. Instead, Bishop Poore permitted them a little gossip through the grating of the window with carefully-selected people. He advised them that it would be better not to run a school for girls - as the majority of anchoresses did by teaching them through the grill - unless by doing so, it prevented them from being taught with boys! (This provides the interesting insight that co-educational schools existed at that time.)

By being sealed into their cells the anchoresses were therefore cut off from the world in a physical rather than a mental way. What was brought out by the *Ancren Riwles* was the manner in which anchoresses were being increasingly considered as the literal and spiritual brides of Jesus, having rejected their traditional role of wife and mother. Bishop Poore compared this religious marriage with all the erotic joy of a worldly wedding:

> "After the kiss of peace in the Mass.....forget there all the world, and there be entirely out of the body, there in glowing love embrace your beloved spouse Christ, who is come down from heaven into the bower of your breast, and hold him fast till he have granted all you wish....."

SAINTS OF DORSET

As well as life in nunneries in Anglo-Saxon times, we also have considerable information about three Dorset women who became Saints in those times. Two of these, Wita and Judith, probably spent all their lives here; the other one, Walburga, was in Dorset for many years before going to Germany where she is far better known than here.

ST JUDITH/JUTHWARE

Although this Saint has taken her full place in the Calendar of Saints (July 13), and her fate is well known - an Italian friend of the author could relate every detail - very few people outside Halstock in Dorset are aware that this is the site of her death and martyrdom.[13]
    The name Halstock is believed to be derived from Halgan Stone or Holy Place, and by the 6th Century there is evidence that it was visited by monks who found a few devout Christians gathered there, giving instruction in the new faith of Christianity which was just starting to gain a tenuous hold in England.[7,12] As well as religious instruction the small community also taught handicrafts. Thus Halstock is supposed to have become a place of pilgrimage by the time of Judith.
    In spite of the knowledge of Judith's fate and subsequent martyrdom that has passed down to us, one crucial fact is missing - the date when it happened. It certainly occurred at some time between the 6th and 10th Centuries, probably nearer to the former date. As with so many stories of long ago, it is difficult to be certain which bits are fact and which are legend that may or may not have a grain of truth in them. In her book on the history of Halstock,[13] Pam Lemmey had researched the subject of Judith (or Juthware as she is also known) and come up with a story that appears most consistent between the different sources as follows.

Judith is said to have been a very pious Christian and befriended any pilgrims who came near her home in Halstock. She had a brother, Bana, and three sisters, Sidwella, Wilgitha, and Edwara: the latter three also later became Saints in Cornwall. After their mother's death they all continued to live at their father's home, even when he subsequently remarried. The new step-mother was said to be very jealous of her pious step-daughter Judith, and was always seeking ways to make trouble for her. A chance came one day when Judith complained of pains in her chest - probably a result of her prolonged devotional vigils in the Church, and repeated fasting. Her step-mother suggested that the pain would be relieved by the application of newly-made cheese to her chest, and Judith dutifully followed the advice.

The first stage of the step-mother's plan had gone well. Now she went to Judith's brother Bana, who was reputed to have a short temper, and told him that the virtuous Judith was pregnant. Bana straightway challenged Judith with this accusation as she was coming away from Church. In spite of her denial, Bana had the "evidence" of her guilt - the front of her undergarment was wet with milk (from the cheese). Full of rage at her apparent wrong-doing, Bana drew his sword and beheaded Judith.

At this point the body of Judith is said to have picked up her head and walked back into the Church where she laid it upon the altar to offer it to God. She was buried at the Church in Halstock, but in the 10th Century her relics were disinterred and taken to St Wulfstan's Church in Sherborne for final burial. Many miracles are said to have taken place at her tomb.

What is traditionally believed to be the site of Judith's death in Halstock - Abbot's Hill - is still known locally as Judith's Hill and, according to legend, this is the place where her ghost may still be seen, a young woman walking along carrying her head. Near the top of Abbot's Hill is a field known as Chapel's Close where formerly were ruins of a Chapel and a Priory, said to have been built on the site of Judith's home.

While these may or may not be the sites connected with Judith, there is one definite reminder of her in the village of Halstock - the inn sign. The village pub is known as *The Quiet Woman* [24] and the inn sign depicts Judith carrying her head.

ST WITA

Whatever our religion - if any - we should feel a little awe at the shrine of St Wita in the Church at Whitchurch Canonicorum, for this is the only intact shrine in the whole of the country apart from that of Edward the Confessor in Westminster Abbey. Such shrines played a large part in the lives of our ancestors, and here in this quiet village Church we can see exactly what they saw all those centuries ago. The shrine stands in the North Transept of the Church; it contains a large cavity below, with three large oval apertures into it.

Above this is the tomb with a reliquary or lead casket sealed within. The casket contains bones which are almost certainly the bones of St Wita, believed to have died in the 9th Century. (The present tomb dates from the 13th Century.)

Who was St Wita, and why did her shrine come to be in a quiet and peaceful valley among the tumbling hills of West Dorset? It is quite amazing that although her shrine remains perfectly intact after many centuries, there is great uncertainty as to who she actually was. Christine Waters[14] has carefully examined the main contenders for the Saint whose shrine rests at Whitchurch Canonicorum, and has presented convincing evidence to exclude two of the principal and all the minor contenders.[25]

She has come down firmly on the side of Wita being a local Saxon hermitess who was killed by the Danes, probably during their major invasion at Charmouth in 831 A.D. She has suggested that a temporary chapel would have been built to house Wita's remains, and the probability that a more permanent building was erected about fifty years later at the instigation of King Alfred the Great. This King is known to have taken a great interest in those who had been martyred for their Christian faith at the hands of the pagan Danes. The present shrine was probably reconstructed in the 13th Century, but how it escaped obliteration at the Reformation in the 16th Century will never be known.

During the winter of 1899-1900 there was some movement of the walls and floor of the Church in the area of the shrine, and a crack that had been in the tomb for centuries widened. A piece of the broken stone was removed prior to repair, and within the tomb, lying on its side,was found the lead reliquary, whose presence had been completely unsuspected. This lead casket was nearly two and a half feet in length, and on its top was inscribed HIC REQESCT RELIQE SCE WITE ("here lies the relics of St Wita"). Inside the casket were the bones of a woman, probably about forty years of age: it would appear that the relics formed a complete skeleton, certainly at least a thousand years old.

What was this hermitess Wita doing in this part of Dorset prior to her death? It has been suggested that apart from her daily religious devotions she may have helped to take care of a nearby Holy Well - subsequently known as St Wita's Well and visited by all the pilgrims who visited her shrine. It has also been suggested that Wita maintained a beacon at the top of nearby Golden Cap, the highest point in the neighbourhood, and a landmark for sea-farers. She may also have acted as a guide for travellers. But all this is mere supposition, for the truth will never be known. All we have with certainty is that a shrine was built to contain her bones, the surest proof that this Dorset woman existed.

ST WALBURGA

Unlike the other two Dorset Saints just described who probably lived their whole lives in the County, Walburga was born in Devon and spent the last thirty-five years of her life in Germany. In between these two parts of her life she spent twenty-seven years in Dorset. She has already been mentioned briefly as one of the nuns who went from Wimborne to help Boniface, alias Winfrith in his missionary work in Germany.[1]

Walburga (Walpurga) was born in Devon in the 8th Century, her father being the Saxon chieftain Richard. It would appear that she came from a very religious background: her two brothers Winnibald and Willibald (both later to become Saints also) were Christian missionaries; her uncle was to become the great St Boniface; and an aunt, Lioba was already a nun at Wimborne when Walburga entered it at an early age (see pedigree 2.1 earlier). During Walburga's long stay at Wimborne, her two brothers accompanied their uncle, Boniface, as missionaries to try to convert the heathen of Northern Europe, principally in what is now Germany. As described earlier, Boniface eventually wrote to Abbess Tetta of Wimborne asking for a group of nuns to go out and help them in their task. Ten nuns were sent in about the year 750, and included in their number were Walburga and her aunt Lioba.

Walburga's two brothers had founded a monastery at Heidenheim in what is now Germany, and it was to this place that she went to become Abbess of the nuns attached to it. When her brother Winnibald died ten years later, the Bishop of Eichstatt appointed Walburga to be Abbess of the whole monastery, monks as well as nuns. In addition to her life of devotion within the monastery, Walburga became best known and loved for her work outside the monastery, caring for the sick. She had a wide knowledge of the medicine of the time - herbal and other natural cures - learned during her time at Wimborne. It is for this reason that she is usually depicted carrying an ampulla of healing oil.

After her thirty-five years work in Germany she died in the year 779, but it was not until 1 May 870 that her bones were translated to Eichstatt to be buried beside her brother Winnibald. When her bones were disinterred it was observed that an oily substance was dripping from them, which was subsequently shown to have healing properties. The oil has continued to flow during the centuries since, usually between October and March, and it is regularly collected by the nuns who bottle it into tiny phials and send it around the world to effect cures. Through this, St Walburga has become one of the best known Saints.[4]

But Walburga has also given her name to a very un-Christian event.[4] The date of her translation from Heidenheim to Eichstatt - the first day of May - has become known as her feast day. It is very likely that the choice of this date had something to do with the Church of those times trying to "Christianize" pagan festivals.

In pagan times the night preceding the first day of May was known as Beltane, one of the occasions when witches flew around casting their evil spells, while the day itself had always been a great one for celebration. Substituting the feast day of St Walburga may therefore have been aimed at eliminating the pagan element but still permitting the day to be one of celebration. Unfortunately for them old traditions died hard, and the night of 30 April/1 May, known as *Walpurgasnacht* or *Walburga's Night* is still associated with witches, although the name of St Walburga herself is said to give complete protection against evil spells.

RECUSANT WOMEN OF DORSET

INTRODUCTION

Although the word "recusant" had been in use for many centuries to mean a person who "refused to submit to authority or to comply with some regulation or request" it took on a more specific meaning in the 16th Century when England was turned from the Roman Catholic to the Protestant religion at the Reformation. "Recusancy" acquired a legal definition in the first year of the reign of Queen Elizabeth I when anyone who failed to attend Church without a reasonable excuse was fined 12 pence for every offence, or £20 for every month that elapsed between attendances.

Thus at Dorchester on 12 December 1632, Ursula Ball was fined one shilling for absence from Church "although she was amending her stockings".[n] Poor Ursula! She didn't want to appear in Church with holes in her stockings and ended up having to pay a fine that would have kept her in stockings for many a year to come!

Gradually the word "recusant" began to apply specifically to Roman Catholics, for whom the laws were much more severe. They were fined up to one hundred marks (£66-13s-4d) for hearing Mass, doubled if they were the one saying it, and they were also liable for up to a year's imprisonment. Anyone convicted of recusancy was also prevented from inheriting lands and property, keeping or teaching in a school, or travelling more than five miles from their home without a special licence: neither could they hold any public office or bring any action in law.

The case of Elizabeth Tregonwell of Milton Abbey has been described elsewhere (see Chapter 1), where she was reported to the authorities for recusancy - probably by her grandson - and had to undergo an examination by five Justices of the Peace. Almost certainly the authorities were perfectly aware that she and her family - and many other local families - were practising Roman Catholics, but they turned a blind eye until someone made an official complaint. As the principal families were all inter-connected by marriage anyway, it probably explains why Lady Tregonwell got off the charge so lightly. (Other cases are described in Rachel Lloyd's book *Dorset Elizabethans*.[j]) Unfortunately, most of the Catholic records of these times relating to Dorset were accidentally destroyed. It was not until 1829 that the Catholic

Emancipation Act finally granted toleration to Roman Catholics. Although the worst of the persecution of Roman Catholics in the 16th Century ended with the death of Queen Elizabeth I in 1603, everyone was still required to take an oath of loyalty to the new King, James I, swearing to accept him as the head of the English Church - which Catholics were unable to do as it denied the spiritual sovereignty of the Pope. Additionally, everyone was required to make at least one attendance a year at their Parish Church and to receive Communion there. The enforcement of these laws varied from place to place and from time to time. Dorset appears to have been very tolerant, and it was probably to escape from some kind of persecution that the Brereton sisters left their home near Taunton to come and reside in West Dorset.[15]

THE BRERETON SISTERS

In 1620 the Brereton sisters, Winifred and Elizabeth, purchased Benville Manor just south of Corscombe. Their choice of Benville may have been influenced by its proximity to Toller Whelme, the Catholic "stronghold" owned by the Penne family. On an October day in 1626, one of their servants, Robert Warham, was out on business when he was told by a neighbour from nearby West Chelborough, that the latter had just come from the *Swann Inn* at Evershot, a little under three miles away: while there he had heard a troop of soldiers planning to visit Benville Manor "to fetch out a seminary priest". Thus forewarned, Robert Warham was able to get back to the Manor and warn the sisters.

The Brereton sisters were aware of the ever-present danger of being attacked in this way, and had made plans accordingly. They locked all the doors and windows and put up barricades behind each. They were just in time, for up to the house tramped nine soldiers accompanied by two chapmen (salesmen) and with the tapster from the *Swann Inn* acting as their guide. When the front door proved too strong, they began an onslaught on the back door. As it began to give way, the Brereton sisters and their staff retreated up the wide staircase and barricaded themselves behind furniture and bedding, prepared for the worst. One of the servants fired a gun out of a window, hoping to attract the attention of neighbours who would come to their help, but to no avail.

When one of the defenders called to the attackers to ask what they wanted, they replied that they were going to kill everyone in the house and "have out the old friar". Among the terrified defenders only Winifred Brereton kept her head. She wrapped several gold coins in a cloth and threw them out of the window to fall at the feet of the attackers. They had got what they were really after, for as soon as they realised what the cloth contained, they were off to the nearest inn at Rampisham, and peace came back to Benville Manor.

It is a similar case to Lady Tregonwell in that it appears that all the local people were fully aware that the Brereton sisters were Catholics, but nothing and nobody had interfered with them in the six years they had been living at Benville, until some visiting soldiers became the worse for drink. Somehow the talk at the *Swann Inn* must have turned to Catholics and presumably it was the tapster who told the soldiers about the Breretons. It is noticeable that the attacking party contained no local men - apart from the tapster - and it was a local man who warned the Breretons' servant about the impending attack. On the other hand, although no local people joined the attackers, neither did any of them come to the aid of the defenders, either in advance of the arrival of the attackers or in response to the firing of the gun from the window,

The following morning the evil-doers were first arrested by their Commanding Officer and then handed over to the local Constable, who in turn took them to Dorchester Prison. Or at least he would have committed them if he could have got them there, for he only arrived with two soldiers and the two chapmen, the rest either having run away or been rescued by their fellow-soldiers. The records of the outcome of their trial have not survived: it would have been an interesting problem, for they were being prosecuted for trying to "arrest" a suspected Roman Catholic priest, who was still "illegal" at the time.

But that is not the end of the Brereton sisters and a Court case. Some years later Winifred Brereton married George Arundel (of the well-known Chideock Catholic family) and went to live at Brinsham Farm in Netherbury, leaving Elizabeth on her own at Benville Manor. Her servant Robert Warham - the one who had received the advance warning of the attack - also steps back into the picture, for it is two of his kinsmen, John and George Warham, who persuade Elizabeth Brereton to enter a religious community of Augustinian nuns at Bruges in Belgium. On behalf of Elizabeth's sister, Winifred Arundel, her husband now brought an action against George and John Warham in the Chancery Court in London, claiming that they illegally held some land that had formerly belonged to Elizabeth by virtue of having been left to her in her mother's will.

At first sight this appears to be just one of the many thousands of such cases brought to determine the rightful owner of land or property. This is a case with a difference, for the Dorset litigants - both claimants and defendants - were all Catholics at a time when an open declaration of Catholicism could still result in serious penalties, and Catholics were still not able to bring any action in law (see earlier). It has been suggested[15] that even though it was widely known in Dorset that all parties were Catholic, this information may not have been passed to the Chancery Court in London. One difficulty of this explanation, however, is that the Chancery Commissioners actually went to Bruges to take a deposition from Elizabeth Brereton, where she could hardly have hidden the fact that she was a nun. The Warhams eventually won the case, principally on Elizabeth's evidence that she had indeed made the estate over to them.

OTHER LAY RELIGIOUS WOMEN OF DORSET

INTRODUCTION

Prior to the Reformation it was very common for widows, particularly if they were older, to enter a monastery to end their days in peace, but without becoming a nun. Many chose this because they had no wish to be remarried: others chose it perhaps to make way for their son and daughter-in-law to succeed to their inheritance without interference from an unwelcome member of the older generation. Again, some may have entered a nunnery because they may have felt the need to atone for misdeeds in their life. After the death of her husband, Ela of Canford retired to the Abbey she had founded at Lacock, where she eventually became its Abbess (see Chapter 1). Many others neither took the veil nor went to live in a nunnery, but still devoted the later years of their lives to religious works. Such a one was Margaret Beaufort.

MARGARET BEAUFORT

Anyone visiting Wimborne Minster cannot fail to be impressed by the beautiful tomb in the Chancel erected by Margaret Beaufort to her parents, the Duke and Duchess of Somerset.[16,17] It is rapidly approaching five hundred years since it was built (about 1498) and yet apart from minor damage, it still stands in a very good state of preservation, a testimony to the great quality of the Purbeck marble used in its construction and to the high standard of craftsmanship at that time. Perhaps the most striking and certainly the most unusual feature of the tomb is the way that the husband and wife are quietly holding hands between them - a sure sign of the affection that they held for each other. Or is this tender love sign just wishful thinking on the part of their only daughter, who erected the tomb fifty-four years after the death of her father, a father she barely knew?

Margaret Beaufort was born in 1441 on her father's estate at Kingston Lacy. She was not quite three years old when her father died in 1444 at the age of thirty-nine, and was buried at Wimborne, then still a monastery. Almost immediately afterwards Margaret Beaufort and her mother, also Margaret, departed to go and live with her mother's family, the Beauchamps, on their estates in Bedfordshire. Her mother had already been a widow with two sons at the time of her marriage to John Beaufort, Duke of Somerset, having previously been married to Oliver St John (see Chapter 6). A few years later she was to marry for a third time.

Margaret Beaufort's connection with Dorset was therefore severed at a very early age, when it is unlikely that she had any memories of either the place or her father. She was not to return until towards the end of her life when, apart from the tomb to her parents, she also founded the Grammar School and endowed a Chantry and Almshouses in Wimborne. It would be interesting to know what brought Margaret Beaufort back to Dorset after so many years, particularly when one considers the life she had been forced to lead in the intervening years. She was betrothed at the age of seven and married at fourteen to Edmund Tudor (see pedigree 6.2 in Chapter 6).[19] Within the year she was widowed and shortly afterwards in 1457, gave birth to a son Henry (later to become King Henry VII). Those were very troubled times, for it was the middle of the Wars of the Roses and Margaret Beaufort and her son were closely caught up in them.

By the time Margaret's son Henry was three years old, the Yorkist Edward IV was on the throne (1461-1483) while Margaret of Anjou was rallying the Lancastrian forces on behalf of her weak and insane Lancastrian husband, Henry VI, and her son Edward (see Chapter 6). Leaving her young son to the care of his uncle, Jasper Tudor, Margaret Beaufort married a second time, to Lord Stafford the eldest son of the Duke of Buckingham. Before long she was widowed and married for a third time, to Lord Stanley, a high figure in the Yorkist administration. The full story of these marriages will probably never be known, but they were almost certainly both political marriages, for Margaret was fully aware that after the deaths of Henry VI and his son Edward in 1471 (see Chapter 6), her son Henry - through her - was the heir to the Lancastrian claim to the throne.

Through these years of the Wars of the Roses the young Henry and his uncle Jasper Tudor, lived at the Court of Brittany. There was constant communication between mother and son, often in very difficult circumstances, that kept Henry Tudor and his uncle fully informed of what was happening in England, and she also gave them much advice. At last in 1485 when she was only forty years old she had the great delight of seeing her son land in Wales and go on to the Battle of Bosworth where he defeated King Richard III and became crowned as King Henry VII. She probably played a major part in planning his marriage to the Yorkist Princess, Elizabeth Woodville, that finally brought the Wars of the Roses to an end.

Before long her son granted Corfe Castle to Margaret Beaufort for her life: he repaired the Castle with a grant of £2,000 from Parliament to pay for it, and it was here that she based her home. She did spend time at Court however, and also helped to found two Oxford Colleges. She became a patron of William Caxton who introduced printing to England, and also of his successor Wynkin de Worde. She also found time to translate Thomas a Kempis' *The Imitation of Christ* into English for the first time, and saw it printed.

In spite of her enormous vitality, she was rapidly beginning to wind down her public life and devote herself more and more to religious and other charitable works. She died peacefully in 1509 at the age of sixty-eight, three months after the death of her beloved son in whose cause she had devoted so much of her life. She did make one brief return to public life just before she died when she became an adviser to the new King, her grandson Henry VIII, who was only aged eighteen when he succeeded to the throne.[q] It is said that it was from her that he probably inherited his enormous energy and zest for life.

In later life Margaret Beaufort always dressed as a nun and wore a wimple.[18] After the death of her third husband she even took a vow of chastity. As well as building the tomb to her parents in Wimborne Minster, she also planned to found a Chantry at Wimborne with a priest to say Mass for the souls of herself, her son Henry VII, and her parents. She died before this was done, but her grandson, Henry VIII, gave permission to her executors to carry out her wish. Her grant of lands and property to this endowment paid for the services of the Chantry priest. She also wished this priest to teach the children of the town of Wimborne at no charge, all costs to be borne by her endowment, thus laying the foundations of the Free Grammar School. It is almost certainly this close association of Margaret Beaufort with Wimborne Minster that preserved the Church from damage at the time of the Dissolution of the monasteries, carried out at the instigation of her grandson.

UNSAINTLY BEHAVIOUR

INTRODUCTION

Earlier in this chapter some insight was given into what life was like in nunneries in the early centuries of the Christian Church in England. Strict observance of religious services, devotion and study were very prominent parts of the life of these nuns. Occasionally there is a suggestion that all was not as it should have been: the novices who danced on the grave of their novice-mistress, for example.

It is well-known - or certainly believed by many - that these original high standards did not last down the centuries, but only occasionally do we have reports of actual misbehaviour. For example Hutchins[h] cites the instance of "the disreputable Abbot of Abbotsbury, Walter de Stokes, who kept many more than three women". No doubt many misdemeanours were covered up or, if they were recorded, then the records were lost at the time of the Dissolution. The many legends that have come down to us of the existence of underground passage-ways between nearby nunneries and monasteries suggest that local gossip was aware of "goings-on" between the two establishments.

The following examples are only a very minor part of the total lives led in the various monastic establishments, and the reader will appreciate that they do not represent the majority, who led unblemished lives. Nevertheless, these examples do show that all was not well all of the time.

KIDNAPPED NUNS OF WILTON

Two nuns made a visit to Dorset at the end of the 13th Century, but we will never know whether they came willingly or unwillingly.[dn] They were abducted from the nunnery at Wilton and brought to Shaftesbury where they, together with their abductor, were subsequently brought before the Archbishop of Canterbury, when he paid it a visit in the year 1285. From the nature of the punishment meted out, it would appear that the nuns were not exactly kidnapped, but had been more than willing to leave their nunnery. Their names, their ages, and their backgrounds are not disclosed, so we do not know whether, for example, they had entered the nunnery wishing to dedicate themselves to God or, as is more likely, they had been sent there merely to be educated.

Life in a nunnery at that time may not have been entirely what we expect. We have a contemporary description of life at nearby Amesbury, the so-called "Royal Nunnery" because it was favoured by many members of the royal family in those days - at one time there were five in residence there. One of these was Mary, born in 1278 as the sixth daughter of King Edward I. She "made her profession" at the age of five, together with thirteen similarly-aged daughters of the nobility who had been chosen to accompany her. It is recorded that this royal princess was frequently allowed to make visits outside the nunnery, being always present at weddings, baptisms and other celebrations of members of her family: she made frequent visits to shrines in various parts of the country: she often stayed with relations for prolonged visits: her bed-linen and table cloths were of the finest linen: she had green cushions filled with down to ease the hardness of the wooden benches in her cell: she played dicing games for money and she encouraged minstrels, play-writers, etc.

Hardly a life typical of what one would expect of a nun? And if that was going on at a nunnery a few miles away, it is very likely that a similar way of life at Wilton may have played a large part in contributing to the willingness of these two nuns to be "abducted" to Dorset.

The "abductor" was Sir Osbert Gifford, and presumably on the complaint of the Abbess, he was excommunicated by the Archbishop, but this was absolved on the following conditions:

- that he should never come into a nunnery or into the company of nuns,
- that he should, for three Sundays together, be stripped and whipped in his Parish Church of Wilton, and as many times in the market and Parish Church of Shaftesbury
-that he should fast for a certain number of months,
-that he should not wear a shirt for three years,

-that he should not take upon himself the habit or title of a knight,
-that he should not wear any apparel but of a russet colour, with lamb
  sheepskins
-that he should restore the nuns to their convent to undergo like punishment.

It is a pity that we do not know the end of the story. Did the two nuns undergo their punishment without a murmur? Did they suffer any remorse? Did they remain at the nunnery for the rest of their lives or, having once tasted freedom, did they decide that they would prefer life outside?

MISTRESSES AT CERNE ABBEY

Some women in Cerne seem to have been living in quite comfortable surroundings in the first part of the 16th Century. They were well-housed, well-fed, well-clothed, and their children were well-looked after too. The only thing wrong was that they were living in the cellars of Cerne Abbey, and their food, clothing and child-care came from monastic funds. For these were the mistresses of the last Abbot there.

Their comfortable life came to an abrupt end in 1535 when the conscience of one of the monks at Cerne Abbas became too much for him and he reported the state of affairs to the Bishop. The Abbot was accused of "a great outburst of fertility", that he had squandered monastic funds on his progeny, and that he had openly solicited women in the streets, many of whom had ended up in his harem. The Abbot wasn't alone in his misbehaviour for other monks were accused of openly consorting with prostitutes and, even worse, had celebrated Mass without prior confession of these sins.

The women were ejected from the Abbey, and the Abbot and his monks were ordered to remain within the confines of the Abbey. The Abbot was later permitted to ride out from the Abbey so long as he was only on official business. The restrictions on all the monks were not to last for long, however, for it was only four years later when everyone was ejected from the Abbey as Sir John Tregonwell took possession of it for King Henry VIII. Presumably there were no longer any women in residence in the cellars then, but what had become of them?

3
CRIMES AND WOMEN
OF DORSET

INTRODUCTION

If one considers various crimes and the criminals who commit them, it is the subject of murder that arouses most interest: so it has always been down the centuries. In recent years the one major change has been the abolition of the death sentence for murder, but what changed greatly over previous centuries was the manner in which suspected persons were tried and the verdict arrived at, in all trials including that of murder.

The jury system only started in Norman times, but it was based on an earlier process whereby if the accused could produce enough witnesses who would swear on oath that the accused was innocent, then that verdict was accepted. An alternative was usually trial by ordeal. One version of this has been described elsewhere in this book (see Chapter 5) when Emma, the mother of King Edward the Confessor, underwent such a trial by walking over heated ploughshares. They were red-hot and if she was able to walk over them unscathed - as she did - then she was immediately deemed innocent. Similar trials by ordeal involved plunging a hand into a cauldron of boiling water, picking up a red-hot iron bar and holding it while walking three paces. The hand was then bound for three days: when unbandaged, the presence of a blister larger than a walnut was taken as a sign of guilt.

Trial by ordeal was abolished in 1219, but the equally-ancient trial by combat survived for another three centuries. The accused would attempt to establish innocence by challenging their accuser to a duel. A substitute could be used in the case of women and priests, the old and the sick. [Such a duel was fought by (a substitute for) the Bishop of Sherborne to establish rightful ownership to the Castle.] The judges in these earlier forms of trial were the persons in whose jurisdiction the crime had been committed: the King, a baron or a Lord or Lady of the manor. It may be remembered that the Abbess of Shaftesbury shared this duty with the King for the Manor of Shaftesbury (see Chapter 2). In many cases it was realised that fining people rather than punishing them was a large source of revenue to the person who had the jurisdiction, and again the Abbess of Shaftesbury was one who benefited in this way from fines, and also outlawry and the confiscation of goods of the convicted felon.

71

Lesser crimes were punishable in the stocks, the pillory and the ducking-stool. While people sat with their legs confined in the stocks, they had to stand with their necks and wrists in the pillory, when it was not unknown for people to die. In some cases a concession to women given a sentence in the stocks required them to put only one leg in the stocks, thus preserving their dignity and enabling them to defend themselves against sexual assault. A typical sentence to the stocks, from Dorchester in 1631 reads "Alice Cox of Dorchester was ordered to be placed in the stocks for drunkenness," but the sentence was forborne for a week, she "being unfit to be stocked, and since was stocked". [Perhaps she was too drunk to appreciate the sentence and needed to sober up first.]

"Scolding women are to be placed in a Trebucket, commonly called a Cucking-Stool, [or Ducking-Stool] placed over some deep water, into which they are let down and plunged under water thrice to cool their choler and heat." is a 17th Century description of the Ducking-Stool as used for "immoral, nagging and scolding"women.[1] Every town and village would have had its ducking stool, and no doubt they were used frequently. Two examples of its use in Dorchester are:

"May 1631. Mary Tuxberry of Dorchester, for scoulding at the Sergeants when they did goe about for mersements [fines] was ordered to be plounced [ducked] when the weather was warmer." What considerate magistrates!

"January 1632. Four women are declared to have spent the most part of two days in scoulding and ordered to be plounced [ducked]."

There was no comparable punishment for men, but then it was very much a man's world in those times and hence no man would be charged with "scolding" his wife! Even a century later if a man was found guilty of murdering his wife, he was hanged; but if a wife was found guilty of murdering her husband then she was sentenced to be burned alive, occasionally being strangled by the executioner before being burned. Such was the sentence passed on Mary Channing of Dorchester in 1705.

MURDERS

MARY CHANNING

Lurid descriptions of public executions abound in the literature, with immense crowds of rich and poor alike jostling to obtain the best view-point, their mood varying according to whether their sympathies were with the criminal. To us this is repugnant, and we wonder how ordinary people could watch such a spectacle. But if a similar event was shown on television today, would we switch it off? Can we therefore honestly say that if we had been in Dorchester in 1705, we would not have been one of the crowd who flocked to watch the public execution of a 19 year-old-girl, Mary Channing?[din]

For centuries until as late as 1767, the old Roman amphitheatre at Maumbury Rings in Dorchester was the site for public executions. The arena with tiers of seats on all sides provided everyone with a good view and allowed a large crowd to be kept under control - as was the original purpose of the amphitheatre in Roman times.

On that day in 1705, the crowds started assembling in the early morning, although the execution was not scheduled to take place until later in the day. It was unlikely that anyone in that excited, expectant crowd had any sympathy for the young woman who was soon to meet her end, for she had been convicted of the deliberate murder of her innocent husband.

Mary Brooks, was born in 1687, the only child of Richard Brooks, a prosperous merchant of Dorchester, and his wife Elizabeth. She had been brought up in a manner that should have ensured her a good marriage. As well as being educated "with a proficiency suitable to one of her sex", she had also been taught social graces and dancing. She had seen something of the world on prolonged visits to both Exeter and London.

Returning to Dorchester at the age of eighteen, she embarked on a round of visiting, and attended innumerable parties, frequently using her neighbours as an alibi to her parents. At one party she met an (unnamed) young man with whom she fell madly in love. It is recorded that she wined and dined the young man at her own expense, bought him presents, and held a Ball in his honour. All this cost a lot of money, far more that the generous allowance made to her by her father, and she soon resorted to stealing from her parents to pay for her indulgences. Eventually her parents tried to put a stop to her behaviour by forcing her to marry, and they let it be known that she would have a large fortune as her marriage portion (in the event this never materialized).

Thomas Channing, a grocer of Dorchester with very respectable parents in Maiden Newton, asked for her hand in marriage, and he was accepted by Mary's parents. But Mary refused, believing that her lover would marry her. The young Lothario had other ideas, for he realised that if he married her against her parents' wishes, she would be cut off without a penny. It seems that Mary now found that she was pregnant with her lover's child, but being rejected by him, she gave in to her parents' wishes and agreed to marry Thomas Channing, primarily to be free of her parents' control. The wedding was arranged for Sunday 14 January 1705, but Mary had cold feet at the last minute, and cancelled it: mainly due to her mother's persistence, the marriage went ahead the next day.

Immediately after her marriage she reverted to her former life-style - even taking a new lover by the name of Mr Naile within three months of her marriage. In a very short time she had spent all her husband's money, and finding him very dull - and now penniless - Mary Channing determined to be rid of him. She used poison, believed to be white mercury, giving it to him on Monday 16 April in a glass of rice wine: when that didn't work, she gave him a much larger dose in another glass of wine, and he succumbed.

Mary Channing was promptly arrested, tried, found guilty of murder and sentenced to death. She pleaded pregnancy and her execution was delayed until after the birth of her child. Eighteen weeks later, in spring 1705, the sentence was carried out.

According to a contemporary newspaper record: "After the under-sheriff had taken her some refreshment, she was brought out of the prison, and dragged by her father's house, to the place of execution. She manifested nothing of alteration [confession of her guilt] when fixed to the stake, but justified her innocence to the very last, and left the world with a courage seldom found in her sex [!]. She being first strangled, the fire was kindled about five in the afternoon, and in the sight of many thousands of spectators she was consumed to ashes."

CHARLOTTE BRYANT

Charlotte Bryant was an illiterate Irishwoman in Londonderry when she met her future husband who was serving there as a British Military Policeman during "The Troubles" earlier this century. She returned with Frederick Bryant to Dorset where he worked as a labourer, and settled into an isolated cottage at Coombe, near Sherborne.[5,6] She was of slovenly habits and was later to be described as having nymphomaniac tendencies: she was also soon to become a well-known figure in the local public houses. Five children were born in rapid succession, but her husband appears to have turned a blind eye to her goings-on, even when it involved a lodger, Leonard Parsons. Like her husband, he was of a gypsy nature and stayed with the Bryants intermittently between 1933 and 1935, by which time Charlotte was thirty-three years of age.

In May 1935 Charlotte's husband was taken ill with what the doctor diagnosed as gastro-enteritis; within a few days he was able to return to work. His illness recurred on 11 December and yet again on 20 December. The day before this latter occurrence, Charlotte Bryant had visited a gypsy encampment near Weston-super-Mare in search of Leonard Parsons. He wasn't there and she received much abuse from his common-law wife, Priscilla Loveridge, and her mother, Mrs Penfold. How much this incident contributed to her action on the following day is uncertain, but her husband was then taken so violently ill that he was removed to hospital where he died two days later. *Post mortem* analysis revealed four grains of arsenic in his body. Although a tin containing arsenical weed-killer was found in a rubbish dump behind the house, the local police were unable to decide who was the murderer and called in the newly-formed Murder Squad of Scotland Yard.

Charlotte Bryant and her five children were removed to the local workhouse - the Sturminster Newton Institution - while the detectives gave her home a detailed search. They swept the dust from every cupboard, shelf, and other possible container, and tested all for the presence of arsenic [there must have been a lot of dust if Charlotte was as slovenly as made out to be]. Traces of arsenic were found in a pocket of one of Charlotte's coats, and when it was discovered that she had purchased the weed-killer a year earlier, she was arrested.

The following May Charlotte Bryant was tried for murder at Dorchester Assizes, found guilty and hanged at Exeter Prison on 15 July 1936. There was one light-hearted event in the trial, produced by the appearance of Parson's common-law wife, and in particular by her mother, Mrs Penfold. The latter made a colourful appearance in Court, wearing a trilby hat and "full of violent oaths against the accused". Doubt was later cast on Charlotte Bryant's ability to plead. She was of very limited intelligence, and did not understand many of the words put to her. She was unable to follow the proceedings of the trial and appeared to have little comprehension of what was happening to her. She would probably not have been brought to trial nowadays.

CONSTANCE KENT

It is extremely rare for a murderess (or a murderer) to leave a permanent mark behind them for all to see many years later. But that is exactly what has happened on the Isle of Portland. A visit to St Peter's Church in The Grove close by the former prison, reveals a building constructed entirely by erstwhile inmates. But walk inside and look at the mosaic paving in the Chancel, and you are looking at the workmanship of a self-confessed murderess, Constance Kent.[3]

Constance Kent was born in 1846 to the first wife of Samuel Kent, reputed to be the illegitimate son of the Duke of Kent, father of Queen Victoria. In 1854, after the death of his first wife, Samuel Kent married Miss Pratt, governess to Constance and her younger brother William. By 1860 another five children had been born and a further one was on the way. Constance, aged sixteen by this time, was later reported telling school-friends how unhappy she was at home.

On the night of 29-30 June 1860, Constance's four-year-old half-brother was taken from his bed in the nursery and next morning was found murdered in an outside privy. The child's nurse, Elizabeth Gough, who had been asleep in an adjacent bed in the nursery, was promptly arrested, but released due to lack of evidence. A blood-stained nightdress belonging to Constance was found, and in spite of no apparent motive, she was arrested: the magistrates released her on 27 July due to lack of conclusive evidence, on her father's security of £200. In September the nurse was re-arrested, and again released.

Shortly afterwards the Kent family moved to Wales from their home in Road, Wiltshire: Constance did not wish to accompany them and entered a convent at Dinant in France, where she lived for the next three years. Returning to England in August 1863, she entered another convent in Brighton.

On 27 April 1865 an astonishing letter appeared in *The London Times* from a doctor, which contained a copy of a confession to the murder made by Constance before Bow Street Magistrates. She had come voluntarily from Brighton, accompanied by a Reverend Wagner, the curate attached to the convent where she had been living. (It was afterwards suggested that great pressure had been brought upon her in Brighton to confess.) The doctor who wrote the letter to the newspaper had been asked to examine on her mental state, which he judged normal. The explanation for the murder was purely one of jealousy of the second family of her father, which she felt was highly-favoured to the detriment of her brother and herself.

Constance Kent appeared before the Assizes at Salisbury where, without a jury or a single witness being called, she was found guilty; the sentence of death was commuted to life imprisonment. And so Constance Kent found herself on Portland where, at some time between her arrival in 1864 and her release in 1885, she was responsible for the mosaic paving in St Peter's Church on the Isle of Portland that still greets the visitor today.

MRS HARBIN

An iron sun-dial on a wooden base stands by the side of the pathway leading to the Church at West Parley. It is said never to tell the correct time because of its gruesome association with a murder perpetrated by a Dorset woman in 1803.[4] Mrs Harbin had been told by her farmer-husband, William, that he intended to cut her out of his will. She determined to prevent him from doing so in the most brutal way possible, and persuaded her son and a male accomplice (said to be her lover) to murder him. They were soon caught, tried and found guilty.

A part of the gallows used to hang them was made into the wooden base of this sun-dial and presented to the vicar of West Parley. A gruesome reminder of an all-too-familiar love-triangle. [It is the same delightful little Church tucked away at the end of a long cul-de-sac that contains the heart of the Lady of Lydlinch mentioned elsewhere - see Chapter 9.]

WAT PERKINS

One of the most unusual solutions to a Dorset murder came with the help of a ghost.[9] Early in the eighteenth Century an (unnamed) widow lived at a cottage called Kit Whistle, close to the mansion of Chantmarle. She helped to make a living by serving refreshments to passers-by. One day a Scottish peddler had the misfortune to go along the road and made the fatal mistake of entering the cottage in search of refreshment. Exhausted by his travelling and warmed by the fire, he fell asleep, resting his head on the end of the settle. The sight of the drapery being carried in the peddler's pack proved too much for the poverty-stricken widow and she brutally cut his throat. She hid his head under the hearth-stone, and buried his body close by, in a ditch under a hedge.

Twenty-two years later, two workmen were clearing the ditch when they came across the skeleton, minus its skull. They told the widow at the nearby cottage of their discovery, and she is reported to have replied that if they kept quiet about it, then she would give them her best cow. As happens in rural areas, news of this event soon leaked out and eventually reached the ears of the authorities. When they investigated, the widow immediately confessed to the murder, telling them where she had hidden the head. She was arrested, tried, found guilty and suffered the death penalty.

And the ghost? For several years before the discovery of the skeleton, a ghost was heard in the Great Hall of nearby Chantmarle, on a date that was believed to coincide with the anniversary of the peddler's murder. On each occasion it is said to have called out three times, "Search for Wat Perkins!" The news of the ghost must have reached the old widow in the nearby cottage. Did it prey on her mind? Was the peddler's name Wat Perkins? Is this why she panicked and immediately confessed to the crime when challenged, especially as there could have been no possible evidence to link her with the crime after all those years? It is unlikely that a search involving lifting the hearth-stone to reveal the skull would have been instigated.

It is said that after her arrest the ghost of Chantmarle was never heard again!

MARTHA BROWN OF BIRDSMOORGATE

On 9 August 1856 Elizabeth Martha Brown was hung in public at the gates of Dorchester Prison.[7,8] Two weeks earlier she had been found guilty of the murder of her husband, an act committed on the preceding 6 July. It was a relatively-simple wife-battering case, as we would call it today, combined with an extra-marital affair, but there are several incidents that make it of interest. We have a verbatim account of the confession of Martha Brown, made the day before she died: the hanging was witnessed by the young Thomas Hardy and it was to make a lasting impression on him: and finally there is an anecdote of its connection with the illness known as "The King's Evil".

Martha Brown lived with her husband at Birdsmoorgate, and it was in their home that his dead body was found on 6 July 1856 with severe head injuries and covered with blood. Martha claimed that his injuries were caused by being kicked by his horse, a story which she later changed to him falling down stairs. A few days after the inquest and *post mortem* examination, Martha was arrested on a charge of murdering him. Less than three weeks later her case came up at the Dorchester Assizes. The defence made a very poor showing, with Martha clinging to her story that her husband had fallen down the stairs. It seemed such a clear-cut case that the jury didn't even leave the Court to consider its verdict, merely turning around to consult briefly with each other, before returning a verdict of guilty. The death sentence was pronounced on Martha Brown.

Additional evidence was brought out at the trial concerning an affair between John Brown and a neighbouring woman by the name of Mary Davis (or Davies). There was a strong outcry throughout Wessex that a crime of this nature - a *crime passionel* - should not be punished with the death sentence, Martha Brown having had to put up with a lot of strife due to her husband's misbehaviour. The *Dorset County Chronicle* of 1 August 1856 published a long article using Martha's case to advocate the abolition of capital punishment altogether. A petition for Martha's reprieve was hastily gathered and presented to the Home Secretary, but to no avail, and the sentence was duly carried out on 9 August 1856.

Martha Brown had been visited regularly in prison by both the chaplain and her own vicar, and on the day before her execution it was to these men that Martha Brown made her confession of what had actually happened a month earlier.

'Elizabeth Martha Brown states that:- My husband John Anthony Brown came home on Sunday 6th July at 2 o'clock, in liquor, and was sick. He had no hat on. I asked him what he had done with his hat. He abused me, and said "What is that to you? Damn you!" He then asked for some cold tea. I said I had none, but would make him some warm. His answer was - "Drink it yourself, and be damned." I then said "What makes you so cross? Have you been to Mary Davis's?" He then kicked out the bottom of the chair on which I had been sitting, and we continued quarrelling until 3 o'clock, when he struck me a severe blow on the side of the head, which confused me so much that I was obliged to sit down. He then said (supper being on the table at the time) "Get it yourself and be damned," and reached down from the mantelpiece a heavy hand-whip with a plaited head, and struck me across the shoulders with it three times and every time I screamed out. I said "If you strike me again I will cry 'Murder'". He replied, "If you do I will knock your brains through the window" and said "he hoped he should find me dead in the morning," and then kicked me on the left side, which caused me much pain. He immediately stooped down to unlace his boots and being much enraged, and in an ungovernable passion at being abused and struck, I seized a hatchet that was laying close to where I sat, and which I had been making use of to break the coal for keeping up the fire to keep his supper warm, and struck him several violent blows on the head - I could not say how many - and he fell to the fireplace and he never spoke or moved afterwards. As soon as I had done it. I would have given the world not to have done it. I had never struck him before after all his ill-treatment, but when he hit me so hard at this time, I was almost out of my senses and hardly knew what I was doing.'

When one reads this confession, one has great sympathy with the life that Martha Brown must have led with her husband - as have countless other wives over the centuries. But murder was murder and the Law said she was to hang. The newspapers of the time go into great detail about the execution which took place at the gates of the Prison, detailing that she only had a cup of tea for breakfast, that she walked from her cell to the gates of the Prison, declining the use of the prison van to transport her that distance, that she was accompanied by the Prison Chaplain and her vicar as well as the Prison officers, that there were eleven steps up to the "pinioning room" where her arms were tied together, and then another nineteen steps to the scaffold.

As mentioned at the beginning, this hanging made a great impression on Thomas Hardy who had witnessed it as a young boy. So much so that in later life, he contacted many of the local villagers around Birdsmoorgate who had been alive when the murder occurred. He found that almost unanimously they declared that Martha Brown should not have been hung, but that the "other woman", Mary Davis, should have been hung in her stead. It was also recalled by the villagers that on the day of the execution Mary Davis had to be forcibly restrained from going to attend the hanging, for it was feared that if she was seen there, it was quite likely that a lynch mob would take its revenge.

In the *Dorset Chronicle and Swanage Times* for 13 January 1936 there is an article about Martha Brown and this murder, written by a Mr A.C.Cox. He wrote that while researching the article, he had talked to an elderly saddler, Mr Mills of Dorchester, who told him a story about his father and the execution. When Mr Mills Senior was a young boy, he suffered from the disease known as "The King's Evil".[11] Although in earlier centuries it was believed that a cure for this disease was being touched by the King - hence its name - by the middle of the 19th Century, this had been replaced by the touch of a murderer (or murderess).

Accordingly, the young Master Mills was taken from his home at Martinstown to witness the execution, and afterwards his neck was rubbed with the dead hands of Martha Brown. The disease was cured. But as the writer Mr Cox said, the cure was more probably from the shock of the terrible experience on the young boy.

SARA GUPPY

Many people achieve fame by being "first" in a particular field, others by being the "last". Sara Guppy of Stoke Abbot was one of the latter group, but she was totally unaware of her fame on 10 August 1858, for by then she had been dead for just over three months.[2]

Twenty-three-year-old Sara was not very tall, and although slightly deformed, she was said to be a quick, lively, and intelligent person. She and her mother lodged with a labourer called Seale and his twenty-year-old son, James, in one of a pair of cottages in Anchor Lane. The other cottage was occupied by Seale's landlord called John Hutchings.

On Friday 30 April neighbours suddenly became aware that Sara's house was on fire. It was quickly put out and then they were horrified to discover her dead body lying in the kitchen with her throat cut. P.C.Lavender was assigned to the case and suspicion quickly fell on the young James Seale who had already served a four month sentence for robbing a child. He was arrested, tried and found guilty. He was hanged at the gates of Dorchester Prison on 10 August. It was in this way that Sara Guppy achieved her "last", for her murderer was the last person ever to be hanged in public in England.

MARY HOUNSELL OF POWERSTOCK

On various occasions when the relics of a Saint were translated - the remains dug up from their initial burial site and removed to their final resting place - it has been claimed that the body was in a perfect state of preservation, even after many years. This "lack of corruption" of the body has been taken as an indication of the sanctity of the person involved. But when the body of Mary Hounsell of Powerstock was disinterred in 1839, three months after its initial burial, and found to be completely preserved, the cause was entirely different. She had been poisoned with a large dose of arsenic.[10]

Mary was the wife of a cattle-doctor, John Hounsell. Over a period of nearly three weeks in November 1838, she was repeatedly taken ill with gastric pains and vomiting, and had twice been treated by a doctor. She eventually died on 16 November and was buried shortly afterwards, with apparently not the slightest suspicion attaching to the manner of her death.

During her illness Mary Hounsell had frequently been tended by a neighbour, Elizabeth Gale, who prepared herbal medicines for her, as well as encouraging her to eat a little food. This kindly neighbour was herself widowed soon afterwards when her husband, James Gale, died the following January. Again, not the slightest suspicion appears to have attached to his death.

But only two weeks later this new widow, Elizabeth Gale, and the widower, John Hounsell, approached the vicar of Powerstock, Rev George Cookson, with the request that he publish the banns of their forthcoming marriage. Apart from causing immediate local gossip, their indecent haste to remarry also seriously disturbed the vicar. So much so that he took it upon himself to employ someone to forbid the banns at the second publication, in order that a proper investigation might be made. Accordingly, he laid the matter before the County Coroner, who ordered the disinterment of both bodies.

On the night of 19/20 November 1839, the coffins of both the deceased spouses were dug up from the churchyard at Powerstock ready for the inquest and *post mortem* examination. The latter was particularly gruesome, not just from the nature of its findings, but from the manner in which it was conducted and in particular the site where it took place. The autopsy room was the Chancel of the adjacent Parish Church and the dissecting table was the Communion Table. Among those present in the Church, apart from the Coroner, the Jury of local men, and the Sexton, were half a dozen doctors from the area, most of whom had come out of pure curiosity to watch their two colleagues perform the *post mortem*. In addition there were several onlookers who watched the proceedings through the Chancel window - including the anonymous author of the report that subsequently appeared in *The Dorset Chronicle*.

It can be imagined what a shock it must have been to everyone present when the Sexton, after much persuasion, finally opened the first coffin and the body of Mary Hounsell was found in a complete state of preservation, even after three months in the ground. It was therefore with virtual disbelief that the second coffin, that of James Gale, revealed the horrific sight of a decomposed body consistent with its three weeks' burial.

Even when the perfectly-preserved body of Mary Hounsell left no-one in any doubt that she had been poisoned by arsenic, the adjourned inquest had to await the official analysis of the organs removed at the *post mortem* examination. These confirmed that Mary Hounsell had received many times the dose of arsenic needed to kill her, and without a moment's hesitation the Coroner's jury brought in a verdict of "Wilful Murder" against her husband, John Hounsell.

The second body, that of James Gale, confounded everyone's suspicions, for not only did it show the expected amount of decay, but the subsequent analysis revealed not a trace of arsenic. The local people - and perhaps the authorities also - remained convinced that he had been poisoned by some untraceable poison, but in the absence of any direct evidence, no charges could be brought against his widow.

John Hounsell was brought to trial at the Summer Assizes at Dorchester. It was clearly established that he had made repeated purchases of arsenic, but this was shown by the defence - with supportive evidence - to be a common medicine used in the treatment of diseases in cattle as part of Hounsell's work. After a straightforward but weak case for the prosecution, the defence set to work to show that there was an alternative explanation for Mary Hounsell's death. The arsenic, together with other drugs and medicines used by Hounsell, were kept on a shelf above the bed occupied by himself and his wife. It was suggested that Mary Hounsell herself, after nearly three weeks of sickness and fearing that she was dying, had taken the arsenic to save herself from a lingering death. When combined with the fact that there was no direct evidence to connect the husband with the administration of the arsenic, this alternative explanation threw enough doubt into the minds of the jurors, that they returned a verdict of "Not Guilty".

Much to everyone's surprise, the remaining banns of marriage between Elizabeth Gale and John Hounsell were read in the Church at Powerstock, but there is no record that the marriage subsequently went ahead, or indeed of what happened to the bereaved widow and widower.

KIDNAPPING

MARY SQUIRES

The story of Mary Squires is not of a crime committed by or against her in Dorset, and yet the County featured largely in a 1752 Court case in which she was involved. The wanderings of Mary Squires around Dorset have been examined in great detail by Darton in his book *The Marches of Wessex*[d] published in 1923: his analysis of the affair makes interesting reading, and he reaches a new conclusion to explain the Dorset part of the affair - that the Squires family were involved with the smuggling trade. Although Mary was only in Dorset for two weeks on this particular visit, she had obviously been here many times before and was well known to many of its inhabitants. She was a very distinctive person, or rather a person with a very distinctive feature. Mary Squires was about seventy years of age at the time of this incident, tall and dark with a stoop, and very swarthy in appearance: in fact easily recognisable for the gypsy that she was. The distinctive feature was an enormous lower lip, said to be "of a prodigious size" and "as big almost as a little child's arm".

Her travels through Dorset were a major part of the alibi used in her defence at a trial in London, a trial that was to be described as the most famous in the 18th Century. It concerned the four week disappearance of a London girl, Elizabeth Canning, from 1-29 January 1752. She claimed that she had been kidnapped and kept in a house at Enfield, north of London, by a woman called Mother Wells, with the assistance of several gypsies, one of whom was identified as the very ugly, seventy-year-old Mary Squires.

When arrested, Mary Squires produced the alibi that at the time of the abduction and imprisonment she had been travelling through Dorset, Wiltshire, and Hampshire, with her son George and daughter Lucy. In spite of witnesses being brought from Dorset to support her alibi, both Mary Squires and Mother Wells were found guilty. The latter was branded and Mary Squires was sentenced to death. The three witnesses from Dorset who had travelled up to London to give evidence of Mary's behalf, were then arrested and tried for perjury. They were acquitted for lack of evidence.

Then a surprising person came to the rescue of Mary Squires; no less a dignitary than the Lord Mayor of London. He came down to Dorset seeking further witnesses, and as a result of what he found, he petitioned the King. In a dramatic about-turn, this resulted in Elizabeth Canning - the girl who claimed to have been kidnapped - being tried for perjury. After hearing evidence from thirty-seven Dorset witnesses, she was found guilty and sentenced to three years' transportation. [It was now believed that her "disappearance" was due to time spent having an abortion.] Mary Squires was given a free pardon. The unfortunate Mother Wells could not be unbranded!

Darton[d] examined the evidence for the Dorset part of Mary Squires' alibi, and also that of the thirty-seven witnesses who gave evidence in support of it at the subsequent trial of Elizabeth Canning. He covered the route supposed to have been taken by Mary Squires and visited the places at which she is supposed to have stopped (see accompanying time-table, Table 2, and map). He came up with the interesting explanation that the gypsy Squires family were very much involved in the highly-lucrative smuggling trade of the day, and that the so-called witnesses were in fact members of the same smuggling fraternity or could easily be bribed by it.

There appear to be several flaws in the arguments used by Darton in his analysis of the situation, and he neglected to pay much attention to the fascinating insight the whole story gives into many aspects of the way of life in those times. For example, on Monday 1 January, at the Old Ship Inn at Litton Cheney, Mary Squires and her family ate two boiled fowls. At the later trial, the London lawyers considered this luxurious, but the inn-keeper in evidence said that "we don't eat roast meat in the country but very little", and George Squires stated that "he often ate fowls because they could be purchased in that district cheaper than beef or mutton". The total bill for board and lodging at the Old Ship Inn was 3s-6d, excluding the two fowls which George had purchased for sixpence each.

The emphasis in the whole story is on walking everywhere, the distances covered and the times they took. For example, Darton lays great stress on the fact that it would have been quite impossible for the seventy-year-old Mary Squires to have covered fourteen miles in four and a half hours - including several hills - in the middle of winter and over wet, muddy ground. (The particular journey was from Winyards Gap to Litton Cheney.) It is likely that Darton was used to travelling on horse-back, in a carriage or even by motorised transport. By his time, and even more so for us, people had forgotten what it was like when most poorer people walked everywhere. (Note in Chapter 8 how only half a century later Clotilde and William

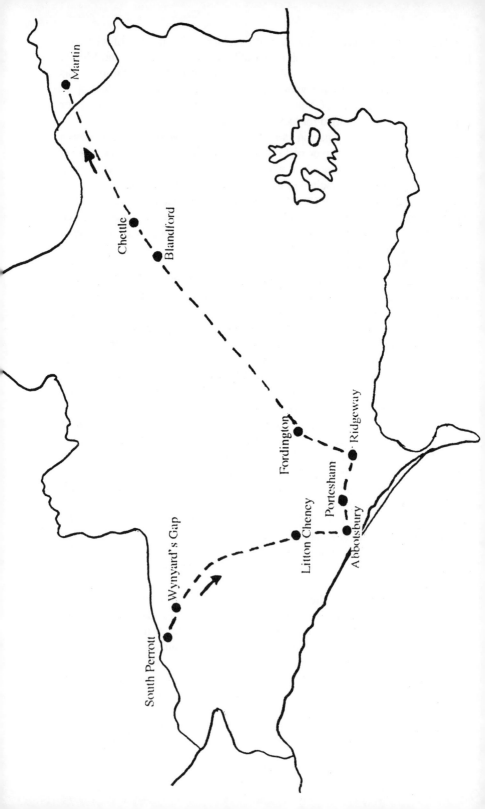

Table 2
The Dorset Itinerary of the Squires Family
(as used for an alibi in the subsequent kidnapping case)

Friday 29 December 1751
Mary Squires and her daughter Lucy and son George spent night at the Red Lion, South Perrott.

Saturday 30 December
Breakfasted between 8 and 9am at the Three Horseshoes, Wynard's Gap. They left there between 9 and 10am and arrived at Litton Cheney at 2pm.

Sunday 31 December
Mary and Lucy stayed at Litton Cheney while George went to William Clarke's at Abbotsbury where he stayed the night.

Monday 1 January 1772
George and William returned to Litton Cheney and then all the family went to Abbotsbury where they danced all evening. The Squires family remained at the Ship Inn at Abbotsbury, until 9 January.

Tuesday 9 January
All the Squires left Abbotsbury with William Clarke and spent the night at the Chequers Inn, Portesham.

Wednesday 10 January
In very bad weather they reached Ridgeway on the Dorchester to Weymouth road between 9 and 11am. They stayed here for the rest of the day and the night at the Ship Aground.

Thursday 11 January
William Clarke returned to Abbotsbury. The Squires family reached Fordington by 11 am where they encountered deep floods. They spent the night at an unknown place on the road to Blandford.

Friday 12 January
They passed through Blandford and spent the night in a barn near Chettle there being no inn nearby.

Saturday 13 January
They left Chettle between 10 and 11am in pouring rain and reached Martin where they spent the next night, also in a barn.

Sunday 14 January
The Squires family left Martin for Coombe Bisset in Wiltshire, *en route* for London.

Lawrence walked an average of over thirty miles per day travelling from Bristol to Glasgow.) In the author's youth there were many Romany gypsies living where she grew up, and they could certainly cover the ground faster than healthy young children - even their elderly women. They were used to it, non-Romanies weren't!

There is also great emphasis on precise timings of Mary Squires' journeyings, in an age when there were virtually no clocks, let alone watches. People lived by the daylight hours and the striking of church bells. They just didn't live their lives regulated by time as we do: it was only when something coincidental occurred that it might be remembered - somebody arriving as people were coming out of church, for example. The witnesses who many months later gave evidence of the times of arrivals and departures of Mary Squires were most unlikely to have been aware of exact times: they would probably not have had much idea on which days Mary Squires was there if it had not coincided with New Year celebrations! One certainly begins to wonder how much of this alibi was rigged - as believed by Darton.

It is interesting that no one seems to have questioned why Mary Squires was tramping around Dorset in the middle of winter, at such an unpleasant time of year. Her son George was carrying a peddler's pack of materials, some of which he sold along the way to help pay for their lodgings. Her daughter Lucy was said to have been with them as she wished to see her sweetheart William Clarke, a shoemaker of Abbotsbury, whom she had not seen for four years. But no reason was given as to why Mary Squires accompanied them. If, as Darton suggests, the Squires family was part of a large smuggling distribution network, then it suggests that Mary was head of her family in these dealings. Her son must have been at least into his thirties and surely able to do any necessary negotiations without dragging his old mother along - unless she was in charge! Mary could have been tucked up for the winter in front of a fire at some friend's or relative's home. Or was it that after spending a life in the open air, she wished to continue doing so, in spite of what we would consider hardship and terrible weather, but which would be quite normal for an out-of-doors person?

Reading the story of Mary Squires in Darton's book is certainly fascinating, but even better is to retrace the steps of Mary Squires and judge for yourself what you think of her alibi.

SEDUCTION

MISS TILLEY OF POYNTINGTON

A few sentences in the law records, a charge brought against someone, perhaps a verdict, and a few names. How often that is all we can ever learn about a Court case of the past, or the history and background of the people involved. But these were actual people, they really lived and the events recorded did happen. Unfortunately that is all we will ever know of a story. Such was the case of Miss Tilley of Poyntington and John Meere of Sherborne.j

      Miss Tilley - we are not even told her Christian name - was the eldest, or possibly the only, daughter of George Tilley of Poyntington, a Justice of the Peace. In 1582 he accused a fellow Justice, John Meere, of committing a felony at the house of the Marquis of Winchester at Hooke. (We know quite a bit about John Meere by comparison with Miss Tilley. He was a troublemaker, who had persuaded himself that "he had a mission from God to torment and plague the men of this world". By 1584 it was said that "he had slandered the most part of the knights, magistrates and best-appointed gentlemen in the County of Dorset". He was later employed by Sir Walter Raleigh. John Meere was of a well-known Sherborne family, and at this time he was Collector of the Bishop of Salisbury's rents.)

      The case brought against John Meere by George Tilley had been referred to the Quarter Sessions at Bridport, but before the case came to court, Miss Tilley had been seduced by Meere. And he not only seduced her, but planned to elope with her two days before the case came up at the Quarter Sessions.

      But we will never know the full story. It seems quite remarkable that George Tilley would not have mentioned to his family that he was bringing a charge against a fellow Justice. So did Miss Tilley really not know what Meere was like: surely his character must have been discussed if he had upset practically everyone in Dorset? Or was she trying to take some kind of revenge on her father, as was Meere? Or was it a case of love being blind on her part? Who did she confide in about her planned elopement? Someone must have known, for her mother in turn either found out or strongly suspected what was going to happen. The planned elopement was foiled by Miss Tilley's mother sitting up all the night in question and preventing it taking place. What a pity we do not know the full story of all the intrigues that must have gone on at the time.

All however was found out, and John Meere was duly brought to trial, with more charges being laid against him; apart from the seduction of Miss Tilley, there was one by a Mary Andrews "for a rape on her". Meere was found guilty and put into the stocks at Poyntington, situated right next to a foul-smelling dung-hill. No doubt some of the dung found its way onto John Meere during his fourteen hours sojourn there. Whether Miss Tilley or Mary Andrews threw anything at him is not known, but Miss Tilley's father obtained his revenge by releasing his pigs to come rooting around the entrapped man in the stocks.

4
WORKING WOMEN
OF DORSET

INTRODUCTION

With the exception of royalty and members of the upper classes, there will be very few women who can be described as "non-working". Apart from domestic activities, many women have excelled at innumerable other occupations, some for which Dorset became famous - embroidery, tapestry work, lace-making, silk-working, glove and stocking-making. Sadly, the products of their labours have usually not survived the years, or there is no knowledge of the craftswoman involved, to identify them specifically to Dorset.

The trade of button-making by hand (described later) has died out completely, as has precise knowledge of how they were made, but collections such as that at the Dorset County Museum, Dorchester, bear witness to the skill that was required.

One doesn't normally think of women of the past as running their own businesses, but searching among the archives reveals the names of many such women - running ale-houses in a room of their cottages and brewing the beer in an out-house, working in occupations that are nowadays known as district nurses and midwives (there was even a female doctor in Dorchester in 1654 by the name of Canander Huggard[n]), and shop-owners. The list goes on and on, but we usually only learn the names of these women; nothing was written of their everyday lives, their problems and triumphs.

Now and again there is much more information about a particular person, and some are described here: the Coades, Mary Anning, the Philpot sisters and Lady Charlotte Guest/Schreiber, not forgetting what must have been a colourful sight - the Reddle Woman, Mary Bull.

MRS COADE OF LYME REGIS

One woman who has left permanent marks not just in Dorset but all over the United Kingdom and as far afield as Russia, Poland, U.S.A. and Brazil, was Mrs Eleanor Coade of Lyme Regis. Yet apart from a few specialists, practically no one has heard of her, or of the artificial Coade Stone she is believed to have invented and certainly manufactured for over fifty years from 1769.[1,2] Coade Stone resembles a creamy-coloured natural stone, but it is far more durable and permanent than the real stone for which it is frequently mistaken. As will be described later, it is unlikely that there is a single person who has not looked at a piece of Coade Stone, although completely unaware of what it is or of the story behind it, a story that has its origins in Dorset.[13]

No autobiography was written by Mrs Coade, and the subsequent lack of authentic facts has led to much misinformation about this lady, particularly when combined with a very misleading description published by a writer on ceramics, Llewellyn Jewitt, in the 1880's from which subsequent writers have frequently quoted. The principal piece of misinformation is that there wasn't *a* Mrs Coade, but *two* of them, mother and daughter, both called Eleanor. To make confusion worse, the daughter who never married was referred to by the courtesy title of "Mrs" Coade, very essential to a business-woman in Victorian times: hence in the various articles about Coade Stone, it is often difficult to decide which Mrs Coade is intended.

At the time their London factory opened in 1769, the elder Mrs Coade was already sixty-one years of age, and therefore unlikely to have played a major part in running the business. She did, however, live for another twenty years until her death at the age of eighty-eight in 1796: by coincidence, her daughter also died at the age of eighty-eight in 1821, having been aged thirty-six at the time the factory was opened.

An exhaustive investigation of the two Eleanor Coades and their work has recently been published by Alison Kelly,[1] and does much to separate facts from the fiction and myths that have grown up concerning these women. Thus in the absence of direct evidence it had previously been presumed that Mrs Coade senior grew up in Lyme Regis. The researches of Alison Kelly, John Fowles, John Havill and others (cited in [1]), now show that she came from Tiverton, Devon, and at the time of her marriage to George Coade of Lyme Regis they moved to Exeter where they remained for thirty years.

Subsequently the family removed to London, where the rest of their lives were based and where each in turn died and was buried. However, the connections of the Eleanor Coades with their relatives in Lyme Regis always remained strong, and were reinforced in 1784 when Samuel Coade presented his house there to his niece Eleanor (the house was originally called Bunter's Castle and renamed Belmont).

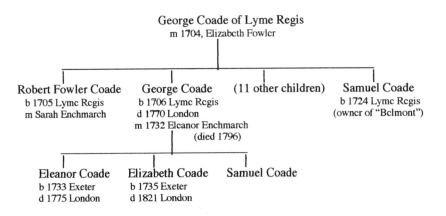

George Coade of Lyme Regis
m 1704, Elizabeth Fowler

Robert Fowler Coade
b 1705 Lyme Regis
m Sarah Enchmarch

George Coade
b 1706 Lyme Regis
d 1770 London
m 1732 Eleanor Enchmarch
(died 1796)

(11 other children)

Samuel Coade
b 1724 Lyme Regis
(owner of "Belmont")

Eleanor Coade
b 1733 Exeter
d 1775 London

Elizabeth Coade
b 1735 Exeter
d 1821 London

Samuel Coade

Pedigree 4.1   The Coade Family

Eleanor Coade was born Eleanor Enchmarch in Tiverton, Devon (see accompanying pedigree 4.1), and had at least three sisters: Sarah who married George Coade's elder brother Robert; Mary, who was married to James Sealy (or Seely) who later became a partner in the Coade Stone business in London; and Frances, married to Walter Oke who was in some as-yet-unknown way related to William Croggon (or Croggan) who was also later connected with the Coade Stone factory.

Eleanor herself, as stated above, moved to Exeter in 1732 with her new husband, where he became a prosperous merchant in the wool trade. Three children were born there in the next few years, Eleanor in 1733, Elizabeth in 1735 and Samuel at an unknown date - he was known to be alive in 1748, but probably died soon afterwards.[3] In 1759 the decline in the wool trade brought George Coade to bankruptcy, and apart from a deed of 1761[3] where he is described as "late of Exeter", he is next heard of in 1762 where for one year he became a Fellow of the Society of Arts and Manufacture in London (now the Royal Society of Arts). At some time in the next few years he regained possession of his Exeter property, but this was sold when he went bankrupt for a second time in 1769: he died the following year in London.

In the meantime, his thirty-three-year-old daughter Eleanor had successfully established herself as a linen-draper in the City of London by 1766, and her sister Elizabeth had lodgings with her. It was the same year as her father died, 1769, that Eleanor and her mother established the factory in Lambeth that was soon to become famous for producing Coade Stone.

91

Much mystery surrounds the opening of this Coade factory, particularly the financing of it and also where the knowledge of Coade Stone manufacture originated. Alison Kelly[1] has done much to dispel the myths surrounding it, but the full story will probably never be known. While most authorities agree that the financing of the factory probably came from members of the Coade family - especially Samuel Coade of Lyme Regis - there is no consensus of opinion over the latter point. The fact that Eleanor Coade the younger was running her linen-drapery business in London makes unlikely the often-repeated story of the two Eleanor Coades having a pottery shop in Lyme Regis. Here, it is said,[2] they invented their own modelling material that subsequently formed the basis of Coade Stone, and also met a convalescent artificial stone manufacturer, Richard Holt of Lambeth, whose factory they were to take over. While it cannot be excluded that the Coades (on holiday from London) met Holt (convalescent from London) at Lyme Regis, Kelly has presented clear evidence in her book demonstrating that the Coade and Holt factories were entirely separate businesses, and although both were situated in Lambeth, they were on completely different sites.

Although there are great similarities between the formulae of the artificial stones formerly produced by Richard Holt and that of Coade Stone, there are very important differences. Holt's contained lead, Coade Stone did not; titanium was used in Coade Stone, but not in Holt's. Although the constituents of Coade Stone are known, the precise details of its manufacture are now uncertain: it is known to contain china clay, felspar and potash, as well as titanium oxide.[14] Whatever the ingredients and process of manufacture,[15] it produced a creamy-coloured stone that was said to be the ultimate in weatherproof stone and was so realistic that even today it is frequently mistaken by experts for the natural stone. It has great stability and its small rate of shrinkage made it far superior for working to the very fine tolerances required by architects, with the advantage that its resistance to weathering compared with natural stone, gave it a durability that could last for centuries. This is well displayed by two prominent landmarks in Dorset - the large statue of George III in Weymouth, while "Belmont", the house in Lyme Regis used as a country home by the Coades, well illustrates how Coade Stone was used.

Coade Stone was extremely versatile, being used as exterior decoration on buildings - the frieze around Buckingham Palace for example, Somerset House, the Royal Opera House, National Gallery, Brighton Pavilion and many other buildings of Regency times both in London and scattered all over the country and abroad. It was used as interior fittings too, for it was soon taken up by Robert Adam and his successors for chimney pieces, pedestals, candelabra and chimney-piece ornaments. It was used for statues both indoors and outside; for busts, many of which were "bronzed" and are indistinguishable from real bronzes; at least fifty church ornaments can still be identified. Captain Bligh of *Bounty* fame was so impressed with Coade Stone that he ordered his tomb to be made of it. Innumerable heraldic coats-of-arms were made of this material - both for families and for the compulsory display of the Royal Coat-of-Arms in

Churches, and even for the "By Royal Appointment" insignia, one of which was used by Mrs Coade herself.

Gardens the length and breadth of Britain "sprouted" articles made of Coade Stone, most of them probably still surviving, unrecognised, to this day. Apart from garden statues there appeared urns, sundials and even fountains - examples can be seen in Kew Gardens, Wardour Castle and Petworth, Sussex. Perhaps the most impressive example is the rood screen in St George's Chapel at Windsor.

But all this was to be in the future, and presumably could not have been foreseen when Mrs Coade and her daughter started in business in the 1760's, under enigmatic circumstances. In 1767 a Daniel Pincott opened a factory making artificial stone in Narrow Wall (now called Belvedere Road) just behind the site of the present-day Royal Festival Hall. Two years later in 1769 he was joined by Mrs and Miss Coade (whether or not George Coade joined them too is uncertain; he died the following year). There must have been some relationship between the Coades and Pincott - whether family or business is not known, but they were all Dissenters which may have given the necessary introduction. But from the time the Coades arrived it was definitely *their* factory and Pincott was an employee: he was sacked by Mrs Coade in 1771. This parting of the ways between Pincott and the Coades must have been very acrimonious, for the following appeared in several newspapers on 11 September 1771:

> "Whereas Mr Daniel Pincot has been represented as a Partner in the Manufactory which has been conducted by him; Eleanor Coade, the real Proprietor, finds it proper to inform the Publick that the said Mr Pincot has no Propriety in this Affair; and that no Contracts or Agreements, Purchases or Receipts, will be allowed by her unless signed or assented to by herself."

This was followed three days later by a further notice:

> "Eleanor Coade gives notice that Mr Daniel Pincott having now no further Employ at her Manufactory at King's Arms Stairs, Narrow Wall, Lambeth; all Orders relative to the Manufactory are desired to be sent to Eleanor Coade at Mr Demar's, Bridge Head Lambeth."

It is known that Miss Coade was running the administrative side of the business from at least 1771 onwards, for there are bills signed in her name from that date.[1,2] Exactly what part the mother and daughter played is not known, but as Mrs Coade was in her sixties by then, she is unlikely to have taken a major active part. She died in 1796 and three years later Miss Coade made a partner of her cousin, James Seely, who had already been working there for some years. Seely died in 1813, by which time Miss Coade was in her late seventies, and she now employed a distant cousin William Croggon as manager.

After Miss Coade's death in 1821, Croggon found that she had not left the business to him and he started a costly action with her executors, although still carrying on the business until he went bankrupt in the 1830's - probably as a result of unpaid debts of over £20,000 from the Duke of York. Although Croggon's son re-founded the firm in 1835, and a former employee also established himself as a successor in Coade Stone manufacture, the last recorded production was in the 1850's. As recently as 1992 a firm in Little Venice, London started making replicas of Coade Stone items in reconstituted stone: these reproductions sell from just under £100 for a ram's-head fountain-mask, up to £5,000 for a pair of sphinx gateposts. The two Mrs Coades would have been amazed to learn that their originals can now fetch over £50,000![2]

Today, as was said earlier, practically no-one has heard of Coade Stone, although throughout the country and especially in the vicinity of Lyme Regis, stand lasting memorials to the two Eleanor Coades, far-seeing businesswomen in an age when women were not noted in this sphere.

MARY ANNING

Less than two hundred years ago the sciences of geology (rocks) and palaeontology (fossils) were virtually unknown. In general people believed in the Biblical time-scale. It had even been precisely calculated that the world and all contained within it, including man, had been created in the year 4004 BC. It was only in the early years of the 19th Century that scientists were beginning to accept the long time scale of the earth's development, and the fact that fossils could be used as a possible means of dating it. Thus began a demand for fossils, at first a trickle and then an unprecedented requirement for specimens from the British Museum, the Geological Society, and various Universities.

It was into this atmosphere that Mary Anning of Lyme Regis was born and bred, and it seems that it was a case of her being "the right person in the right place at the right time".[4-8] Deposits containing fossils are found in many parts of this country, as well as in Europe and other parts of the world. Lyme Regis was, and still is, an ideal place to find them since its fossil deposits are found in its cliffs: the action of the sea and storms are therefore continually exposing new fossils. The place was right, the scientific world was ready to appreciate the finds, and Mary Anning was the ideal person to obtain them.

Mary Anning was born in 1799, two years after her brother Joseph. Her father was a carpenter, but his health gradually deteriorated over the next few years until his early death of consumption in 1810. He had eked out his living as a carpenter by selling "curiosities" to people passing his shop in Bridge Street, Lyme Regis - Jane Austen mentioned him in her diary of 1804. On a table in front of his shop he displayed these curiosities, known locally as "crocodile bones", "Indies fingers" and "John Dories". There was no shortage of customers, for since the opening of the nearby Dorchester to Exeter turnpike in 1758, Lyme had become a very popular holiday place for fashionable people especially from Bath.

After their father's death, Mary and Joseph decided to carry on selling these curiosities to passers-by. Ever since they could remember, the two children had accompanied their father along the beach collecting fossils: they were well able to continue this in spite of their young ages - Mary was ten and her brother twelve.

It was the same year, 1810, that her brother uncovered the massive fossilised head of what he thought was a crocodile, but it was to be another year before tides and weather permitted further investigation. It was Mary who then uncovered the rest of what was to be the first complete *Ichthyosaurus* seen. (A few fragments had been discovered over a century earlier by the Welsh naturalist, Llhyd, and fully described in his book *Lithosphylacii Britannia Iconographia*, published in 1699.) Mary sold the fossil for £23 to the nearby Lord of the Manor of Colway, Mr Henry Henley. He exhibited it in William Bullock's Museum of Natural History in Piccadilly, and a full description of it was published in the *Transactions of the Royal Society* in 1814. It was about this time that Mary was greatly encouraged by a boy, Henry de la Beche, not much older than herself, and who was to become a lifelong friend. His educated background complemented Mary's practical experience and willingness to find the fossils.[16]

Money was still very short in the Anning home, and Mary and her family were barely making a living in spite of her discovery of the *Ichthyosaurus*. It was now that another man came to their financial rescue. While paying frequent visits to Charmouth, Lieutenant-Colonel Birch of Lincolnshire had purchased many fossils from Mary to add to his collection. In 1819 he became aware of the poverty in which the Annings were living: he sold his large collection of fossils for £400 and gave the entire proceeds to Mary. This helped to put the twenty-year-old Mary Anning on her feet, and she never looked back.

In 1824 came Mary's next "first", an almost perfect fossilised skeleton of a *Plesiosaurus*, a similar-sized reptile to the *Ichthyosaurus* but with an elongated neck and very small head. This specimen was sold for over £100 to the Duke of Buckingham. It was followed four years later by the third of Mary's "firsts". This time it was the flying (or rather gliding) reptile, a *Pterodactyl*, a land animal whose remains are rare even now. In 1832 Mary was fortunate to find an even larger specimen of *Ichthyosaurus* - the one on view in the Natural History Museum in London.

For most of her adult life, Mary Anning lived in reasonable comfort, first in Bridge Street and then in Broad Street, but she was never a wealthy woman. She was known to complain of the many people who visited her to pick her brains of her knowledge of fossils, and then went away to write of it to their pecuniary advantage while she - the supplier of the information - received nothing.

She seems to have spent the whole of her life in Lyme Regis (with the exception of one brief visit to London), dedicating herself to collecting fossils, analysing them, and acquiring a vast knowledge on the subject plus, of course,

95

still continuing to sell them in her shop. She received many visitors of high scientific intellect, and from her letters it appears that she thoroughly enjoyed debating with them. She enjoyed their visits and gave them any help she could quite willingly: she also maintained a large correspondence with people from further afield. This was many years before Charles Darwin's *Origin of Species* was published and yet, from her letters, it seems that Mary was already thinking along the same lines herself.

Mary Anning appears to have had an abrasive nature though, taking likes and dislikes to people: in 1832 she was described as "a prim, pedantic, vinegar-looking, thin female, shrewd and rather satirical in her conversation". For most of the years she was noted for being a solitary person, especially when out scouring the beaches and cliff-faces for new specimens. In her last few years it began to be rumoured that she had taken to the bottle, but sadly this was a misinterpretation of the fact that she was taking larger and larger doses of laudanum to deaden the pain of cancer. In 1847 she died of this disease, and was buried in the churchyard at Lyme Regis with other members of her family.

In July 1846, a few months before her death, Mary Anning was made an honorary member of the Geological Society - of whom her life-long friend Sir Henry de la Beche was now the President - in recognition of the help she had given to many geologists during her life-time. The Royal Society contributed to a stained-glass window to her memory in the Parish Church at Lyme. It is very surprising that there is no statue to Mary Anning in Lyme Regis however, for apart from her scientific reputation, she has done much to attract visitors to Lyme in the century and a half since her death.

THE MISSES PHILPOT

In recording the story of Mary Anning as gleaned from a variety of sources, she is presented as *the* fossilist of Lyme Regis, the principal attraction for visitors to the Town at that time. But that does not give a true picture of what was happening in Lyme at the beginning of the 19th Century, and in particular it pays great disrespect to the work of other female fossilists of the time, especially the Philpot sisters, Mary, Margaret and Elizabeth.[4,6] They started their fossil-collecting at Lyme Regis before Mary Anning, but in the academic world they appear to be as well-known as - if not better-known than - Mary Anning. Rather than being rivals, the Philpot sisters seem to have been on very good terms with Mary. It is strange therefore that they have been virtually forgotten, while Mary's name lives on as *the* fossil-collector of Lyme Regis.

The explanation for this discrepancy may well be in their respective fossil collections. Mary Anning collected and sold fossils for a living in a shop visited by all and sundry, and hence would have become well-known to the populace in general. The Philpot sisters, on the other hand, only collected fossils to add to their personal collection: this was displayed in their home and was only open for inspection to a limited number of selected visitors. At least that was so in their lifetime, for in 1880 their brother's daughter-in-law, who had acquired the whole Philpot collection on the death of her husband, bequeathed it to the University of Oxford, where it can now be viewed by all.

The three Philpot sisters, Mary (1777-1838), Margaret (?-1845) and Elizabeth (1780-1857), first came to Lyme Regis in 1805. They arrived initially for a holiday with another sister and their only brother who was a solicitor in London. While the rest of the family returned to London, the three sisters decided to remain at Lyme and stayed for the rest of their lives. They lived at Morley Cottage (later re-named 'The Nest') in Silver Street. It should be remembered that Mary Anning was only five or six years old at this time, having been born in 1799.

Specimens in the Philpot collection are known to have come from Wiltshire and other places, indicating that they had already started collecting fossils before they came to Lyme. It may very well be that this was the reason that they came to Lyme Regis for their initial holiday - to go fossil-hunting - for it was already well-known (to scientists anyway) for its fossils before Mary Anning's time. It was Mary's subsequent finding of the large dinosaur fossils that elevated it as a collecting-place.

A description of how the Philpot collection was displayed[4] tells of the dining-room containing many glass-topped cabinets with shallow drawers down the front. The collection continued into their parlour and also upstairs onto the landing. Although the three sisters helped with the collection, it appears to have been the youngest, Elizabeth, who was most actively involved. All three went out fossiling and were happy to conduct visitors on collecting expeditions.

By 1817 the first illustration of one of the Philpot fossils appeared in print (Sowerby's *Mineral Conchology)* and many more were to do so in the future - an indication of the contacts the Philpots had with scientific circles. In 1828 Mary Anning found the first complete fossil of a *pterodactyl* - the gliding reptile - but its presence in the locality was already being talked about in University circles from part-specimens in the Philpot collection gathered early in the 1820's. A similar specimen had also been described as existing in about 1810 in the collection of a Mr Rowe at Charmouth: further evidence for a group of fossilists in this area of Dorset at that time, prior to Mary Anning becoming very active in the field.[7,8]

Other references to the Philpot collection make mention of the "ink-bags" of fossilised squid-like animals: when powdered these both resembled and could be substituted for the sepia ink used to tint pictures. (Sepia is so-called after the name of the present-day squid from whose ink-sacs the ink is obtained.)

From references that were made to the Philpot collection, it is obvious that everything was cleaned to show to best advantage. They were also carefully classified, but regrettably not labelled with exact details of the sites where they had been found. Many specimens were lent to academics so that they could be drawn and used for illustrations in publications. Now on display in Oxford, they are a lasting memorial to the Philpot sisters who so carefully and lovingly collected them. Poor Mary Anning has no such memorial, for most of the fossils she collected were sold as fast as she could find them in order to provide her with a living. On the other hand, there are few people who do not remember entering the Natural History Museum in London and being greeted by that massive fossil dinosaur: unfortunately, the name of the Dorset woman who found it, Mary Anning, is not equally well-remembered.

LADY CHARLOTTE GUEST

The Manor of Canford features several times in this book for it has been in the hands of a surprisingly large number of women. The Manor House itself has taken many forms during its existence since Norman times, but the present building, that now houses a Public School, reached its peak of magnificence in the middle of the 19th Century when it was extensively altered and enlarged by the new Lady of the Manor, the remarkable Lady Charlotte Guest.[5,9]

Just how extraordinary she was, may be seen by the following list which links various aspects of her life: running the largest iron works in the country; Benjamin Disraeli; collections in both the Victoria & Albert and the British Museum; mufflers for London cabbies; the Chartist movement; Queen Victoria's uncle, the Duke of Sussex; railways in Russia and the United States; translation of Welsh folk legends into English; archaeological remains from Assyria; embroideries by Turkish refugees; the Duke of Wellington; life at Court, and many others. And if all that seems a lot for one woman, she also found time to raise ten children and have two long and happy marriages!

The woman in question was born Lady Charlotte Bertie in 1812, the only daughter of the ninth Earl of Lindsay by his second wife Charlotte Layard. She first came to live at Canford in 1846 as Lady Charlotte Guest, the wife of Sir John Guest, and it was at Canford that she died in 1895 as the widowed Lady Charlotte Schreiber. In order to understand how one person could pack as much into her life as Lady Charlotte did, it is necessary to go back to her early life, pre-Canford.

It is difficult to know how much of Lady Charlotte's later achievements were due to the character with which she was born, and how much was consequent on her home life after her father's death. He died when she was six years old and her mother remarried soon afterwards. Her new stepfather, Rev. Peter Pegus, was of violent temper and a heavy drinker, and her mother turned against her. She withdrew more and more into herself, finding her only consolation in reading. She had two mentally-retarded younger brothers, and it was after they were put in charge of a private tutor that her intellectual abilities rapidly expanded. From this tutor she learned French, Italian, Latin, Greek, Hebrew and Persian: he encouraged her musical abilities on the piano and harp. She also indulged in the outdoor activities of riding, hunting and shooting and learned the art of copper-etching, but this latter was probably self-taught. It can therefore be seen that she had a much higher than average intellect, but it was the abnormal family life that allowed her to develop this potential, for it was only by immersing herself in all this learning that Lady Charlotte was able to escape her otherwise traumatic home life.

Whenever possible, Lady Charlotte visited various relations, and especially delighted in going to London. It was on one of these visits in 1833 at the age of twenty-one, that she was introduced to a young man who apparently became very enamoured of her and started escorting her about Town. The affection was not returned by her to the same extent. The twenty-eight-year-old man - whose name was Benjamin Disraeli - was already a frustrated novelist: he had failed in an attempt to enter Parliament, and now he was to suffer a further frustration when he introduced the object of his affections to another man who became her husband within three months. It was to be another fifty years before Lady Charlotte and Disraeli were to sit down together in Berlin, and reminisce about the time she had rejected him, and all that had happened to both of them in the intervening years.

Her new husband was Josiah John Guest, a man of forty-eight to her twenty-one. There was not only a vast difference in their ages, but also a great difference in their respective social backgrounds. She came from a titled family - hence she was *Lady* Charlotte in her own right - while he came from a business background, greatly looked down upon by the upper classes of the day. His grandfather had established an iron works at Dowlais, near Merthyr Tydfil in South Wales, which had prospered greatly, until *Mr* John Guest was now a very rich man. A year before their marriage he had become M.P. for Merthyr Tydfil, a seat that he was to hold for another twenty years. Over the next twelve years Lady Charlotte was to have ten children, five boys and five girls.

It was in 1845 that Lady Charlotte and her husband - now Sir John - first came to look at Canford. At that time it was still an estate of over 13,000 acres stretching right down to the sea at Canford Cliffs - now the built-up area between Poole and Bournemouth. After prolonged negotiations, it was purchased for £335,000 and Lady Charlotte immediately set about planning its alterations. These were to take several years to complete and the estimated cost of £6,000 soon rose to £14,000 and finally exceeded £30,000 as more and more grandiose ideas were put into effect to produce a vast Gothic-style mansion.

Sir Charles Barry was employed to draw up the plans. He had recently completed the Gothic-style Houses of Parliament, and this no doubt influenced the changes at Canford. In fact he was probably chosen for just that reason. The new building incorporated a large tower at its entrance, closely resembling the Victoria Tower at Westminster (not Big Ben, the other one). The Great Hall was created by going up through four stories, and there was also a magnificent oak staircase. The whole area of the house was enlarged to change it from a modest-sized building to a large irregularly-shaped mansion. With small additions in the 1880's it still presents a pleasant prospect, enhanced by the battlements and heraldic beasts that appear at every possible opportunity.

It would appear that one of the principal driving forces that led Lady Charlotte to pursue such a grandiose scheme for her new home at Canford was as a result of the conflict she experienced with regard to her social status in Society. From her birth into a titled family and her various relations, she was fully acceptable into Society, and had been so up to the time of her marriage. But her husband was "in trade" and as such was distinctly looked down upon, even though he was an M.P. There was also a second conflict in that although she wished to be accepted in Society, she was far from approving of the frivolous, empty lives led by the females of the day.

In the earlier years of her marriage she had exploited her family position to try to obtain an entrée into Society for her husband. In 1838, at the age of twenty-six she had been presented at Court and had attended and given all the necessary parties for the Season. By the end of the year her husband was created a Baronet, a great distinction for someone of his background, but considerably less than Lady Charlotte had hoped for, or believed was due to her husband for the business he had created and income earned for Britain. Nevertheless, as a Baronet, Sir John Guest could now take a place in Society in his own right even though neither of them particularly enjoyed the social activities. It was at this time that they became very friendly with the Duke of Sussex, uncle to Queen Victoria, probably mainly due to the parallel of socially-unacceptable spouses. The intimacy led to Lady Charlotte's sixth child being named Augustus after the Duke who was his god-father. They were also delighted when the "Lion of Society", the Duke of Wellington attended one of their Balls; his seal of approval considerably advanced their social acceptability.

Lady Charlotte also pursued the possibility of obtaining a position at Court for herself, but when informed that the most she could hope for was the minor post of Lady of the Bedchamber, she did not follow up the idea. In fact she seems to have given up London Society more and more, and devoted herself to helping in her husband's business.

Her husband's health was not good and he was in almost continual pain. In 1844 he had an operation for a stone in his bladder, which was not completely successful. It was his declining health that persuaded Lady Charlotte that they should find a new home in more congenial surroundings, and hence came the move to Dorset, when she was thirty-four and her husband sixty-one. Sir John Guest still retained control of the Dowlais Iron Works, but it had increasingly been run by his wife in the previous few years. She was to continue doing this more and more in the remaining six years of her husband's life. After his death she took over complete control until her eldest son came of age and was able to take control for himself in 1856.

Lady Charlotte had taken an interest in the Iron Works from the first year of their marriage, when she went to live nearby. At about the same time the two of them had travelled on the newly-opened Manchester to Liverpool

Railway: when this was combined with the terrible "overland" journeys experienced by Sir John in travelling between South Wales and London on his Parliamentary duties, they decided that a nationwide network of railways was going to be the thing of the future. The Dowlais Iron Works was therefore turned over to the manufacture of railway lines. What a wise decision! Their foresight was well-rewarded and Dowlais expanded as never before to supply lines for the vast expansion of railway-building that now exploded everywhere. They supplied railway lines not just within Britain but also in ever-increasing amounts to first Russia and then the United States. Lady Charlotte did much of the work in the firm. She wrote all her husband's letters; she took charge of the account books; she wrote all necessary reports; and she also negotiated new contracts herself, in the face of her husband's declining health. She had also travelled abroad with her husband on working-holidays, visiting iron works and other factories equally with art galleries and museums.

In between acquiring all this business and technical knowledge, she was also producing a new baby annually, and still found time to learn Welsh so that she could talk to the employees at Dowlais. She became so proficient in Welsh that she made the first English translation of ancient Welsh stories known as *The Mabinogion*. This not only required a knowledge of Welsh, but also a complete understanding of Mediaeval Welsh. (It may be remembered that she showed a flair for languages as a child.) She worked on the translation for eight years and it was published in parts between 1838 and 1846. Anyone else would probably have been content to be known only for this magnificent achievement of effecting such a difficult translation, but as it turned out, *The Mabinogion* is only remembered as one of the lesser things of Lady Charlotte's life.

One thing was marring the success of the Dowlais Iron Works, and that was the negotiations for its new lease. The existing lease was due to expire in 1848, and negotiations for its renewal had started seven years earlier. When the Guests received the proposals for the new lease in 1845, the demands of the landlord, Lord Bute, were so exorbitant as to make them believe that the Works would have to close. It was this belief, combined with the increasing ill-health of her husband, that made Lady Charlotte persuade Sir John that they should look for a new home. The same year they viewed Canford: it was purchased the following year, but it was to take another three years for all the alterations to be completed. They lived there intermittently for the next three years while re-building was in progress, and in 1850 they finally moved in. Sadly, Sir John died the following year, and it was only two days before his death that the new lease for Dowlais was finally agreed: signing it was almost the first task performed by Lady Charlotte when she assumed total control after her husband's death.

By the time they had purchased Canford, another member of Lady Charlotte's family had made his mark in the world. This was Henry Layard, a cousin on her mother's side, seven years her junior. With no detailed knowledge or experience but with plenty of enthusiasm, he had gone out to

Assyria to search for the lost city of Nineveh in 1839 at the age of twenty-two. On his first day of digging, he struck lucky and started uncovering what became such an enormous find of archaeological treasures that even the British Museum was unable to accept it all. The surplus was to come to Canford. Lady Charlotte had taken up her distinguished relative with great enthusiasm, showing him off in London Society, and he was a frequent visitor to Canford. All the family were very fond of him, so much so that he eventually ended up marrying one of her daughters, Mary Enid, born 1843, and twenty-six years his junior. But that was in the future. In the meantime he was bringing all these archaeological treasures to England, and the surplus was being transported to Canford. Lady Charlotte persuaded her husband to let Sir Charles Barry build an extension to form a museum that could house these treasures, and a small museum, the Nineveh Porch, was added at the eastern end of Canford. Layard went on to have a distinguished political and ambassadorial career, ending as British Ambassador in Turkey. He is to recur later in Lady Charlotte's story.

Twenty years of great happiness for Lady Charlotte came to an end on 26 November 1852, when her beloved husband died in her arms at Canford. He was then sixty-eight years of age to her forty. She was heart-broken, but life had to carry on and within two days of his death she signed the new lease for the Dowlais Works. Her eldest son, Ivor, was only seventeen when his father died and shortly due to go up to Cambridge. She wished him to proceed with this, while she would continue running Dowlais until he came of age in four years time. In the meantime she set about employing a tutor for Ivor for the time before he went to Cambridge, and accordingly appointed a twenty-seven year-old Fellow of Trinity College for this job, by the name of Charles Schreiber. Little did she realise how profoundly this appointment was to affect the rest of her life.

Almost immediately she was taken up by troubles with the workmen at Dowlais. For several years there had been industrial unrest in South Wales, following the activities of the Chartist Movement, an organisation dedicated to improving the lot of the working class. The higher cost of living had made the men determined to seek a correspondingly higher wage. Although the men of Dowlais and its associated coal mines had been very loyal to the Guests, Lady Charlotte worked with the other Iron Masters: in the end everything was settled without either the troops being called in or the threatened lock-out - which she was very much against. It is remarkable that as a woman she was able to play an equal part in all these negotiations, both with the other employers, and with the workmen.

Back at Canford she was faced with another crisis when Charles Schreiber, her son's tutor, was taken seriously ill and lay at death's door for several days. She personally nursed him, and it was while he was seriously ill that she finally admitted to herself what she had been trying to hide - that she was in love with this young man thirteen years her junior. Her love was returned, but not unnaturally, there was great opposition from all members of her family to their romance. To the end of her life, Charlotte's eldest daughter,

Charlotte Maria, never became reconciled to it. After much turmoil of mind, the couple did go ahead and marry in 1855, when Lady Charlotte was forty-three and her new husband was twenty-nine. The next four years were to prove a little traumatic for Lady Charlotte as she both adjusted to her new marriage and had to deal with the problems of the children of her first marriage. Her son Augustus was a complete failure at Cambridge and had been sent down: he was packed off to Germany to study metallurgy. Her son Monty did not get on very well in his army career, and eventually resigned his commission: her other son Thomas became involved with a very unsuitable young lady from whom he was finally disentangled. There were stormy scenes with her unreconciled eldest daughter, Charlotte Maria, only solved by her marriage in 1859. But her eldest son, Ivor, fulfilled all her hopes for him. He obtained a First-Class degree at Cambridge and was well able to take on the task of running the Dowlais Iron Works.[17] Lady Charlotte was therefore very happy to hand it over to him, and devote herself to her new husband.

After handing over both Canford and Dowlais to Ivor, Lady Charlotte and Charles Schreiber moved to live full-time at their London house, but in 1865 they rented it out and returned to make their base at Canford. Charles Schreiber had persisted in a political career and after several unsuccessful attempts, he finally won the seat for Cheltenham in 1865. But Lady Charlotte found that having resigned control of Dowlais to her son left a large hole in her life, and before long she had found something to fill it - collecting 17th Century English china. This was to occupy her for over twenty years, and involve her in prolonged trips abroad every year in search of additional items to add to her collection. Her husband always accompanied her, planning their trips to fit in with his Parliamentary career.

She threw herself into this new occupation with as much enthusiasm as she had devoted to her previous business interests. She did nothing by halves. There was no existing work of reference for her new hobby, so within a very short time she had become the authority herself. Before long she added other interests to her collecting enthusiasms; enamels in the form of medallions; tea-caddies; snuff-boxes; buttons; cuff-links; and thimbles. Later she was to add fans and playing cards to her collections. Along with collecting the actual items, she also sought out every piece of documentation that she could find, that would both authenticate the pieces, and provide a history of their manufacture.

Every year they were away for several months, visiting all the European countries at different times; no junk shop was left unvisited by them, as well as the smarter antique shops and private collections. They built up quite a remarkable collection, simply because of her foresight in choosing to collect what was unfashionable at the time; hence they could pick up items at very reasonable prices. At the end of her life Lady Charlotte was to present these collections to the Nation, and her china collection can be seen at the Victoria & Albert Museum, (The Schreiber Collection), and the playing cards and fans at the British Museum. But that was a long way in the future.

During all her visits abroad, and indeed for most of her life, Lady Charlotte kept a Journal, which today makes remarkable reading. Every facet of her journeys from North Africa (Tunisia) to Scandinavia is listed. It was on one of these visits to Berlin in 1870 that at a reception at the British Embassy Lady Charlotte met her former sweetheart, Benjamin Disraeli, now Lord Beaconsfield, and they reminisced over the lives they had led since their first meeting forty-five years earlier. The following year Lady Charlotte was delighted when her eldest son, Ivor, received a peerage - an honour that had been denied to her husband. It was almost certainly due to the intervention of Disraeli that the family was so honoured, and she was fully aware of her own part in this achievement.

But age was at last beginning to catch up with Lady Charlotte, and she was confined to the house at Canford for several weeks during the hard winter of 1881. Although she was now nearing seventy, she still had all her old enthusiasm and used this time to start cataloguing her vast collections spread through the many rooms of Canford. But while being involved in this monumental task, she still found time to explore a new interest. Her daughter Mary Enid Layard was now living in Turkey with her Ambassador husband. She had sent her mother several samples of embroidery work done by Turkish refugees from the Balkan Wars. Lady Charlotte was a good embroideress herself [when *had* she found the time!], and recognised their superb craftsmanship. She persuaded some of the big London stores to sell them - obtaining many more samples from her daughter - and was able to raise over £1,000 in this way to help the plight of the refugees.

The last of Lady Charlotte's china-collecting trips was to be in 1881, for she was now faced with a decline in her husband's health due to lung problems. His doctor suggested a trip to South Africa, which at first seemed to work wonders, but then he deteriorated rapidly and she was advised to take him home. He never made it back to England, for he died in Lisbon in Portugal where they had disembarked to recover from a particularly bad sea voyage. Just before he died on 6 January 1884, Lady Charlotte received a letter from her eldest son Ivor informing her of a disastrous fire at Canford that had damaged most of the Great Hall and totally destroyed the magnificent oak staircase.

It was therefore with great sadness that Lady Charlotte returned to Canford for the funeral of her beloved husband, and also to see the ravages caused to her home by the fire. It was after this that she decided to give her vast collection to the Nation, and it was to its cataloguing that she devoted the rest of her life. She was now seventy-two years of age and this was to occupy her for the remaining ten years of her life, although she still found time to perform one more charitable work. She had always been impressed by the many kindnesses and courtesies she had received over the years from London cabbies. As her sight began to deteriorate, she started knitting long red mufflers for the cabbies, and also persuaded her son Arthur to have a shelter built for them at Langham Place which she personally supplied with daily newspapers for them to read at her expense.

In the last few years of her life she was based at her London home, but made many prolonged visits to Canford. She did manage two holidays in 1887 and 1890 to stay with her daughter and son-in-law, the Layards, in Venice where they had retired. That was to be the end of her travels, and the last five years of her life were spent quietly with her youngest daughter Blanche, Countess of Bessborough. But it was at her beloved Canford where she died. and was buried in 1895 at the age of eighty-three. She was buried in the Parish Church there, the Church that dates in part from Anglo-Saxon times and therefore links Lady Charlotte with all those other female predecessors at Canford whose stories over the centuries have contributed to these pages.

JANE GIBBS AND HER STARCH

"This is to certify that Jane Gibbs of the Isle of Portland has in her possession two hundred weight of starch made from roots dug in the common field, which roots are not the food of man; and the said Jane Gibbs will produce any quantity of the starch whenever required: the said roots were dug, and the starch made in the present year."

J. Payne, Rector
William Pearce, Churchwarden
Edward Pearce, Churchwarden
Portland
December 22nd, 1796

This certificate accompanied a letter from Mrs Jane Gibbs to the Royal Society of Arts in London.[10][18] She was claiming the prize they had offered (a gold medal or 30 guineas alternative) to anyone who could provide a method of preparing starch from some material other than food. Mrs Gibbs duly won their prize, and a letter describing how her starch had been produced was published the following year in the Society's *Transactions* (volume 15, 1797).

Why should that eminent body, the Royal Society of Arts be offering a prize for a kitchen recipe of an alternative method of preparing starch? And how did Mrs Jane Gibbs of Portland come to achieve her success? There had been a gradually increasing demand for starch during the previous two centuries, for use with clothing, table napery and bed linen. The principal source of this starch was wheat flour. But in the 1790's a series of poor harvests had increased the price of wheat to unprecedented levels, and the dramatically-reduced amount of available flour was required for the production of bread. Hence the necessity for some alternative non-food source of starch, and the Royal Society of Arts' offer of a prize. (It is quite indicative of the values of those times, that when flour was short, the prize was for the luxury of starch, and not for some means of providing alternatives to bread or flour for the poor!)

How Mrs Gibbs came to hear of the prize is not known, but as she was the landlady at the *Portland Arms* it is probable that she heard of it from a visitor from London. What is surprising about her winning the prize is that the recipe she used was widely known throughout the country and had been in use for many generations. Her starch was prepared from the roots of *Arum maculatum* commonly known as Lords and Ladies, Cuckoo-Pint or Wake Robin, a very common flower of the hedgerows.

In a second letter written on 2 January 1797, Mrs Gibbs gave details of her method of production. The Royal Society of Arts had obviously written to her for further information, but she was unable to answer one of their questions. This letter - which was the one later published - ran:

> Sir, In consequence of your letter I have made enquiry concerning the quantity of roots of the plant from which my starch had been prepared, necessary for the making of a given quantity of starch but do not find any of the roots have been weighed so that I cannot ascertain what proportion of starch is yielded by them. It is believed a peck of roots [two gallons dry weight] will make about four pounds of starch, though, in operation, a less quantity is yielded by some roots than from others; the starch is sold at about eleven pence a pound; the plant from which it is prepared is here called Lords and Ladies; the roots are found in the common fields, and being cleansed, and pounded in a stone mortar with water, the whole is then strained, and after settling, the water being poured off, the starch remains at the bottom, which being dried becomes a fine powder. It may be advisable during the preparing of the roots of this plant, to be careful of handling them lest their acrid quality may injure the hands.
>
> The two hundred weight of starch I have prepared as mentioned in the Certificate is equal to the sample now sent.
> I am,
> Your humble servant,
> Jane Gibbs
> Portland Arms,
> Portland,
> Dorsetshire, January 2nd, 1797.

Although Mrs Gibbs won the prize, there was a little deceit in the whole affair. Whether or not the rector and the two churchwardens were party to it will never be known, but Jane Gibbs could not have been unaware of it. The prize was offered for a method of preparing starch from a *non-food* source.

While the recipe clearly did not use wheat flour, she must have known that a food was extracted from the self-same roots of *Arum* - arrowroot. Although practically unheard of today, Portland arrowroot was widely used then as a food for invalids. It was a powder which, when dissolved in boiling water, formed a fine jelly that was very palatable to weak or convalescent people. (It was called Portland Arrowroot to distinguish it from true arrowroot which comes from a different plant, *Maranta aruninacea* grown in tropical America and the West Indies.) Portland Arrowroot could therefore be described as a food - although limited in application - and Jane Gibbs could hardly have been unaware of the fact!

In her letter, Mrs Gibbs emphasised the careful handling required during the preparation of the starch, to prevent injuring the hands. This was a well-known complaint among laundry-maids and had been referred to as long ago as 1597 in a book on botany: "the most pure and white starch is made of the roots of the Cuckoo-Pint; but most hurtfull to the hands of the launderesses that hath the handling of it, for it chappeth, blistereth, and maketh hands rough and rugged, and withall smarting."[11]

At the time that was written, two hundred years before Mrs Gibbs won her prize, starch was relatively new to England, having been introduced to Queen Elizabeth I by Flemish immigrants only about thirty years earlier. Thus had been born the new fashion of ruffs, first by Elizabeth's courtiers and then copied by ordinary folk. Alongside it was born the art of starching by launderesses, for not only ruffs needed stiffening, but also the lace trimmings on cuffs and elsewhere. Without doubt a large number of Dorset women learned and used this new craft, and also were employed in the manufacture of starch, but their names are not recorded. How many millions of hours must they have spent in starching ruffs, the large lace collars of the Stuarts, the plain Puritan collars, Regency frills and cravats, the stiffened collars of Victorian men's shirts that persisted into the present century: and how many table cloths, sheets and other linen must literally have passed through their hands? It was only Jane Gibbs of Portland who clearly profitted by it !

THE REDDLE WOMAN

Mary Ann Bull certainly made her presence felt in no uncertain terms at the turn of this century, for she could always be heard a long way off, well in advance of her appearance. Children would run in fear as the clanking and banging got louder and louder. Then along the road would appear the source of all this noise - a horse and two-wheeled cart with pots and pans strung along the sides, driven by Mary Bull. And the sight proved just as frightening as the sound when the cart drew closer, for every bit of the horse, cart, driver and her dog were a bright red colour. The Reddle Woman had arrived![12]

Mary Franklin had been born into a gypsy family of north-east Dorset and had married another gypsy by the name of Bull. What happened to him is unknown, but from quite an early age she had lived a solitary life with her horse and cart. For innumerable years she had become a familiar sight to villagers and farmers as she wandered around Dorset, straying occasionally into Somerset and parts of Wiltshire. She made a meagre income by selling "reddle" (or "treddle" as it is sometimes called), which she obtained from the Poole area. This was an impure oxide of iron which, when mixed with clay or chalk, was used for marking sheep. It was this bright red, powdery "reddle" that covered Mary and all her belongings and made her such a fearsome sight. She also sold silver sand and brick dust for burnishing horse harnesses, etc.

Mary Bull was a small woman, being only about five foot tall, and she had the typical dark, penetrating eyes of a gypsy. She always wore a long grey overcoat that almost reached the ground, boots, and a man's felt hat tied on with a scarf. Many an evening she was to be seen sitting by the side of the road, smoking an old clay pipe, but if passers-by stared at her she would always respond with the words, "Ave 'ee zeed enough? Mind yer eyes don't drop out!" Her sleeping arrangements were very simple: she just let some sacking down from the sides of her cart and crawled under to sleep, with her dog snuggled up by her side.

She was always very kind and gentle with her horses, and there is a story that when one of them died, the villagers where it happened clubbed together to buy her a replacement. However, this was almost certainly not out of the kindness of their hearts, but more from a fear that she might cast her "evil eye" over them. She had earned this reputation some years earlier at the village of Shillingstone, when her request for a glass of water had been refused. In a temper she had turned to a young woman in a nearby group, and told her that bad luck would follow her wherever she went. This woman married shortly afterwards, but her husband had died in a short time, and bad luck had indeed followed her in all sorts of ways.

But Mary Bull had one weakness, she liked to drink, and most of her money earned from selling "reddle" went in this way. Many a time she found herself in the hands of the police on charges of drunkenness. It was this drinking that led to her final downfall, for one day in the bitter winter of 1917 she was found in a drunken sleep, frozen stiff under her cart on Sydling Hill. She was taken to Cerne Abbas Workhouse but died of pneumonia shortly afterwards. She was subsequently buried at Sydling - the parish in which she had died - and her horse, cart, and other possessions were sold to defray the expenses of her funeral.

BUTTON-MAKING

It is impossible to estimate exactly how many women of Dorset worked in the button-making industry at the height of its production in the 18th and 19th

Centuries - there were over 4,000 women and children in the Shaftesbury area alone in 1793.[12] Button-making was a cottage-based industry, and although it primarily involved females, other members of the family - and particularly children - could join in to make extra money. Women could earn an average of two shillings a day, compared with the nine-pence a day they might expect from farm-work, the only real alternative for these women.

Although a major factor, it wasn't just the money that attracted so many females to the industry. There were many other advantages. Working indoors was certainly preferable to being out in the fields in all weathers. It enabled women to be at home, for example to look after young children, especially if they were sick. If they were doing farm-work. then they would have to find someone to look after them - expensive - or take them out into the fields with them while they worked. It meant that the housewives could prepare and cook a meal for their husbands' return at the end of the day, or at lunch-time if preferred. It meant that the wives could go on working and earning money into the last days of pregnancy, or while they were injured in the foot or legs, again an impossibility with working on a farm.

Apart from these direct benefits, there was at least one indirect benefit that was very important when money was tight. Their clothes, and particularly their shoes, didn't wear out at anything like the rate they did when worn in the fields in all weathers. It was therefore no wonder that poorer women in towns, villages, hamlets and isolated cottages, flocked to join in this new cottage industry.

Although button-making had been going on in a very small way here and there, it was Abraham Case of Shaftesbury who put it on a more business-like basis in the reign of Queen Anne (1702-1734). The buttons were made from a disc of the horn of Dorset sheep, covered with a piece of cloth and then overworked with a fine tracery of linen thread. The diameters of the buttons ranged from half an inch down to the almost unbelievable size of an eighth of an inch (3 mm). [What on earth was such a minute size used for?]

Twenty years later there was a great revolution in the button-making industry when Abraham Case's grandson started importing metal rings from Birmingham to use as the base for the button instead of horn. They were far easier to work with - and cheaper. The industry now spread out in all directions, reaching as far south as Bere Regis and Morden.

The centre of the industry shifted from Shaftesbury to Blandford when, after the fire of 1731, a Mr Robert Fisher opened a "Button Depot" at his draper's shop in Market Place, Blandford. The out-workers could bring or send their completed buttons at any time; and the depot was regularly visited by travellers who bought them in bulk. Cloth-covered buttons were sold at between eight-pence and three shillings a dozen, while the women workers averaged about two shillings a day for making approximately six or seven dozen buttons. Each size and type of button had its own name: trite, bird's eye, vest, shirt, jam, waist, outsize, and extra outsize.

109

The industry thrived throughout the 18th and 19th Centuries, still run primarily by the Fisher family of Blandford. Many families lived in relative comfort, and were able to survive the loss of the male breadwinner, something that had been very difficult in times past. But then the bubble burst. At the Great Exhibition of 1851, a Mr John Aston demonstrated a button-making machine. It was a disaster for the cottage-industry of Dorset. Now buttons could be made at a fraction of the cost of hand-made ones, and at a far more rapid and reliable rate, all exactly identical.

Near-starvation hit most families, especially those with widowed bread-winners, who had depended totally on their earnings from making buttons. The introduction of more mechanisation on farms since the Agricultural Revolution meant that there was far less requirement for unskilled labour. There was no Social Security or Government subsidies in those days: people just starved to death. A few of the local gentry came to the rescue of some, and many hundreds of families were helped with the cost of emigration to America and Australia. But for others, especially the elderly, it was the Workhouse; a sad end to the lives of these women who had known better days with the button-making industry.

5

WOMEN OF THE DARK AGES

For most of us, English history begins with the arrival of the Normans in 1066. Before that time we may have faint memories from schooldays of learning about the Romans, the Stone Age and, of course, that era beloved of all children, the age of prehistoric monsters. The Dark Ages - those from the departure of the Romans to the arrival of the Normans - are rapidly skipped over in our minds, with just a hazy recollection of Alfred burning the cakes. But those interested in the history of Dorset, and especially the women of those times, should pay a little more attention to the Dark Ages, for a number of women made their mark in Dorset during those few centuries. While the exploits of Boudicca (Boadicea) of East Anglia in leading her troops into battle have come down to us from distant days, there is scarcely a mention of the fact that at least *three* Queens of this region similarly led their troops into battle. But who has heard of the Saxons Sexburga, Ethelburga and Ethelfleda?

The events of this period were virtually unrecorded, and it is only with difficulty that we can delve into the history of that time - hence their name of the Dark Ages. Events occurring during the earlier Roman occupation of England were well recorded by their efficient administrative system, and by their scholars and writers. After the departure of the Romans, and the various invasions by the Vikings, Angles and Saxons, there was no recorded history, except for odd jottings in the annals of the various monasteries that were beginning to spring up after the arrival of Christianity. These notes recorded such things as the death of a King, a battle, an invasion or a similar major event. Since they were written by monks, everyday events and particularly the affairs of women, were usually not noted.

It was only at the end of the 9th Century at the instigation of Alfred the Great that these isolated scraps of information were brought together to form a retrospective history of England. Scholars of more recent times have therefore had to try to piece together what was actually happening during these Dark Ages, and attempt to separate fact from legend (King Arthur and the Knights of the Round Table, for example).

Even with these reservations about the sources of the material, quite a few stories of women who left their mark in Dorset history emerge from these Dark Ages, and these tales certainly deserve to be brought out into the light of day. In particular they show that it wasn't completely "a man's world" as many subsequent historians would have us believe!

111

WOMEN OF THE WEST SAXONS

With regard to Dorset, the Dark Ages can be divided into two parts which will be referred to as the West Saxons and the Anglo-Saxons, separated by the reign of Alfred the Great. (It was under Alfred's grandfather, King Egbert (802-839), that the Saxons and Angles became united to form the Anglo-Saxon Kingdom of Wessex that was soon expanded to include the whole of England.) During the three and a half centuries that form the first part - the West Saxons (519-873) - at least three women were involved in major events; two led their armies into battle and one murdered her husband, the King. The lack of detailed history means that none of these events involving females can be precisely locatd to Dorset, merely to the Kingdom of Wessex, which initially consisted of what is now Dorset, Hampshire and Wiltshire. The Royal Courts were necessarily peripatetic, travelling to wherever uprisings or invasions were occurring, or where new conquest of land could add to the Kingdom of Wessex. Since these three women must certainly have spent considerable time in this County, they are included as "Women of Dorset" - otherwise to which county *would* they belong?

The two women who led armies, Sexburga (Sexburh)[5] and Ethelburga (Aethelburh), were both Queens of Wessex, the wives of Cenwalh (643-675) and Ina (688-726) respectively (see accompanying pedigree 5.1). They were also Royal Princesses in their own right, being descendants of Cerdic (519-534), the original Saxon invader who settled in the Isle of Wight and Hampshire, and from whom all subsequent members of the Royal Family of Wessex were descended. Although successive Kings were always chosen from these descendants, there was no automatic right of succession from parent to offspring as we have today. The sons of these Kings were frequently under age at the time of their fathers' deaths, and it was much more likely that a brother or uncle with a proven record in battle would be chosen to succeed. On the death of a King, there would be intense rivalry between all Princes of the Blood-Royal who had the necessary experience, often leading to actual fighting between the contenders. It was to avoid just such a situation arising on the death of her husband, that the first of our Saxon women came to the fore.

SEXBURGA

Sexburga was widowed in 675 on the death of her husband, Cenwalh, without children, and she immediately seized the reins of government in her own right. She had in fact been ruling jointly with her husband for the three years prior to his death, but in exactly what capacity is not known. By her quick action she

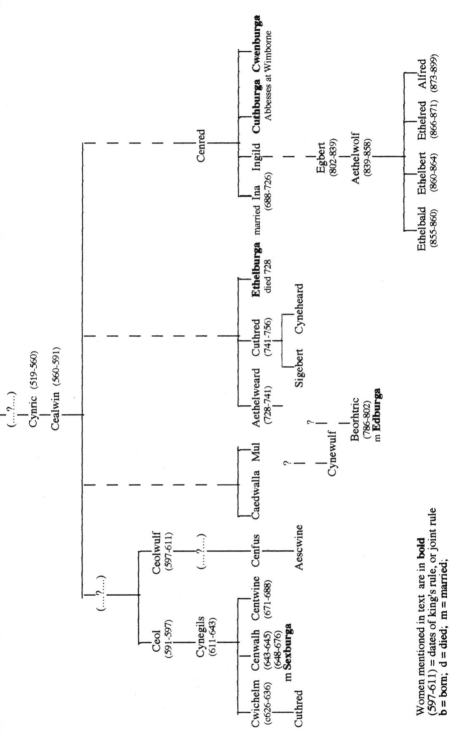

Pedigree 5.1 The Saxon Royal Family from Cerdic to Alfred

Women mentioned in text are in **bold**
(597-611) = dates of king's rule, or joint rule
b = born; d = died; m = married;

113

was able to suppress the rival contenders for the throne. She had obviously been playing an active part in co-ruling Wessex - which at the time consisted only of Dorset, Hampshire and Wiltshire - for Sexburga was immediately able to lead an army against the Kings of the neighbouring Kingdoms who had taken the opportunity of the death of the King to attack Wessex.

Although Sexburga was successful in defending her territory, she was not equally successful in winning over her subordinates within Wessex. It is recorded[x] that they didn't take kindly to being ruled by a mere female and she would soon have been deposed, had not the problem been solved for her subjects by her death within the first year of her becoming ruler in her own right.

Sexburga was therefore the first ruling Saxon Queen of England, and although neither was her reign a long one, nor was it popular with the men once peace had been established, we should be proud to claim this "first" for Dorset/Wessex. Two hundred and fifty years later, Ethelfleda, one of the daughters of Alfred the Great, repeated the action of Sexburga in assuming the role of leader on the death of her husband (see later): this time a mere woman was apparently accepted quite happily as ruler of a "kingdom", and she went on to achieve great things. This apparently demonstrates a clear change in the attitude towards women as leaders in these two and a half centuries, but the discontent towards Sexburga may have been due to personal antagonism, for it was only a short time after her death that the second of our Saxon women led an army, but under slightly different circumstances.

ETHELBURGA

The second Queen who led her troops into battle, Ethelburga (Aethelburh), did so during the life-time of her husband. In 720, the childless King Ina of Wessex had been on the throne of Wessex for thirty-two years - a long time in the life of his potential successors - and it was an insurrection from one of these aethelings (princelings) that drew Ina to Sussex, which by that time had become part of Wessex. The previous year Ina had erected a strongly-built fortress at what was to become Taunton, to help guard his western frontier in the newly-conquered valley of the River Tone. Another aetheling, Ealdbriht, took advantage of Ina's absence to raise a second rebellion and seized this castle at Taunton. Undaunted, Queen Ethelburga raised another army and went to Taunton where she took the fortress by storm and levelled it to the ground. She then drove Ealdbriht across Wessex to Kent where he was killed by her husband, Ina.

It certainly throws an interesting insight into the role of women in those troubled early Saxon times that Ethelburga was obviously well-accepted by the people as a natural leader in time of need, like Sexburga only forty-five years before. But we shall never know whether Ethelburga would have been accepted as overall leader had her husband died, or if like Sexburga there would have been plans to depose her had not Ina returned to rule instead.

The end of Ethelburga's story is very different from that of Sexburga, for eight years after this incident at Taunton - in 728 - she accompanied her husband (after he had relinquished the throne of Wessex to Ethelburga's brother, Aethelheard) on the strenuous overland journey to the Holy City of Rome. The couple must have been quite elderly for those times to make such a journey, and they both died within a year of their arrival in Italy.

But just to show that all women of those times were not dashing around leading armies into battle, it should be remembered that at some time between 704 and 720, Ethelburga's sisters-in-law, Cuthburga and Cwenburga, were busy founding the Abbey at Wimborne (see Chapter 2). Indeed, it was the same year as Ethelburga was leading her troops into battle at Taunton - 720 - that Cuthburga died peacefully at Wimborne.

EDBURGA

Seventy-four years after Ethelburga and Ina died in Rome, the last of this trio of early Saxon women came on the scene. She was Edburga (Eadburh), a royal princess in her own right, being the daughter of King Offa of Mercia (he of Offa's Dyke). She was married to Beorhtric, King of Wessex (786-802) - see previous pedigree 5.1. Having been well trained in deviousness and ambition by her father, she is said to have ruled her husband, mainly by the use of her temper. Little is known of the events of her husband's reign apart from the manner of his death - poisoned by his wife. It appears that Edburga had become jealous of her husband's friendship with Worr, a young ealdorman (nobleman) and the latter's increasing influence on the King. Edburga resolved to eliminate Worr by the simple expedient of poisoning his drink. By one of those twists of fate that she certainly couldn't have foreseen, her husband drank from the same goblet as Worr and died alongside his favourite.

Edburga managed to escape to the Continent with her treasures. There the Emperor Constantine offered her an opulent monastery where she was able to live as its Abbess, but her scandalous behaviour soon resulted in her expulsion. After much travelling and further adventures, this former Queen of Wessex ended her days begging in the streets of Pavia in Italy. We will never know whether or not the poisoning affair occurred in Dorset, for its actual site went unrecorded.

ANGLO-SAXON WOMEN OF DORSET

While there remains uncertainty as to how much of the lives of the trio of Saxon Queens just described was actually spent in Dorset, there is no doubt of the sites of all the events occurring from the time of Alfred the Great onwards.. For these historical records we have to thank not just Alfred but also his mother, for it was this very learned and literate woman who ensured that Alfred could read and write, and also imbued him with a love of learning.

Prior to Alfred's reign, as mentioned earlier, events of any note had merely been recorded in a haphazard fashion in the records of various monasteries. During his reign and at his instruction, this material was brought together to form a preface of retrospective history to the *Anglo-Saxon Chronicles.* Thereafter the *Chronicles* commenced a more detailed history of England, starting with Alfred's father, Aethelwulf, and continuing for many centuries after Alfred's death. Many more details of history may therefore be gleaned from these *Chronicles* than in previous centuries, but there is one cautionary note - particularly where women were concerned - and that is that they were invariably written by monks with virtually an inbuilt bias against the "weaker sex".

During the one and a half centuries from the reign of Alfred the Great to the arrival of William the Conqueror and the Normans, at least six Anglo-Saxon females left their mark in Dorset. But if we try to locate references to them in books on Dorset, it is found that most are disposed of in perhaps one or two sentences. The first example is typical.

ETHELGIVA

> "...the great Benedictine nunnery at Shaftesbury, the foundation of King Alfred, whose daughter was its first Abbess." [1]

Searching through the reference books on Dorset will give us the further information as to the date, 888 A.D., her name, Ethelgiva (or Aethelgiva/Aethelgifu/Ethelgeda), and the fact that she was Alfred's middle daughter. Further investigation of general history books gives us the background information that Alfred, born 849, was King of Wessex from 871 to 899, and in about the year 880 he built the town of Shaftesbury where he founded this Abbey eight years later.

We therefore have a picture of Alfred the Great ordering a small town to be built at the top of the hill, and founding the Abbey there for his daughter to live quietly and peacefully with her group of nuns, devoting themselves to a religious life. Nothing could be further from the truth!

Alfred came to the throne of Wessex in 871 at the age of twenty-one, when he was already married with a young family. For the next few years he fought battle after battle against the Danes attacking from the North and West, and by sea from the South. By 878 he was all but defeated, and with a small band of followers retreated into the Isle of Athelney in Somerset - where grew up the legend of his burning the cakes. After a year or so of guerrilla tactics and a final battle at Edington, the Danes surrendered and a treaty was arranged between them - the Peace of Wedmore. The Danes were to retain Northumbria, East Anglia and half of the Midlands (East Mercia) - the Danelaw; Alfred retained Wessex, which by that time included London and Kent. In 883 West Mercia also acknowledged Alfred as King.

From 879, therefore, Wessex was comparatively secure, but experience had taught that a fresh set of invaders might appear at any moment - as did happen. To try and guard against this threat, Alfred had a large fleet built to guard his coast-line, and on land he set about choosing strategic sites where he could raise permanent settlements guarded by earthworks and stockades. Each town - in general they were hardly larger than a small village of today - was garrisoned by a few experienced soldiers, capable of keeping the enemy at bay until Alfred and his main army could reach it with aid. Some of these towns were built on the sites of former Roman cities - Winchester (the capital), Rochester, Exeter, Chichester and London, for example; others like Shaftesbury were usually new sites, perhaps having formerly been used by Celts prior to the Roman invasion.

So why did Alfred found the Abbey at Shaftesbury in 888, and put his daughter Ethelgiva in charge?   Shaftesbury was a front-line defensive town, built on a 700-foot-high hill standing out above the surrounding forest and swamp-land. Alfred's last major sea-battle had been fought in 885 - although at the time he didn't know that it would be the last. There were still occasional raids and more serious attacks, with the most severe yet to come in 897 when a mighty Danish army arrived in Kent in 330 ships. Did Alfred think that his daughter and her companions in the Abbey would be safe there, protected within the wooden stockade by a few experienced soldiers? The pagan Danes had no mercy on any Christian they encountered in their way, and had established an horrific record of how they treated monks and nuns.

Or was Ethelgiva able to defend herself, with sword and axe if necessary? We are led to believe that young ladies of those times were weak and defenceless against the invading hordes of blood-thirsty Danes. But no-one seems to consider Ethelgiva's sister Ethelfleda - the Boudicca of her time - or indeed the two West Saxon Queens, Sexburga and Ethelburga, just described.

Ethelfleda had grown up in Wessex but was married to Ethelred, ealdorman of West Mercia, who was Alfred's trusted aide and a proven soldier. (It is possible that Ethelred was Alfred's nephew, for Alfred's wife was Ealswitha, a daughter of another Ethelred, Earl of Mercia - see accompanying pedigree 5.2.) The last major invasion of the Danes in 893 had been defeated by Alfred, his son Edward, and his son-in-law Ethelred of Mercia: this was followed eight years later by the death of Alfred and the accession of his son Edward (the "Elder"). In 910 a Danish rising on the northern frontier accompanied by an invasion on the south coast again saw Edward and Ethelred in action, and this time they determined to eradicate the Danes totally from the Danelaw. But hardly had they begun than Ethelred died in 912, leaving his wife Ethelfleda as sole ruler in Mercia. While Edward tackled East Anglia, Ethelfleda led her forces in establishing fortifications along the western frontier

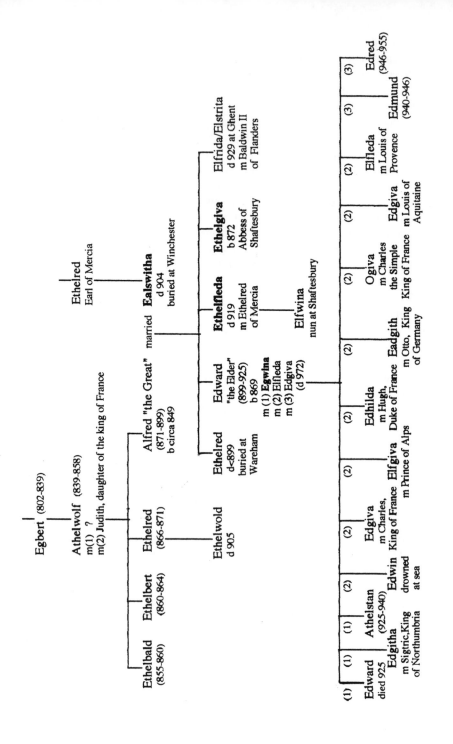

Egbert (802-839)

Athelwolf (839-858)
m(1) ?
m(2) Judith, daughter of the king of France

Ethelbald (855-860)
Ethelbert (860-864)
Ethelred (866-871)
Alfred "the Great" (871-899) b circa 849   married   Ealswitha d 904 buried at Winchester

Ethelwold d 905

Ethelred Earl of Mercia

Ethelred d<899 buried at Wareham
Edward "the Elder" (899-925) b 869 m (1) Egwina m (2) Elfleda m (3) Edgiva (d 972)
Ethelfleda d 919 m Ethelred of Mercia   Elfwina nun at Shaftesbury
Ethelgiva b 872 Abbess of Shaftesbury
Elfrida/Elstrita d 929 at Ghent m Baldwin II of Flanders

(1) Edgitha m Sigtric.King of Northumbria
(1) Edward died 925
(1) Athelstan (925-940)
(2) Edwin drowned at sea
(2) Edgiva m Charles, King of France
(2) Elfgiva m Prince of Alps
(2) Edhilda m Hugh, Duke of France
(2) Eadgith m Otto, King of Germany
(2) Ogiva m Charles the Simple King of France
(2) Edgiva m Louis of Aquitaine
(2) Elfleda m Louis of Provence
(3) Edmund (940-946)
(3) Edred (946-955)

118

with Wales, and then laid siege to, captured, and subdued to her own rule, the Danish strongholds of Tamworth, Stafford, Warwick, Derby and Leicester. She had made Mercia secure!

The relatively limited information about Ethelfleda indicated that she was not just a strategist, but actually led her troops "from the front". If we stop and consider this, it produces some surprising results. Ethelfleda could - and did - use sword and axe. Where had she learned how to use them? We are taught that these were very male-dominated times, where strength and might conquered all. And yet we have Ethelfleda not just using weapons, but leading her troops - and they obeyed! Battle-hardened male soldiers taking orders from a woman over and over again!

Additionally, how did Ethelfleda come to be accepted as the leader of the Mercian troops when her husband died? All the history books lead us to believe that when a leader died, whether he was a local chieftain or a king, the new leader was chosen on the basis of being a strong man with a proven "track-record". Surely Ethelred had a deputy leader that fitted this description? Or had Ethelfleda been her husband's deputy all along? Was that why the Mercians were only too willing to accept her as their leader? Had she been trained in military arts from childhood in order to defend herself?

And if one daughter of Alfred the Great's had been so trained, what about his other daughter, Ethelgiva, the first Abbess of Shaftesbury? Had she also been trained in military arts from childhood? Was that why she was put at Shaftesbury? As well as following her religious life as Abbess, was she also put in charge of the defenders of the town? After all, she was the King's daughter, and we know that her sister was able to give orders and be obeyed.

But is it likely that a young woman who was going to devote her life to religious service would learn to use weapons? To answer this question we have to look more closely at the early life of Ethelgiva. If we consider her age when she became Abbess in 888, it is extremely unlikely that she was less than sixteen years of age at the time, and hence born no later than 872. But her father Alfred was only born in 849, and it is unlikely that he started producing legitimate children before he was fifteen or sixteen years of age, (864/5) and there is evidence that he was not married until 866.[1] We also know that Ethelgiva was his middle daughter, and hence had at least one older sister. Ethelgiva must therefore have been born between 866 and 872, probably nearer the latter date, and the year 871 has been suggested as the most likely.[1]

In 878, as mentioned earlier, just about the whole of England was over-run by the Danes, and Alfred with a few followers retreated to the Isle of Athelney, Somerset. Presumably his family were with him, for nowhere else in England was safe for them. So at a time when Ethelgiva was still a child there was virtually nothing between her and the extreme danger of the advancing hordes of Danes. This now puts into a better perspective the likelihood that both Ethelgiva and her sister Ethelfleda, along with their young brothers, would have been taught to defend themselves at that time of great danger.

Additionally, it is very unlikely that at this tender age, Ethelgiva would have known that she would later wish to follow a devout and religious life. This latter statement is reinforced by the fact that in Alfred's will, believed written in the mid-880's,[4] he left Ethelgiva property in her own right without referring to her as a nun, suggesting that she had not even taken the veil by that time. (Prior to becoming an Abbess, she would have had to receive instruction at some religious establishment, possibly Wimborne Abbey if it had not already been destroyed by the Danes, or at Winchester in the Abbey founded by her mother, Ealswitha.)

There is no record that Shaftesbury was attacked by the Danes during these early years from its foundation, before peace was finally established. (It was attacked and repaired by Canute at a later date.[1]) It therefore appears that Ethelgiva was never called upon to perform this military role that has been theorized for her, so we will never know if she was capable of so doing. But perhaps it is all wrong, and she was in fact simply a very devout young lady with no thought in her mind of fighting, preferring to leave that to the men-folk. Infuriatingly, the record books tell us nothing about the matter. But then they were written by monks - usually celibate - who had no love for, or perhaps an active dislike of, the "weaker sex".

The life at Shaftesbury Abbey, started by Ethelgiva in those troubled times of the fear of Danish invasions, went on for another seven centuries until it abruptly ceased to exist at the Dissolution. This later history is told elsewhere (see Chapter 2). At the beginning of this story of Ethelgiva it was mentioned how most reference books on Dorset dispose of her in one or two sentences. Perhaps this exploration of the background of Ethelgiva and the context of the times in which she lived, may have added some "life" to her story. What a difference it makes to the beginnings of Shaftesbury Abbey to know that it was founded at a time when any moment could bring the enemy to the gates, and that the Abbess was a mere teenager.

EGWINA

"Egwina, the wife of Edward the Elder, was buried
at Milton Abbey, founded by her son Athelstan."[n]

Egwina was the first of the three wives of King Edward "the Elder" (869-925) who ascended the throne in 899 on the death of his father, Alfred the Great. They left a large family: three of the sons who survived them successively ascended the throne, Athelstan, Edwin and Edred; six of their daughters were married to foreign princes, some of them the most powerful in Europe, and the remaining three daughters embraced a religious life (whether any of these latter were in Dorset is not known).

It was Athelstan, the eldest surving son, who founded the original Milton Abbey in 938, and it is here that he and his mother, Egwina, are said to be buried. There are two very old paintings in the Abbey Church, dating from the time of Edward IV (1462-1483), but probably copies of earlier paintings, which are believed to depict the founder of the Abbey and his mother. The lady holds an enormous glove in one hand, and in the other hand is a strange bird, said to be a hawk. Nothing remains of the original Anglo-Saxon Abbey which was founded for secular (married) priests, who were there until forced to give way to Benedictine (celibate) monks in 964 by the founder's grandson Edgar. The original Abbey was replaced by a Norman one, which was in turn destroyed and rebuilt in the 14th Century. Any possibility of identifying the original site of their burial has therefore disappeared long ago.

There is a romantic story about the first meeting between Edward and Egwina, but the truth of it must remain in doubt. It comes not from the reasonably reliable *Anglo-Saxon Chronicles,* but from the writings of the Anglo-Norman monk, William of Malmesbury (circa 1096-1142), and is based on a ballad that had been passed by word of mouth for over two hundred years.

Egwina was the daughter of a neat-herd - a cow-herd appointed by a community to ensure that their cows didn't stray. Even as a child Egwina was reputed to show signs of great beauty, but of more importance to her future was that she had a dream portending that she would be the mother of a great monarch. This report was said to have aroused the interest of the (unnamed) lady who had nursed the children of Alfred; so much so that she took Egwina into her own home where she was reared and educated as if she was her own daughter. What this unnamed nurse no doubt had in mind, soon came to pass. The young aetheling (princeling) Edward came to pay a visit to his old "nanny", saw Egwina, and immediately fell in love with the beautiful young girl. The future King Athelstan was born of this marriage.

So somewhere in the grounds of the public school that now occupies the site, are buried this beautiful young woman, Egwina, and the son, Athelstan, who founded the original Abbey here.

If we look a little closer at the story of Egwina, one little interesting point emerges. Egwina must have died about the year 900, for it is known that Athelstan (born 894) was sent to be brought up by his aunt Ethelfleda (the military one already described) when his mother died. Athelstan didn't found Milton Abbey until 938, the year before his death. His mother had died approximately forty years earlier. Presumably Egwina would have been buried somewhere "suitable" by her husband. So why did Athelstan have the remains of his mother - whom he must have scarcely remembered - disinterred and removed to Milton after all those years?

ELFRIDA

At least one Anglo-Saxon woman of Dorset is given more than half a line in the history books, for every book on Dorset refers to this story of how the wicked Elfrida had her step-son, the young King Edward ("the Martyr"), murdered in order that her own son Ethelred might come to the throne instead. Some of the details have obviously become embellished by subsequent legend, but the essential facts do not appear to be in dispute.

Elfrida was the second wife of Edgar, King of England. On his death in 975, he was succeeded by Edward, his fifteen-year-old son by his first wife, despite Elfrida's efforts to get her own son, Ethelred, elected. Elfrida was still determined to obtain the throne for her son, and her chance came three years later on 18th March 978 at Corfe Castle (it was called Corfe's Gate then). Elfrida had various possessions in Dorset, including a hunting lodge built by her late husband on the site of which now stands the ruins of the later Corfe Castle.

She was in residence there with her son Ethelred when the young King Edward was staying at nearby Wareham to go hunting. On this fateful day Edward had become separated from the rest of his party, and realising that he was close to Corfe, he decided to pay a visit to his step-mother and Ethelred - of whom he is said to have been very fond. As was usual in those times, an important visitor was always greeted at the gate by the owner of the house with a drink. But as Edward was raising the stirrup-cup to his lips, he was stabbed in the chest - by his step-mother say some sources, by one of her servants say other authorities. According to the story that has come down to us, Edward's horse ran away with the wounded King, until he fell dead by the stream that still runs through the village.

Elfrida is supposed to have had Edward's body carried to the home of one of the villagers, an old blind woman, who was to watch over the body without knowing that it was of the dead King. According to legend, this was when the first of the miracles associated with Edward's body was said to have occurred when, during the night, the old lady accidentally touched the dead body. Instantly the room was said to have been filled with a powerful silvery light, and the old woman was cured of her blindness.

The young King Edward was buried at Wareham Church, while Elfrida is reported to have fled to another of her homes at Bere [Regis], her ambition at last fulfilled. For now it was her eight-year-old son who came to the throne, known to us as Ethelred the Unready (Unlearned, or Badly-advised).

Two years later Ethelred decided that his half-brother should have a more fitting resting-place in the Abbey at Shaftesbury, founded by his great-great-grandfather. Accordingly, Edward's body was disinterred from its grave at St Mary's in Wareham - which still claims to have his reputed coffin - and carried in slow procession to Shaftesbury. This was led by the Earl of Mercia, the Bishop of Sherborne, together with the Abbess of Wilton and all her nuns, plus many nobles, their retinues, and many hundreds of ordinary folk.

Tradition has it that Elfrida tried to join the procession for this second funeral, but her horse repeatedly backed away from it. She therefore dismounted and tried to follow on foot, but her feet remained glued to the spot and she was unable to join the rest of the mourners. All that is known of the rest of Elfrida's life is that she restored the monastery at Amesbury, founded an abbey at Reading, and a nunnery at Whorwell in Hampshire, where she subsequently died and was buried.

If we leave Elfrida on one side for the moment, one major detail stands out from this story. Why did they take Edward's body to Shaftesbury? Why didn't they take it to Sherborne, the most ancient bishopric in the area? Why wasn't it taken to Milton Abbey, founded by Edward's grandfather; or to Old Sarum (Salisbury); or to the capital, Winchester, where so many of his predecessors were buried? No, it was taken to Shaftesbury. And what had Shaftesbury to offer? An Abbey, founded for Ethelgiva, Alfred's daughter, and run by females in the century since its foundation. Why did they choose a female-dominated town? All the other places mentioned were run by men. What had Shaftesbury to offer that the others hadn't? Why was the care of his tomb entrusted to the care of females? We are not even told the name of the Abbess at the time!

Another relevant but unanswered question is why did Edward become Edward *the Martyr?* He didn't suffer for his Christian faith. He didn't die for the sake of his country over which he had barely begun to rule. He died because of the jealousy of his step-mother, who wanted her own son to be the King. In those times it was nothing new for a king or other leader to be murdered by jealous relatives, or even for a king to do the murder himself. As we shall see in a moment, Elfrida's second husband, King Edgar - the father of Edward the Martyr - had no compunction about murdering his close friend, Elfrida's first husband, in order that he could marry her himself. So was it because Edward was murdered at the instigation of a female that he was subsequently called a Martyr? (Remember that the records of these events were written by monks!)

Who made the decision that Edward should become a Martyr anyway? Presumably the leading Church-men with the approval of the King and the Pope. However, there is a sneaking suspicion that it was all engineered as a "public relations exercise" by the Abbess of Shaftesbury. Did she foresee that having a shrine to a Martyr in her Abbey would attract thousands of pilgrims, all bringing their offerings? For that is what happened over the next few centuries, so that by the time of the Dissolution, the Abbess was one of the richest women in the country (see Chapter 2).

To return to Elfrida, we are led to believe that out of the blue and on the spur of the moment, she caused the barbarous deed to be done to her step-son at Corfe. Was she really as wicked as she is made out to be? If we look at the little we know of her life at Court, she could not have had an easy time during her marriage to King Edgar "the Peaceful". In the fifteen years of his reign from 959 to 975 he was noted for his religiousness, including the expulsion of all secular (married) monks in favour of Benedictine (celibate) ones. In spite of this, his private life was very different. There were always many mistresses around his Court, and he produced a large number of illegitimate offspring. By the time he came to the throne at the age of eighteen, he already had a bad reputation for being a lecher and no attractive young girl was safe in his presence: he continued in this manner throughout his life. His first son by his wife Elfleda was Edward, born the year of his accession at the age of eighteen. During the life of this first wife, Edgar - the promoter of chastity and celibacy in the monasteries - carried off from the monastery at Wilton a beautiful young girl of noble birth named Wulfrith. She remained his mistress for many years, and they had one daughter, Edgiva.

Within a very short time however, the young King Edgar heard of the great beauty of Elfrida, the daughter of Ordgar, Earl of Devonshire. He schemed with one of his earls, Athelwold, that the latter was to go to Devon and see for himself if Elfrida was as beautiful as the reports claimed. Since the young lady was also a wealthy heiress, Athelwold was instructed that if the reports of her beauty were true, then he was to act on the King's behalf and invite Elfrida to become Edgar's wife - even though his first wife was still alive at the time.

Not only did Athelwold find Elfrida every bit as beautiful as reported, but he was so taken with her that he failed to mention the true purpose of his visit: instead he proposed to her on his own behalf, was accepted and they were married. Meanwhile, he had a message sent to the King that the reports of her beauty were misleading, and that although rich, she was most unsuitable a person to be the wife of a King!

Edgar obviously had his suspicions, for he determined to see the young lady for himself. The fat was in the fire for Athelwold! There was nothing he could do but confess to Elfrida that he had prevented her from marrying the King. He pleaded with her to make herself as unattractive as possible, so that the King might not see her beauty. Not for Elfrida! She made herself as attractive as possible and wore her most beautiful clothes when she was taken to the King's presence. When Edgar saw Elfrida he fell in love with her, and solved the one problem that stood in his way of marrying her by stabbing Athelwold in the back whilst they were out hunting together.[3] What became of the second obstacle in his path - his first wife - has not come down in history. Edgar's long-term mistress, Wulfrith, remained at Court, and it can be imagined that there was no love lost between the new wife and the old mistress. Within the year Elfrida gave birth to their son, Ethelred. Nothing further is recorded of their married life together, until the death of Edgar in 975, nine years after their marriage.

So what can we make of the character of Elfrida? Was she evil through and through as we are led to believe? Did she have to fight tooth and nail for her "rights" and for those of her son during the remainder of their marriage? She certainly had to fight against the active dislike of Archbishop Dunstan who had great influence with her husband - it was mainly due to Dunstan that she was defeated in trying to get Ethelred to succeed upon his father's death. She also had to fight against Wulfrith and the many other mistresses, each trying to push their own child's future interests forward.

But in the end, did Elfrida actually instigate the killing of Edward at Corfe, or could there be any other explanation? If we consider the death of Thomas Becket in 1170, then King Henry II was considered - and believed himself to be - responsible for it, even though he didn't directly order the murder. All he did was speak out loud to the effect that he wished someone would rid him of the Archbishop. Six courtiers took him at his word and killed Becket. Could a similar thing have happened with Elfrida? Her servants would certainly be aware of how much she wanted her own son to be King, and of how her step-son stood in his way. Did one of these servants take matters into his own hands and kill Edward without Elfrida's direct involvement and without her foreknowledge? The history books would have us believe otherwise, for as far as they are concerned, Elfrida was directly responsible.

There is one point that raises further doubt. If the situation after Edward's death is considered, there is one odd thing about it. The new King, Ethelred, was only about ten years old. The government of the country therefore passed into the hands of the great nobles, in whose number was the all-powerful Archbishop Dunstan. Amongst these there must have been many who were enemies of Elfrida - particularly Dunstan - and yet although it appeared to be an accepted fact that Elfrida was guilty, no action was taken against her, not even her restriction within a nunnery. It might be argued that perhaps she sought sanctuary in some religious house where she could not be reached, but only two years later she openly tried to join the funeral procession accompanying the removal of Edward's relics from Wareham to Shaftesbury. Why did no-one try to seize her then?

A more detailed consideration of the political background of those times also throws further doubt on Elfrida's involvement in the death of her step-son. This background centred on Dunstan, Archbishop of Canterbury. During the reigns of Alfred the Great's three grandsons from 925 to 955 (see accompanying pedigree 5.3), Dunstan had risen to become the favourite minister of King Edred in his powerful position as Abbot of Glastonbury. He suffered two complete reversals of fortune in the next generation of Kings. Dunstan favoured celibate monks, but when he fell out with King Edwin and was banished to the Continent, secular (married) clergy were permitted to re-occupy all the monasteries.

Everything was reversed under the rule of the new 18-year-old King Edgar in 959, who was strongly under the influence of Dunstan. The latter was now appointed Archbishop of Canterbury (or probably elected himself) and all the secular clergy were dispossessed and replaced by celibate monks in the monasteries. On the death of Edgar in 975, the secular clergy saw their chance to regain their former superior positions. Edgar's elder son, the 16-year-old Edward (the Martyr) was under the influence of Dunstan, so the secular clergy turned to support Edgar's younger son, the eight-year-old Ethelred (Elfrida's son) in a rival claim to the throne.

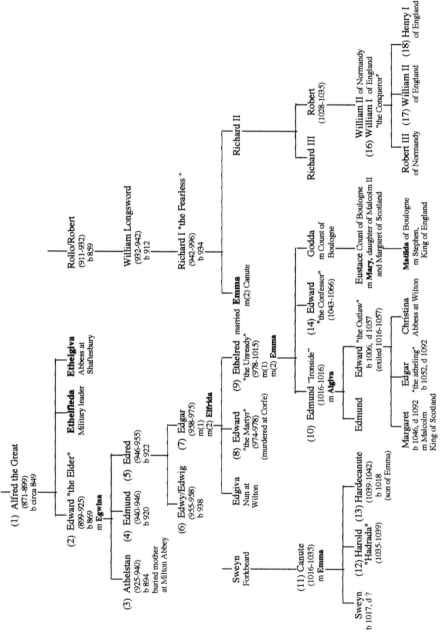

Pedigree 5.3   Later Saxon and early Norman Kings of England, and the Dukes of Normandy

The ranks of the secular clergy in this "Church War" received support in many parts of England from dispossessed monks who reclaimed their former monasteries. They were in turn supported by many of the nobles who were against the great power of Dunstan, including Elfhere, the powerful ealdorman of Mercia.

Elfrida's son was now the figurehead of one side in this "Church War", and although defeated by Dunstan and his supporters when Edward was declared King, the secular clergy and their supporters - particularly the Mercian Elfhere - still continued their intrigues to oust Dunstan from the all-powerful position that he created for himself. And that meant getting rid of King Edward.

If one remembers that the historical accounts of those times were written by monks, then one has to pay more attention to how much bias may have been intoduced into their records, for these authors would have been supporters of Dunstan and his celibate monks. The story of Elfrida that has come down to us presents her as a wicked step-mother who murdered her stepson in order that her own son might come to the throne. But now we see that a large part of England had an equally good reason for wishing to get rid of Edward - for political reasons. Had they been the stronger side in the "Church War" that broke out at Edgar's death, then Ethelred would have been King (there were no other contenders), Dunstan ousted, and the secular clergy reinstated. When this failed to materialize, did the losers all meekly return home and forget the idea? Or did they continue to intrigue against Edward? Could it possibly be that they were directly responsible for the murder of Edward at Corfe when he became separated from his companions? Was Elfrida an innocent bystander and not directly involved in the murder at all?

The foregoing analysis has been based principally on material in 19th and 20th Century publications, and demonstrates that there are several flaws in the evidence for Elfrida's involvement in the murder of her step-son. Ideally, one should always go to original sources to check the veracity of all statements, but this may not be practical in many cases. The author was therefore delighted to find (after the above had been researched) that Alan Miller had investigated this very point in relation to the story of Elfrida[2], and as the following will show, he has produced some surprising results: details from his source material are given in Appendix A.

The only contemporary accounts from the time of Elfrida are the *Anglo-Saxon Chronicles* written by monks. At least seven versions survive, all with slightly different texts, suggesting that they were not all copied from each other. All seven versions give the date of King Edward's murder (18th March 978) and the place (Corfes-Gate) - but none mention Elfrida. The only reference to her is ten years earlier when she married King Edgar.

A clear account of Edward's death was written *thirty years* after the event (probably in 1008) - see Appendix A1 - and again there is no mention of Elfrida. This was the same year that Edward was canonised, and was probably written to celebrate this event.

One hundred years after the event (between 1070 and 1080) another account was written and for the first time Elfrida is mentioned as playing a part in the murder (see Appendix A2). This account is believed to have been written by a monk called Goscelin who lived and worked at the monasteries at Sherborne and Wilton. He was a professional writer of the biographies of saints, and this particular account is believed to have been written for Shaftesbury Abbey.

The mists surrounding the origin of Elfrida's story are now beginning to thin a little! This account was written several years after the Norman Conquest, by which time most heads of monasteries and abbeys had been replaced by Normans. The tomb of St Edward the Martyr at Shaftesbury Abbey was acquiring a reputation for miracles, and the account was written for the Abbey where his tomb was situated. There was no-one still living who had been alive at the time of Edward's death, and the story had therefore already passed down at least three generations.

If one now follows through subsequent stories of the deed written in the 12th Century (see Appendix A3-A7), then what appear to be completely unbelievable flights of the imagination were written as true facts in connection with Elfrida's story: the introduction of a dwarf; poison; a person called Elferius apparently alone, moving Edward's body to Shaftesbury and later being eaten alive by lice; and the assassination occurring at Shaftesbury itself. Were all these embellishments purely imagination on the part of the writers, or had they been misled by someone "spinning them a yarn"? And if these later embellishments of the story are completely fictitious, then what about the earlier ones written a century after the event, when Elfrida is first implicated?

So whose story is one to believe? Accounts written one or two centuries after the incident - perhaps with an ulterior motive in biasing the story - with certain proof of how fictitious versions can develop? Or is one to believe seven contemporary accounts which make no mention of Elfrida's involvement?

As mentioned earlier, there is the puzzling fact that no action was taken against Elfrida. Given the circumstances of the time, there would appear to be no other explanation than that Elfrida was not involved with the murder, which in turn agrees with the *Anglo-Saxon Chronicles*. The balance of evidence appears to be in favour of Elfrida's innocence. What do you think?

The question was posed earlier as to why Edward became known as Edward *the Martyr*, when there didn't seem to be any adequate explanation for his martyrdom. In the light of what has been discussed about the "Church War" is it possible that he was considered to be a martyr for the cause of celibate monks because he died at the instigation of the supporters of secular monks? His canonisation was only thirty years after his death, and would have involved the "victorious" celibate monks!

Tithe Barn and ruins of the Abbey at Abbotsbury founded by Tola and her husband Orc in about the year 1030. In Domesday Book of 1086 some of the lands were being unjustly held by Hadwidia Fitzgrip (Chapter 1).

above: Statues at Lacock Abbey representing Ela of Can▮ (Chapter 1), and her two daughters who became Abbesse▮ Shaftesbury and Romsey (Chapter 2). Ela founded Lac▮ Abbey, and became its first Abbess in 1240. The terra▮ figures are by Alexander Sederbach, circa 1756 *permission of National Trust, Lacock Abbey).*

left: William Longspée, husband of Ela Canford. From▮ tomb at Salisbury Cathedral, of which he and his wife ▮ founders (Chapter 1).

of an old barn at Blynfield Farm (formerly Blynchesfield) near Shaftesbury, that might from the time of Alice Russell's disputed ownership in the fifteenth century (Chapter 1). stone window frames are older, and most certainly came from Shaftesbury Abbey at the solution (Chapter 2). *(By permission of Mrs Hayward).*

old manor house of Wynford Eagle which was the principal prize won under dubious umstances by Ann Michel in the Land Lottery of 1699 (Chapter 1). It was also the scene of murder of Lady Sydenham during the Civil War in 1644 (Chapter 7). *(By permission of . John Best).*

Scene at drawing of a lottery in Mercer's Hall, Ironmonger Lane, Cheapside, Londo[n]
beginning of eighteenth century — the exact situation pertaining to Ann Michel's disputed
in the Land Lottery of 1699 (Chapter 1). It is difficult to see how any fraud could have [been]
perpetrated since in full view of the public the draw was made by Blue Coat boys from Chr[ist]
Hospital, supervised by presiding officials and Trustees of the Lottery, with clerks seated [at a]
lower level in the platform. The rotating drums containing the draw tickets were secu[rely]
locked inside their covers at night. This scene was painted on a vellum fan-mount.

Nuns at Stapehill Abbey (Chapter 2). *(By permission of Rev. Mother Abbess, Holy Cr[oss]*
Abbey, Dyfed).

Saint Judith, based on the former inn sign at the "Quiet Woman" at Halstock (Chapter 2).

Saint Walburga and her companions crossing the English channel on their way to be missionaries in Germany (Chapter 2). *(By permission of Mary Brown).*

Margaret Beaufort, mother of King Henry VII (Chapter 2). *(Mary Evans Picture Library)*

Travelling trunk of Margaret Beaufort (Chapter 2). *(By permission of the Public Record Office, London).*

The mosaic in St Peter's Church, Portland, laid by the murderess Constance Kent (Chapter *By permission of The Governor, The Verne Y.O.I., Portland).*

t: Wooden base of sun-dial in churchyard at West Parley, made from the gallows involved Iarbin murder of 1803 (Chapter 3).

at Birdsmoorgate where the inquest took place into the death of John Brown in July 1856, where his wife was subsequently arrested for his murder (Chapter 3).

Two of the inns used by Mary Squires in her alibi against a charge of kidnapping in 17: (Chapter 3). *Upper*, the Red Lion at South Perrott, now a private house: *lower*, the for Three Horseshoes, now known as the Wynard's Gap Inn.

"...mont" at Lyme regis, the former home of Mrs Coade, illustrating the use of Coade Stone in ...corations (Chapter 4). *(By permission of the owner)*.

...decoration frequently found on Coade Stone (Chapter 4). *(By permission of the owner)*.

Tombstone of Lady Charlotte Schreiber, formerly Guest, née Bertie, at Canford Ch
(Chapter 4).

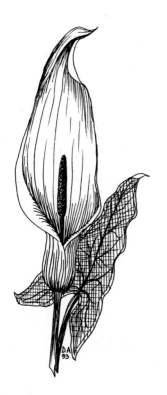

Arum Maculatum, (Lords and Ladies), from which Jane Gibbs of Portland obtained the starch that won her a gold medal in 1797 (Chapter 4). *(By permission of David Arnold).*

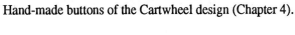

Hand-made buttons of the Cartwheel design (Chapter 4).

Queen Egwina, based on the fifteenth century (or older) reproduction of earlier portrait at Milton Abbey where she was buried by her son, King Athelstan, in 929 (Chapter 5).

The Great Seal of Empress Matilda (Chapter 6).

Queen Margaret of Anjou, wife of Henr
From a window in a church at Angers, Fr
destroyed in the French Revolution (Chapt

Mrs Fitzherbert, formerly Lady Wel
Lulworth, the morganatic wife of the P
Regent, later George IV (Chapter 6). *(I
Evans Picture Library)*.

Lady Bankes, the defender of Corfe Castle during the Civil War (Chapter 7).

Lady Digby, the defender of Sherborne Castle during the Civil War (Chapter 7). *(By permission of the Duke of Bedford).*

Pilsdon Manor where a young lady was assaulted by Roundhead soldiers who "convinced" she was King Charles II in disguise (Chapter 7).

November 15 1725

This is to give notice to all the World that Andrew Tucker and his Son John Tucker are Clowns, and Cowards ———— Witness my hand

Henry ffeilding

Poster left by Henry Fielding at Lyme Regis mocking the guardian of Sara Andrews who had unsuccessfully tried to kidnap. Note that he then spelt his surname "Fielding", and "ff" for "F" (Chapter 8). (By permission of Lyme Regis (Philpot) museum).

...stones of Clotilde Lawrence née Clariet and her husband in Studland Churchyard ...ter 8).

...stones at Worth Matravers of Elizabeth Jesty (inset), the first person recorded as having a ...nation, and of her husband Benjamin, who administered it (Chapter 8).

The house and church built by Adela Curtis at Burton Bradstock (Chapter 9).

Norman burial urn in wall of Church at West Parley, believed to have contained the heart of "the Lady of Lydlinch" (Chapter 9).

ALGIVA

Most reference works on Dorset simply refer - if at all - to the fact that the wife of Edmund Ironside (983-1016) was buried at Shaftesbury Abbey. Occasionally her name of Algiva (Elgiva/Elgifu) is mentioned, and that is all. But she led quite an eventful life! She was probably of noble birth, for the first mention of her is as the wife of Sigeferth, a Danish chieftain in Northumbria. He was one of the Danish settlers who had lived there peacefully for many years until, on 13th November 1002 (St Brice's Day), Ethelred the Unready deceitfully ordered the terrible massacre of all the Danes living in Wessex. Presumably Algiva and Sigeferth were in Wessex at that time, for he was slain while she was confined in the Abbey of Malmesbury in Wiltshire.

Edmund Ironside, the eldest son of King Ethelred by one of his mistresses (see previous pedigree 5.3), demanded of his father the possessions of the murdered earls of Northumbria, Sigeferth among them. When Ethelred refused, Edmund immediately visited Algiva at Malmesbury Abbey and persuaded her to marry him. They soon went to Northumbria where Algiva used her influence on her late husband's subjects to get them to accept her new husband as their chieftain.

At least two sons were born to Algiva in the next few years, first Edmund and then Edward in 1006. None of the events of their married life are reported until the death of her father-in-law, Ethelred, when her husband Edmund Ironside was proclaimed King. It is likely that Algiva and her family spent most of their time within the Saxon stronghold of Wessex, for during the greater part of her married life the Danes came flooding in to take their revenge for the massacre of St Brice's Day, first under Sweyn and then under his son, Canute.

The reign of Edmund Ironside only lasted seven months, most of which were occupied in battles with Canute. A treaty eventually gave some measure of peace, granting Canute rule over the Northern counties and Edmund rule over the South. On Edmund's death, Canute was crowned King of all England. He immediately sought to eliminate the leaders who had fought against him, and also all rival claimants to the throne - of whom Algiva's two sons were very prominent (see previous pedigree 5.3). Edmund's half-brother Edwy was proclaimed an outlaw, pursued and brutally killed. His two half-brothers, Alfred and Edward, were in Normandy with their mother, Emma, and safely out of Canute's reach (see later). That left Algiva and Edmund's two sons, by then about ten years of age. Canute had them arrested and brought before him.

What was happening to Algiva at that terrible time is not recorded. All we know is that at some unknown date she died at Shaftesbury Abbey and was buried there. Had she taken refuge with her sons at the Abbey of Shaftesbury before they were taken from her? Did she then die of a broken heart at the thought of what might happen to them at the hands of Canute? Or did she remain there as a nun for many years to come, until finally she died and was quietly buried there? Let us hope it was the latter, for then she would have known that her sons were safe. Apparently Canute had a weak moment and could not bring himself to be directly responsible for the deaths of the two little boys. Instead, he sent them to his ally and vassal, the King of Sweden, with instructions for him to put them to death. But the King of Sweden also took pity on them and sent them far out of Canute's reach to the Court of the King of Hungary. The elder boy soon died, but Algiva's other son, Edward, lived a reasonably happy life there, before returning with his family to England forty years later (see Chapter 6). It was this son of Algiva that provides the sole link between all the Saxons of Dorset since the time of the arrival of Cerdic, and the present-day Queen.

If we go right back to the beginning of this story of Algiva, one fact stands out. Why was it necessary for Edmund to marry her, and *get her to use her influence* on her dead husband's subjects to accept him as their ruler? Edmund was the son of the King. He could have taken the possessions by force, without the necessity of marrying Sigeferth's widow. He could even have inherited them by right of his marriage to Algiva. But the historians specifically state that *she used her influence* and this doesn't equate with what they have also been telling us about it being a male-dominated society, where the might of the sword ruled. What influence could the widow of a dead earl have under such circumstances? If she had been the "little wife at home", then her subjects would barely have known of her existence, let alone listened to her pleadings on behalf of a new and "alien" husband - or taken notice of them. There is no way that these two viewpoints can be reconciled, unless there is a lot more to the story than has been told.

"The wife of Edmund Ironside was buried at Shaftesbury Abbey" is all the reference books say. What is the rest of the story that they don't tell us?

EMMA

The last of these Anglo-Saxon females who left their mark on Dorset was Emma, the second wife of Ethelred the Unready (see previous pedigree 5.3), and daughter of Richard the Fearless, Duke of Normandy (she was the great-aunt of William the Conqueror). After the death of Ethelred she neglected the children of this marriage and favoured her children by her next husband, Canute, the enemy of her first husband. She was also implicated in the death of one of her sons of her first marriage. What was she really like, her character as well as her looks? At the time of her marriage to Canute, she was about thirty years of age to his twenty. Was she a *femme fatale*, or was it purely a diplomatic marriage, probably at the instigation of her brother, the Duke of Normandy?

The amazing events during her life can be read in any history text-book, and there is only one event that connects her with Dorset. She was not born or married here, she did not die here, nor was she buried here. Her mark on the County is very indirect, but it had a significant effect on an area of Dorset - the Manors of Weymouth, Portland, Wyke Regis, and Elwell.

The ownership of these manors changed because of a false allegation made by Emma's son, Edward the Confessor, in regard to her behaviour with a bishop. To understand how this came about, we have to look at the relationship between ·mother and son. After the previously-mentioned St Brice's Day massacre in 1002, Emma and her husband - King Ethelred the Unready, who had ordered the massacre - fled to Normandy and the safety of the Court of Richard, Emma's brother. They all returned to England, but on Ethelred's death in 1016, Emma and her two sons, Edward and Alfred, again fled to Normandy, leaving Ethelred's eldest son Edmund Ironside (by his mistress) to fight against the onslaught of Canute. As mentioned earlier, Edmund Ironside died within a few months, leaving Canute as sole ruler of England. Emma was back in England within the year for her marriage to Canute, and the following year their son Hardecanute was born.

Emma's son Edward was thirteen years old when they had to flee to Normandy for the second time, and he was to be forty years old when he finally came to the throne of England in 1042. He had no love for his mother! She had:

- left him and his brother Alfred to live in poverty in Normandy, dependent totally on the charity of others,
- married Canute, their father's enemy,
- lavished affection and material gains on her son by Canute, while neglecting him and his brother for nearly thirty years,
- been implicated in luring Alfred to England where he was brutally murdered ,
- set the whole of England against Edward when he had arrived to claim the English throne after Canute's death in 1035: at the time she was promoting her youngest son, Hardecanute (in fact, the latter didn't succeed until 1040, the throne being usurped by Harold Hadrada, an illegitimate son of Canute's),
- refused to advance any money from her very large accumulation of riches, when the poverty-stricken Edward finally came to England to take the throne in 1042.

Not surprisingly, soon after his coronation Edward the Confessor started taking his mother's wealth away from her - he considered it to be ill-gotten. He also insisted that she enter the nunnery of Whorwell. Was this ironical - or more probably deliberate on Edward's part? For this was the nunnery founded by the "murderess" Elfrida, who had been the mother of Ethelred - Emma's first husband and Edward's father!

It was not long before rumours started spreading about Emma's relationship with Alwyn, Bishop of Winchester. By this time Emma was well up in her fifties! Alwyn was a distant relative of Emma's, being a year or so older than her. As a young soldier he had originally accompanied her from Normandy to England when, as a fifteen-year-old girl, she had come to marry Ethelred. He was then acting as her guardian and counsellor, and had retained this latter role ever since. Through her influence he had risen to his present position as Bishop of Winchester.

The rumours of their "affair" grew in magnitude until it became an open scandal. Many letters protesting her innocence were written by Emma to her son, but to no avail. Finally she insisted that she would prove her innocence by undergoing a trial by ordeal. The Witan - the Parliament of the day - met and agreed to the trial by ordeal. Three earls were sent to inform Emma of the time and place, and at the same time they stripped her of everything of value, leaving her completely destitute.

On the appointed day, with her son Edward the Confessor sitting as judge, Emma was brought to the Old Minster in Winchester, where nine plough shares, heated to red-hot were laid on the floor. The person undergoing the trial was blindfolded and had to step over all of them: only if they came through unscathed were they deemed innocent. Probably to just about everyone's surprise, except presumably her own, Emma came through unscathed, with no trace of a single burn. Edward had to proclaim her innocent of the charge and restored some of her possessions to her.

In thanks for her deliverance, Emma gave some of her properties to the Church of St Swithin in Winchester, and Archbishop Alwyn gave an equal amount. Finally, Edward the Confessor gave these Dorset Manors of Weymouth, Portland, Wyke Regis, and Elwell, presumably to recompense for his belief in the false allegations against his mother. The tenants of these Manors now belonged to the Church and not the King: this was to be of great advantage to them only a quarter of a century later when William the Conqueror arrived, as they did not therefore come under a new and perhaps a brutal Norman landlord.

Emma lived the rest of her days in Winchester, mourning the death of her close and lifelong companion Bishop Alwyn in 1047, until her own death five years later, by which time she had reached the age of sixty-five. She had lived in three different cultures, Norman, Saxon, Danish, and then back to the acquired Norman of her Saxon son.

6

ROYALTY AND DORSET

Since Anglo-Saxon times, no Queens or Princesses appear to have been born, married or died in Dorset, but many have paid visits here for varying lengths of time. Most went unrecorded or were of no importance, but now and again there was a particular significance in a visit, or some way in which the female left her mark in Dorset. The events were usually only minimally reported, but that is a reflection of the nature of recorded history, for historians were usually only interested in kings, politics and battles. The social history, family life, and especially stories of women were largely ignored. When men went off to fight, the womenfolk were left to manage in their absence. The wives of Dorset knights were left to manage the estates, having to cope with the problems of raising ransoms should their husbands be taken prisoner, or dealing with all the legal problems of disposing of the estates if their husbands were killed, especially if the heirs were under age. The wives of tenants and servants had to take over their husbands' work in order to provide for their families - there were no hand-outs in those days. So little of such things was recorded, that what has come down to us must of necessity be concerned with the royal families. But even then, we only have part of the story, for no queen or princess would have travelled alone. We rarely hear about members of their retinues, and there must have been many links between these visitors and the local people. Most of this chapter is therefore involved with queens and princesses visiting Dorset, but there are also several stories of how Dorset women were directly involved with royalty.

ROYAL VISITORS TO DORSET

Scotland, being at the opposite end of Britain from Dorset, does not exactly spring to mind as having many close historical connections with this County, and yet such connections undoubtedly existed. As recently as 1981, a Scottish coin of the reign of William the Lion (1165-1214) was found in the road-side spoil during construction of the Bere Regis by-pass.[1] Such a solid example of a Dorset-Scottish link gives only the faintest of glimpses of what must have been innumerable connections, but sadly wery few were recorded or have come down to us: two sisters of a Scottish King imprisoned in a Dorset castle - even getting a mention in Magna Carta; a Scottish Queen and her young daughter being held as hostages in an Abbey; another Scottish Queen being buried in Dorset, at her own request.

An explanation for the surprising number of Dorset-Scottish links in the 11th to the 13th Centuries is illustrated in the accompanying pedigree 6.1, which shows the various links between the English and Scottish Royal Families - five marriages in six generations. It is mentioned elsewhere (see Chapter 5) how the Saxon Queen Algiva was buried at Shaftesbury Abbey while her two sons escaped to the continent from the vengeance of Canute. It was through the marriage of one of her grand-children, Margaret (1046-1092), to Malcolm, King of Scotland that relations were very much improved between England and Scotland. This was further enhanced by the marriage of their daughter Edith (Eadgyth, 1079-1118) to Henry, the youngest son of William the Conqueror, the year before his accession as King Henry I in 1100. After the marriage she was known by the Norman name of Matilda. [Since there are several Matildas within the next few generations, this one will be referred to as Edith/Matilda.] Although the information is not available, it is very likely that Edith/Matilda was a frequent visitor to Dorset for she was the foundress of a Hospital at Christchurch.[h]

EMPRESS MATILDA

It was Matilda, the daughter of Edith/Matilda and Henry I, who was the cause of England being torn apart in the Civil War that accompanied her claim to the English throne in opposition to her cousin, Stephen (see pedigree 6.1 opposite). [This Matilda will be referred to as Empress Matilda from her first marriage to the Emperor of Germany.] Some of the fighting associated with Matilda's struggle took place in Dorset: Sherborne Castle was besieged and then surrendered; Corfe Castle was successfully defended in her name, and she was subsequently entertained there; Wareham was also defended in her name, but was captured by Stephen and the Castle burnt and totally destroyed. So much disruption and death must have occurred to the populace of Dorset during the eight years that the War lasted, before Matilda made her way back to her husband's Court.

At the time of this 12th Century Civil War the Anglo-Scottish Empress Matilda was married to her second husband, Geoffrey, Count of Anjou (one of whose illegitimate daughters, Marie, was later to become an Abbess of Shaftesbury, see Chapter 2). During the lifetime of Matilda's father, Henry I, he had made his subjects swear allegiance to her as his successor, after her brother had been drowned in *The White Ship*. However, on Henry's death in 1135 his nephew Stephen immediately seized the throne while Matilda was in Anjou nursing her sick husband. Matilda had many supporters who upheld her right to the throne - led by her half-brother Robert, Earl of Gloucester, Mabel Fitzhamon's husband - and it was inevitable that a conflict would ensue. This Civil War dragged on for eight wearisome years until Empress Matilda finally relinquished her claim to the throne on the understanding that her son Henry (some say her cousin Stephen's also) should succeed after Stephen.

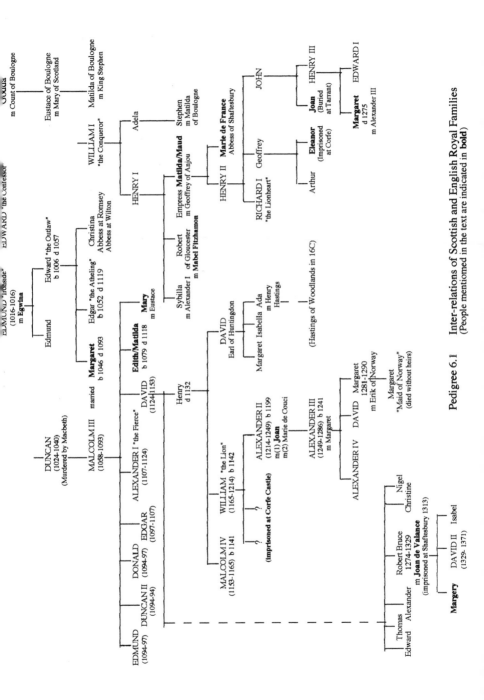

Pedigree 6.1   Inter-relations of Scottish and English Royal Families
(People mentioned in the text are indicated in **bold**)

135

But what of Matilda's visit to Corfe Castle and her entertainment there? Did she live in sumptuous state as befitted the claimant to the English throne, and daughter of the late King? Or did the exigencies of war make limitations? Did she travel with a large retinue of female companions who were light-hearted at that terrible time? Was Mabel Fitzhamon of Cranborne (see Chapter 8) one of her companions? It may be remembered that Mabel was married to Robert of Gloucester, the natural son of Henry I, and hence she was the half-sister of Matilda. Robert had promised his father on his death-bed that he would look after Matilda, and he certainly did so during the Civil War when he was the overall commander of her forces. Did Mabel accompany her husband throughout? She could hardly have stayed at Cranborne, for her husband's position made her a target for being captured and held for ransom. (Her husband was captured at one point and only released in exchange for the imprisoned King Stephen.) Or did Mabel stay at Matilda's Court at Anjou, and accompany her when she arrived at Corfe Castle? Did she take time off to go and visit her estate at Cranborne to see how much damage had been done to it by Stephen's forces?

It wasn't only Mabel and Robert who would have been affected, for many knights and others in their retinue would also have come from their Dorset estates. Did all the other wives who had been left behind come flooding to Corfe Castle when they heard of Mabel's arrival, hoping for news of their husbands? Historians weren't interested in such menial affairs and sadly they went unrecorded. With so much of Dorset pro-Matilda there must have been many more stories that are lost in the mists of time.

TWO SCOTTISH PRINCESSES

There must surely have been royal connections with Dorset during the long reign of Empress Matilda's son, Henry II (1154-1189), and that of his son, Richard Lionheart (1189-1199) but no records are easily available. On the other hand, the reign of Richard's brother, John (1199-1216), opened up many links. He was a frequent visitor to Dorset in order to indulge his love of hunting, visiting Cranborne Chase, Powerstock Forest and the great Pensel Wood among others. But King John must have eyed the stronghold of Corfe Castle with thought, for he often lodged his Crown Jewels there for safety, as well as choosing it as a prison for many a sad person who had offended him.

It was to Corfe Castle in 1209 that John sent the two daughters of the Scottish King, William the Lion (1165-1214): he was holding them as hostages after the settlement of a misunderstanding between William and himself, until an appropriate fine was paid. They were about ten years old at the time of their arrival at Corfe Castle, but virtually nothing is known of their stay there. Were they allowed a Scottish lady to look after them, or were they cared for by the wife of the Constable of Corfe Castle? How were they restricted within the Castle; were they allowed outside for exercise?

Perhaps a little insight can be given by information about another little girl who was being held at the Castle at the same time. This was Eleanor, the daughter of King John's elder brother Geoffrey (see previous pedigree 6.1). When Richard the Lionheart died childless in 1199, the next in line of succession was Arthur, the young son of his brother Geoffrey, followed by this Eleanor. John usurped the throne by the simple expedient of having his nephew Arthur murdered and making his niece a prisoner at Corfe Castle in 1199. She fared better than the soldier-prisoners who accompanied her, for they were simply thrown into the dungeons and forgotten until they starved to death. Eleanor was still at Corfe ten years later when the two Scottish princesses arrived; after the death of John in 1216 she was removed to Bristol Castle where she remained until her death, forty years after she was first taken prisoner.

During these years that Eleanor was held prisoner, relations between John and his Barons deteriorated into open mutiny; it is therefore curious that there is no record of anyone ever trying to rescue her and put forward her rightful claim to the throne over that of John. It certainly appears that she was not kept in close captivity, for included among a list of clothes purchased for her in 1213 is "a saddle with gilded reins",[2] strongly suggesting that she was allowed to ride out from the confines of the Castle - making an ideal time for her to be rescued. Perhaps the memories of the ravages associated with the Civil War between Matilda and Stephen were too fresh in people's minds, and acted as a deterrent. It would appear that there were no trustworthy doctors in Dorset in the early part of the 13th Century, for it is also recorded that when Princess Eleanor was ill, a London doctor, Master J. Beauchamp, was sent to attend her. He was paid the sum of two pounds for this duty, but this also included compensation for his horse, which had died on the journey back to London.[2]

So, if Eleanor was permitted to ride out from the Castle, it is most probable that the two Scottish princesses were also allowed to do so. But while the continued imprisonment of Eleanor made no impression on the English Barons, it was a different matter for the two Scottish princesses. [Their names were not thought important enough to be recorded, but possibly they were Margery and Isabel!] So much did they stir the consciences of the Barons, that they were actually mentioned in one of the clauses of Magna Carta. Thus Clause 58 (referring to them as the sisters of the new Scottish King, their brother Alexander) states:

> "With regard to the return of the sisters and hostages of Alexander of Scotland, his liberties and his rights, we will treat him in the same way as our other barons of England, unless it appears from the charters that we had from his father William, formerly King of Scotland, that he should be treated otherwise. This matter shall be resolved by the judgement of his equals in our court."

It is presumed that this is one of the few clauses of Magna Carta with which King John complied, for soon after his death the following year, Princess Eleanor was transferred to Bristol but there is no further mention of the two Scottish Princesses as hostages.

However, two sisters of Alexander II do feature again in the history of England, but whether they are the same sisters is not stated. One was married to Hubert de Burgh - after he had been married to, and divorced from, Adelicia of Gloucester (and of Cranborne), the cast-off first wife of King John (see Chapter 8). It is also this self-same Hubert de Burgh who carried the lies to Ela of Canford concerning her husband's supposed death, and subsequently poisoned him (see Chapter 1). The hand of the other Scottish sister was later sought in marriage by King Henry III, son of John. All thoughts of this betrothal were firmly ruled out by the Barons who did not fancy such a close relationship as brothers-in-law between the young King and Hubert de Burgh, the deceased King John's obnoxious henchman.

JOAN OF SCOTLAND

The third child and first daughter of King John was Joan (or Joanna), born in 1210. In spite of becoming the Queen of Scotland, she was buried in Dorset according to a request in her will. How did such a Dorset-Scottish connection come about?[cfin]

Joan was the daughter of Isabella of Angouleme, whom John had married after casting-off his first wife, Adelicia of Gloucester, by divorcing her in 1198 but keeping her lands and titles (see Chapter 8). In 1217, the year after John's death, Isabella took her daughter Joan to France to betroth her to Hugh de Lusignan - to whom Isabella herself had formerly been betrothed before her marriage to John - but Hugh preferred his former fiancée and married Isabella instead.

Back in England again, Joan was married by her brother, Henry III, to Alexander II of Scotland. From the time of Henry's accession in 1216, relations between him (born 1207) and the Scottish King (born 1198) had been very friendly, and the latter was often at the English Court. It is therefore not surprising that Henry's favourite sister, Joan, was married to Alexander on 25 June 1221, when she was eleven-years-old and he was twenty-three. Joan is said to have always been of a weak constitution, possibly consumptive, and the frequent journeyings between Scotland and England probably contributed to the total break-down of her health. She died, childless, at Canterbury in 1237. She was buried at Tarrant Crawford in Dorset, as requested in her will.

How did this surprising request come to be made? What connection did Joan have with Dorset? Although her father had been a frequent visitor to the County and was possibly accompanied by his family, Joan was only six years old when he died, so it is unlikely that she would have developed any special love for Dorset by that age. No, it was the newly-refounded Tarrant Kaines Abbey at Tarrant Crawford that was the attraction.

This Cistercian Abbey (for nuns) had originally been founded at the end of the 10th Century (see Chapter 2), but had fallen into disrepair by 1230 when it was re-founded by Bishop Richard Poore. He had been born in the village of Tarrant Crawford, and had been successively Bishop of Chichester, Salisbury and Durham. In his older age he re-founded the nunnery in the Dorset village of his birth and richly endowed it. Soon after this re-founding he presented it to Joan, Queen of Scotland. On his death on 15 April 1237, Bishop Poore was buried in the Church of the Abbey on one side of the altar, and eleven months later, Joan was buried on the other side,

King Henry accompanied the funeral procession of his beloved sister from Canterbury to Tarrant, and wherever the coffin stayed overnight, he made an offering of an altar cloth - twenty-six in all - of rich silk woven with gold for a cathedral or abbey, and of silk of Arras for the churches. After her burial at Tarrant, the King made a request:[f]

> "to cause the marble tomb that Master Elias de Derham [the architect then involved in building the new Cathedral at Salisbury, and the designer of Becket's tomb at Canterbury] is making at Salisbury to be paid for, and to be carried with all speed to Tarrant to entomb there the body of Joan, Queen of Scotland, the King's sister"

The affection that existed between Joan and her brother is evidenced by letters between them which have survived to the present day, and by the fact that even in 1245, long after her death, he was still making donations to the Abbey: presents of herrings, a tun of wine, a "fother" of lead, and 100lb of wax to celebrate the seventh anniversary of her death. The following year he ordered the Sheriff of Dorset to provide two wax candles, one to burn before the Host and one before Joan's tomb. In 1247 he supplied the wood of six oak trees to make stalls in the Church.

As well as Tarrant having this Scottish connection, it also has a Welsh one at virtually the same time and for what sounds like the same reason - the burial there of Joan, the daughter of King John. This latter Joan was a natural daughter, some years older than Joan, Queen of Scotland. When King John was having trouble with the Welsh, he tried to buy the friendship of their leader, Llewellyn ap Jorworth, by giving his illegitimate daughter Joan to him in marriage. There is no obvious reason why this Joan of Wales chose Tarrant as her final resting place,[c] but it suggests a strong affinity between the two Joans in their earlier life.

Nothing remains today to mark the sites of this once-rich magnificent Abbey, or the tombs of these two Joans, one Scottish and one Welsh.

MARGERY, DAUGHTER OF ROBERT BRUCE

The early death of all three of Margaret and Alexander III's children (see previous pedigree 6.1) and also their only grandchild, Margaret, the Maid of Norway, who was betrothed to Edward I's son Edward, meant that this line of Scottish Kings died out with the death of Alexander in 1286. Many claimants to the throne sprang up - at least twelve - and it is the family of one of these that provides the last link between Dorset and Scotland in those times.

King Edward I of England had taken advantage of this disarray in Scotland to try and annex it. In 1306 Robert Bruce (born 1274) had himself crowned King of Scotland in order to provide a rallying point for the nation to unite against the English. He was the youngest of five brothers and two sisters, and had married an English lady, Joan de Valance. (Much of the early life of Robert Bruce had been spent at the English Court.) In 1312 he left his wife, baby daughter Margery, and his two sisters under the care of his brother Nigel at Kildrummie Castle in Mar, but being betrayed, they were all taken captive by the English. Nigel Bruce was executed, one sister was shut up in a convent and the other kept prisoner in Scotland. His wife Joan and her little daughter Margery were brought to England as hostages.

For part of their time here they were sent to the care of the nuns at Shaftesbury Abbey. The King gave them an allowance of £1 per week for their maintenance - a not inconsiderable sum in those days - so they would have been able to live in comparative luxury in the already very rich Abbey. The total defeat of the English by Robert Bruce at the Battle of Bannockburn on 24 June 1314, ensured their freedom after two years of restraint, and they were returned to Scotland. Treves[n] gives a romantic picture of the Queen and Princess being brought into this "abhorred country" of England, and of pacing in the garden of the Abbey, looking to the north where lay their "wild home". He had failed to notice that Queen Joan was born an Englishwoman.

JOAN OF NAVARRE

A very brief passage through Dorset of a Queen left a sufficient mark that it was commemorated in a pageant at Bridport in 1953. This was the 1403 visit to the town by Joan of Navarre when she was journeying from Cornwall to Winchester where she was to be married to King Henry IV. [She had in fact already been married by proxy the previous year in a ceremony that must have been a strange sight, for her male envoy took her place as bride, and the King placed the wedding ring on the man's finger as he made his vows!] Joan of Navarre called herself Queen from the date of this proxy wedding, and it was as such that she made her brief visit to Bridport.

.What a sight this rich and beautiful lady with her very large and sumptuously-arrayed retinue must have been to the folk of Bridport! She was thirty-three years of age, a widow of the elderly Duke of Brittany, by whom she had already had eight children. She was to remain in England for another thirty-four years until her death in 1437, surviving both her husband, Henry IV and her step-son Henry V. (She also made a name for herself by successfully defending a charge of witchcraft.)

Her marriage to Henry was very much a political one, from which many Dorset people must have benefited through increased trade by merchant ships with what is now the west coast of France. Her brother was ruler of Navarre (on the Spanish-French border), her son was Count of Brittany, and her uncle and cousin were successive rulers of the powerful and influential Burgundy.

MARGARET OF ANJOU

Margaret of Anjou was only in Dorset for two weeks in April 1471, but in that time she had to make a major decision that was to dramatically alter the course of history. In retrospect she made the wrong choice, for apart from the direct effects on her family, it was the cause of many lives being lost in the next ten years. For this was the middle of the Wars of the Roses when, apart from the destruction in Dorset, families were wiped out and new families came to this County, and family fortunes were lost - and reinstated - as lands were confiscated by either Lancastrian or Yorkist kings in turn (the author's own family was one).

It was at the height of the Wars of the Roses that Margaret of Anjou, wife of the insane Henry VI returned to England in 1471 with her son Edward, heir to the throne.[3] She landed at Weymouth and went to the sanctuary of Cerne Abbey to gain strength, and to make that decision. While she rested at Cerne, she must have reflected on her life. Daughter of the penniless Rene of Anjou, she had been brought up amid the intrigues of the French Court by her aunt. She was betrothed at the age of seven, and married at sixteen to the twenty-four year-old King Henry VI of England, who had already been on the throne since he was one. No children were born in the first few years of marriage, which were the happiest of her life, before disaster struck in 1453 when her husband became mad. It was to be two years before he became sane again, during which time Margaret had given birth to their one and only child, Edward, in 1453.

The long delay before an heir was born, combined with Richard's madness, had already given Richard, Duke of York, big ideas about the fact that he had a strong claim to the English throne (see pedigree 6.2). Before long (1455) the Wars of the Roses had broken out. For the next eighteen years, Margaret had fought to keep the throne for her husband and her son, the one weak in the head and suffering intermittent bouts of madness, the other an infant; but she had been defeated by the son of the Duke of York who was crowned as Edward IV. She and her son had fled to France, while her husband, now more or less continuously insane, was kept a prisoner in the Tower.

Now, on 13 April 1471, Margaret and her sixteen-year-old son had landed at Weymouth after being at sea for seventeen days in a stormy crossing from Honfleur in France. She was met by many of her supporters, including Cardinal Morton, who was probably the one who suggested she rest at Cerne Abbey, where he had been a pupil in his youth. Apart from the traumatic crossing, by the time she reached Cerne, she had also received the news of the defeat at Barnet of her husband's Lancastrian forces under Warwick, who had been killed there. She who had been so strong for so long must have felt extremely low during those first few days at the Guest House at Cerne (still to be seen). What anguish of mind she must have suffered in that quiet and peaceful valley of Dorset. But then the peace was broken as more and more of her chief supporters came flooding in as they heard of her arrival there.

The future of England now rested on the shoulders of this one woman staying at Cerne. Should she go ahead and unite the Lancastrian forces to fight - and hopefully defeat - the Yorkist Edward IV, and so put her son on the throne that was rightfully his? Or, having lost her chief Commander and so many soldiers at Barnet, should she return to France and hope that a future time might be more auspicious for them? Encouraged by her supporters at Cerne, she made her decision. They would have one last attempt to gain the throne.

Secret messengers were sent out to gather her forces in the Gloucester area, and then, since Edward IV now knew of her arrival, false trails were led as to the route she and her son would take. More messengers were sent out in various directions - Shaftesbury, Glastonbury, Wells, Yeovil, Bruton - as if preparing the way for her party. Meanwhile she and her son accompanied only by a few attendants went cross-country to Bath and then Gloucester.

The end of the story came quickly at the Battle of Tewkesbury two weeks later on 4 May 1471. Margaret of Anjou's Lancastrian forces were totally defeated, her only son was killed, and she was taken prisoner. Her husband died in the Tower on 21 May, probably murdered, and she was eventually released on payment of a ransom by the King of France. She returned to France in 1475 and died there in 1482 of consumption at the age of fifty-three, still mourning the loss of her beloved son. In those last years did she ever give a thought to the peace of Cerne Abbey where her hopes for her beloved son to become the King of England were still alive? Did she regret that decision she had made in Dorset?

The Wars of the Roses dragged on for some years until Edward IV died suddenly in 1483, and the throne was taken by Richard III, who may or may not have been responsible for the murder of Edward's two sons in the Tower. Richard did not last long, for in 1485 he was defeated by Henry Tudor (the son of Margaret Beaufort mentioned in Chapter 2), who became Henry VII. The Wars of the Roses were at an end, and the Tudor dynasty began.

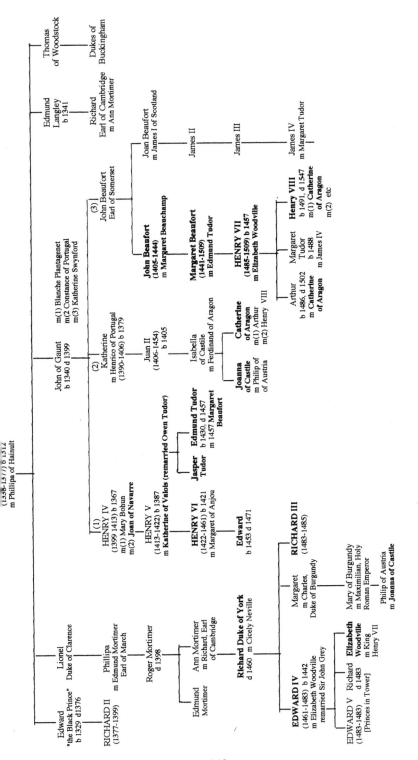

Pedigree 6.2 Family of Margaret Beaufort and simplified pedigree of royalty involved in the Wars of the Roses
(People mentioned in the text are indicated in **bold**)

143

TWO SPANISH SISTERS IN TUDOR TIMES

Two Spanish sisters both arrived in England in the first few years of the 16th Century, but the manner of their arrival was very different. Catherine, the younger one, arrived in Plymouth in 1501 where she was formally greeted by envoys of King Henry VII and escorted through Dorset to Windsor. Joanna, the elder sister, made a completely unplanned visit to Dorset in 1506, and so much was it unexpected that at first she was thought to be part of a French invasion and armed soldiers came against her.

These sisters were Catherine of Aragon and Joanna of Castile, two of the daughters of Isabella and Ferdinand who jointly ruled Spain. They are always treated in history books as merely Spanish princesses, but this is a reflection of the male chauvinism of historians, who never seem to consider the female line in pedigrees, and after all, genes are inherited equally from a female parent as a male one! From the previous pedigree, 6.2, it can be seen that through their mother, these sisters can trace their ancestry from Edward III in exactly the same way as all the Kings and Princes involved in the Wars of the Roses, and also the Tudor dynasty. For example, their mother was a grand-daughter of John of Gaunt as was Henry VII's mother, Margaret Beaufort.

In 1489 it was agreed that Catherine, the third daughter of Isabella of Castile and Ferdinand of Aragon, should marry Henry VII's eldest son, Arthur. They were formally betrothed in 1497, and on 2 October 1501 the sixteen-year-old Catherine of Aragon landed in England on the way to her marriage to Arthur. Poor Catherine, broken-hearted at leaving her parents' home in the sunny south of Spain, had landed in the bleak late autumn in Devon, after a bad crossing of the Bay of Biscay. After a brief rest, she made a slow progress to Windsor via Dorset. One night of her journey was spent at Charmouth, and it is reputed that she stayed at the *Queen's Arms* there, the same inn at which the escaping King Charles II was to stay during the Civil War of the next century (see Chapter 7).[4]

It is again reputed that Catherine spent the next night at Crewkerne in Somerset, before re-entering Dorset to spend the following night at Shaftesbury Abbey, in the care of the nuns. (One of the nuns there was Elizabeth Zouch, its future Abbess at the time of the Dissolution - a direct consequence of the second marriage of this young Spanish Princess, see Chapter 2.) Being a deeply religious girl, this must have been a haven for Catherine, so far from home. The peace of Shaftesbury was not to last for long, for it was on to Windsor and her marriage to Arthur, her widowhood within six months, then the miserable penniless life in England before her marriage to the new King Henry VIII. And we all know where that led!

I wonder how many of the people of Dorset who saw Catherine pass by, could ever have envisaged the trauma that her second marriage (and divorce) would cause to everyone's lives. For there was unlikely to have been a single person whose everyday life wasn't affected in some way by the

Dissolution of the monasteries, and the turning of England from the Catholic to the Protestant religion.

Unlike Catherine of Aragon whose visit to Dorset in 1501 was a natural part of her journey from Devon to London, the arrival of her sister, Joanna of Castile, in Dorset a little over four years later was purely accidental. At the beginning of 1506, Joanna and her husband were sailing down the Channel from Flanders to Spain when their fleet was caught in a violent storm and dispersed. Their ship, although severely damaged, managed to limp into the harbour at Melcombe Regis. Two of the biggest political pawns of their age had landed in the County and were to remain here for the next two weeks. Joanna is always referred to as "Mad Joanna": so was it an insane Queen who had arrived? Also, what on earth was she doing sailing down the Channel in the most dangerous winter months?

Joanna (or Juanna) was born in 1479, the second daughter of Isabella of Castile and Ferdinand of Aragon who jointly ruled Spain.[x] After the death of her brother, her older sister and their two children, all in 1499, she had become heiress to both her parents' kingdoms of Castile and Aragon: following Columbus' discoveries, these also now included territories in Mexico, Peru, Central America and the West Indies, as well as the gold and other wealth flowing back from there. Shortly afterwards, in 1500, Joanna had married Philip, Archduke of Austria, ruler of the Hapsburg lands along the Danube and, through his mother, of the Low Countries (Netherlands, Belgium and Luxembourg) as well. A son, Charles, was born in 1500.

Joanna's mother, Isabella, died in 1504, but since her husband had been born in Aragon he could not inherit her possessions in Castile, and they therefore came to Joanna. It was not a simple succession, and the complications caused by Isabella's will had ultimately led to this journey down the Channel in the middle of winter.

Isabella had recognised what was becoming increasingly apparent, that her daughter Joanna's sanity was suspect. In history she has come down to us as "Mad Joanna", but this is more a reflection of her behaviour in the forty years after her husband's death later in the same year as their visit to Dorset. Certainly there are reports that she was a "strange" child, given to sudden bouts of excitement and melancholia, and there is no doubt that she had an obsessive love for her husband which was not reciprocated in the slightest degree, causing her great distress. She appears to have suffered from manic-depression - treatable nowadays. She certainly became worse after the death of her husband, and her mad behaviour over the next forty years could well have been a true insanity, complicated by her manic-depressive nature. In all accounts of her visit to England there is no mention of her "madness", either in Dorset or later at Windsor. Indeed, King Henry VII went so far as to offer for her hand in marriage after Philip's death, which he certainly wouldn't have done if she had displayed insanity when they met.

Although Joanna had been appointed Isabella's heiress in her will, her mother had added the stipulation that in Joanna's absence or in case of her incapacity through illness, she appointed her husband Ferdinand as sole Regent of Castile until the majority of Joanna's son. This role should normally have fallen to Joanna's husband, Philip, but Isabella had disliked him intensely, and had also condemned his treatment of Joanna, particularly the open flaunting of his mistresses.

On Isabella's death, Joanna was recognised as Queen of Castile, but Joanna herself - then in Flanders - was quite happy for her father to be recognised as Regent in her absence. Not so her husband, Philip. He certainly wasn't happy with the situation and determined to have the Regency for himself. Hence the reason for their journey down the Channel in winter.

When the Spanish fleet was dispersed by storms, they were seen off various points along the coast of South West England. and rumours started to fly around that an invasion was imminent, thought to be the French. When three damaged ships arrived at Melcombe, the Sheriff of Dorset, Sir Thomas Trenchard, hastily arrived with a body of soldiers prepared to make a fight of it.[m] Instead he found a Queen and an Archduke on his hands, ill from sea-sickness and in great distress from the storm. He quickly had them conveyed to his home at Wolverton, just to the north of Dorchester, while he sent an urgent message to King Henry VII at Windsor informing him of their arrival on English soil.

None of the historians recording this event has paid any attention to the situation confronting poor Lady Trenchard when these very distinguished visitors arrived on her doorstep. It was the 6th January, just at the end of the Christmas celebrations, and without a doubt her store-cupboards were sadly depleted. Now she had to cope with Joanna, Philip, their servants, bodyguard and others of their retinue. It would be interesting to know how she solved that problem!

It would appear that Joanna and her husband remained at Wolverton for approximately two weeks. During this time messages were sent to and from Windsor, until the Duke of Arundel arrived with a large company to escort the visitors to the King [more feeding of large numbers for Lady Trenchard to cope with!]. According to State Records, Philip arrived at Windsor on 29 January, and Joanna thirteen days later on 10 February. Ever keen to get away from his wife, Philip's party had ridden on ahead, hunting and hawking their way through Dorset to Windsor [6]. Joanna's party came at a slower speed, she being carried in a litter. Four days after her arrival at Windsor, Philip was off again, bound for Plymouth where some of their fleet had re-assembled to take them on to Spain. Poor Joanna was once again left to trail far behind in her litter. Without doubt, both Joanna and Philip would have come back through Dorset on this journey too, but there are no records of their sojourns here.

THE DUKE OF MONMOUTH'S REBELLION

Most people only think of Judge Jeffreys and the "Bloody Assizes" in linking Dorset with the 1685 Rebellion of the Duke of Monmouth. Although women rarely featured in these Assizes, we do have several Dorset women who were involved with other aspects of the Rebellion. Thus Nan Chafin was kept fully informed by her husband of all the events of Monmouth's progress, and two Dorset women were directly involved in his eventual capture.

The Duke of Monmouth was the eldest illegitimate son and a great favourite of King Charles II; he was born while Charles was in exile before his Restoration. When it became obvious that Charles was not going to have legitimate children by his Queen, Catherine of Braganza, there was an increasing body of support for making this already highly-popular Protestant Duke of Monmouth his successor instead of Charles' very unpopular brother, the Roman Catholic James. On Charles' death in 1685, the Duke of Monmouth landed at Lyme Regis in Dorset in a completely unplanned effort to usurp the throne from the newly-crowned James II, hoping that his supporters would rush to join him. Many did, and within four days he had assembled over two thousand horse and foot soldiers. On 14 June they attacked Bridport, to be confronted by the Dorset Militia. The rebels were dispersed and returned to Lyme Regis. It is at this point that we take up the story of Nan Chafin.

So much is written about battles and the men who fought them, but so little is written about the affairs of women left to manage their homes while their husbands were away. Did they suffer in silence about what was happening to their spouses, or did their husbands keep them fully informed? Such a collection as the *Paston Letters* will probably never come to light again, but here and there we catch a glimpse of correspondence between husbands and wives at such times. We have one such set of "Dorset" letters (only those from the husband to the wife unfortunately) written at the time of Monmouth's Rebellion in 1685.[n] Apart from the historical value of these letters, they give us an insight into the feelings of the husband for his wife, the terms of endearment in which he addressed her - "my dearest creature" and "my dearest deare" for example - and also his concern for the means by which she might return to her home when the Rebellion broke out.

The letters written between June and the end of July 1685, were to Ann "Nan" Chafin, née Penrudock, from her husband, Thomas Chafin of Chettle, near Blandford. They were both in their thirties by this time, and were to have eleven children before his death in 1691, followed by hers in 1705. Ann must therefore have already been the mother of five or six children at the time the letters were written.

On 11 June 1685 the Duke of Monmouth landed at Lyme Regis and, as mentioned above, on 14 June attacked Bridport. The first letter received by Nan Chafin was written after this engagement, where her husband had commanded a troop of Horse of the Dorset Militia. He had returned to Dorchester and this first letter, dated 16 June and addressed from "Mrs Bestlands, Dorchester,'" reads:

> "My dearest creature. I am very well soe far on my journey ... My cos Strangways was killed as he was takeing horse. Mayjor Stiles saved himself in a plat of kidney beans [plot, not plate!]: Mr Churchill of Moston [Mosterton] saved himself by running up into the garrett....I was forced to take Collington [a servant] knowing noe other soe fitt: Therefore if you be pleased to come home you must send to Chettle either for Will Horner or Will Lambert. Horner and the colt would draw you home almost as well. I have Thomas Clements and the gardiner, well armed, with me."

More letters followed as he and his Troop followed the perambulations of Monmouth and his army, culminating in the Battle of Sedgemoor in Somerset on 6 July 1685. Nan is regaled with full details of this battle. Ten days later the last letter of the series was written to her by Thomas, this time from London where he had just witnessed the beheading of the captured Duke of Monmouth (15 July 1685). He concludes this last letter with "Blessing to the bratts. Soe farewell, my dearest deare Nan. I hope to be home of Saturday sennight".

Just a small glimpse into a personal correspondence, but we can still learn a lot. So many letters in the six weeks he was away from her. His terms of endearment, indicating that it wasn't just a "marriage of convenience". He spared her no details of the battles. Even in the first letter when he didn't know what was going to happen with the rebel army, he still found time to be concerned about her means of returning home to Chettle, worried that he had taken the servant who normally accompanied her. He suggested which servants she should send for as an alternative, and even indicated which horse she should ride. What a pity that the letters from Nan to Thomas didn't survive.

While Nan was receiving these letters from her husband about the Duke of Monmouth, she would have been extremely surprised to learn that the person in question was, for a brief period, only a couple of miles from her door (the original house was replaced in 1710).

When it became obvious that all was not going well for him at the Battle of Sedgemoor, The Duke of Monmouth and a few friends fled the field, leaving his army to its terrible fate. They rode in a south-easterly direction intending, it is said, to make for the safety of the New Forest. It was at Horton, only about six miles from Nan's home at Chettle, that he was finally captured, and this was in no small part due to two Dorset women, a Mrs Uvedale, the local Lady of the Manor, and Amy Farrant.

After riding the fifty miles from Sedgemoor, the horses of the Duke's party were completely exhausted and had to be set loose; their saddles and bridles were carefully hidden away and the Duke and his remaining companions separated, to go on foot. Close to Horton the Duke changed clothes with a peasant, but had the misfortune - for him - to drop his gold snuff-box in a pea-field. It was soon found and, being full of gold pieces, was taken to Mrs Uvedale of Horton, who gave half the contents (£15) to the finder. The authorities were now alerted by Mrs Uvedale to the fact that the Duke of Monmouth was probably in the area.

There was a price of £5,000 on the Duke's head, and it was probably this that made Amy Farrant, a local peasant woman, tell the pursuers that she had seen the Duke enter the Horton Plantation on the Woodlands Estate. It was here that he was found, hidden in a ditch, A week later he was beheaded in London, as recorded in Thomas Chafin's letter. Whether Amy Farrant ever received any of the reward is not known, but it was afterwards said by people who knew her [cg] that her family had "fallen into decay and never thrived afterwards".

As stated earlier, women hardly featured in the "Bloody Assizes" where Judge Jeffreys handed out his brutal sentences to Monmouth's supporters. There was one Dorset woman, Ulalia Brown of Lyme Regis, who literally felt the full force of the so-called justice handed out by the Judge. She was found guilty of "treasonable talk" - she had apparently spoken jokingly at the time of Monmouth's landing at Lyme - and was sentenced to be publicly whipped through several market towns.

As an example of the indiscriminate sentences handed out by Jeffreys, Ulalia's should be contrasted with that of her husband's, Bernard Brown. He was also found guilty of "treasonable talk and behaviour" - he had apparently "been accosted with great friendliness by Monmouth himself on the recruiting field, and was regarded as an adherent". Bernard Brown got off scot-free, and to rub salt into his wife's wounds, he was subsequently employed for many years by Lyme Regis Corporation!

ROYAL MISTRESSES

If it had not been for a tragic event that occurred in the early life of a young lady in Dorset in 1775, she would never have achieved fame and notoriety in later life. For less than ten years after this Dorset incident, it was the same lady, then known as Mrs Fitzherbert, who was to bring the expression "morganatic marriage" to the notice of the general public.

Mary (Maria) Anne Smythe was born in 1758, the youngest daughter of Walter Smythe of Brambridge House in Twyford, Hampshire. In 1775, after being educated in Paris, she was married to Edward Weld of Lulworth Castle, and all was set for a rosy future for the young couple as they settled into their new life in Dorset. Sadly, her husband died within a few months of their marriage, and she was left a young, rich, and attractive widow of eighteen. In 1778 she became the wife of Thomas Fitzherbert of Swinnerton in Derbyshire, but he died in 1781, leaving her a widow for the second time before she had reached her twenty-fifth birthday.

Almost four years after the death of her second husband, Mrs Fitzherbert was introduced to the Prince of Wales, later King George IV, and they became deeply attached to each other. The Prince of Wales proposed marriage to her on innumerable occasions, but Maria Fitzherbert was a Roman Catholic and any marriage between the heir to the throne and a Catholic was banned by law. If he went ahead with such a marriage, then he would forfeit his right to succeed (as has Prince Michael of Kent in recent years). Although very reluctant at first, Maria was eventually persuaded into a secret marriage. The ceremony was conducted by a Protestant clergyman, and witnessed by her uncle and brother, on 21 December 1785, when Maria was twenty-nine years old to the Prince's twenty-one.

Rumours of this secret "morganatic" marriage soon began to spread, and in April 1787 his close friend, Charles Fox, was instructed by the Prince to make a statement in the House of Commons that was an unqualified denial of these reports of his marriage. Ten years later in 1795, he was "officially" married to Princess Caroline of Brunswick, a marriage that was to end so disastrously almost before it had begun.

This second marriage caused a deep rift between Mrs Fitzherbert and the Prince, but it was soon healed and with the approval of the Pope, they lived together as husband and wife. As a consequence of his behaviour, they again parted, and she lived the rest of her life in quiet retirement at Brighton until her death in 1837. During this latter period she was treated with great respect by other members of the Royal Family who frequently visited her (several of the Prince of Wales' brothers had also contracted morganatic marriages) and she was also beloved by the general public. She turned down offers of a peerage which were repeatedly pressed upon her, although by the nature of the morganatic marriage, she was not entitled to one.

But what exactly is a morganatic marriage, or a left-handed marriage as it is sometimes called? It is a marriage between a prince, noble or other man of exalted rank, and a woman of inferior rank. Very rarely it is used of a marriage between a woman of superior rank and a man of an inferior one. The distinctive features of a morganatic marriage are that the wife does not acquire the rank of her husband, and any children - although perfectly legitimate - do not inherit the titles or estates of their father.

A morganatic marriage performed by a clergyman is recognized by the Church: if there is a subsequent "regular" marriage, then the Church will only recognize the former morganatic one, while the State only recognises the "regular" one. (The Royal Marriage Act introduced in Britain in 1772 made a morganatic marriage invalid in Public Law.) Such was the situation between Mrs Fitzherbert and the Prince of Wales. However, by publicly denying that such a marriage had occurred - and who would dare to disbelieve a statement made on his behalf in Parliament? - the Prince was able to go ahead with his supposedly "first" marriage to Princess Caroline, and have it accepted by both Church and State.

The custom of a morganatic marriage originated in ancient German law, and was very prevalent among the princes and high nobility of that country, and to a much lesser extent amongst other royal families of Europe. For example, George William, Duke of Zell, married Eleanor d'Esmiers in this manner, and their daughter Sophia Dorothea was later to become the ill-fated wife of the Hanoverian George I of England, the great-great-grandfather of George IV, husband of Mrs Fitzherbert.

The word "morganatic" is usually considered to have come from the Old English *morgengifu* meaning "morning-gift" - a gift made to the wife on the morning after the consummation of a morganatic marriage. This gift was all that the wife could expect from her morganatic husband's estate. An alternative origin has been suggested as coming from the Gothic word *morgjan* meaning "to curtail" or "to limit", and again it is applied to the dowry or gift from the husband to the wife that is considered to be the limit of the marriage portion she will receive.

And the reason that a morganatic marriage is also known as a left-handed marriage? In the marriage ceremony the husband-to-be gives his left hand to the bride instead of his right, when he says "I take thee for my wedded wife".

I wonder if in later years Maria Fitzherbert ever looked back to her youth and pondered on how different her life might have been if her first husband, Edward Weld of Lulworth Castle, had not died so prematurely? Would she have become the mother of a large family in Dorset, entertaining lavishly at the impressive Lulworth Castle, and paying the occasional visit to London, perhaps catching a distant view of the Prince of Wales? What a different life that would have been, instead of her notorious morganatic marriage to the future George IV.

Two other royal mistresses are frequently referred to as being "of Dorset". These are Arabella Churchill, for ten years the mistress of the Duke of York, later King James II, and Lillie Langtry who for four years at the end of last century was the mistress of the Prince of Wales, later King Edward VII. Both have been excluded from these pages on the grounds that Arabella belongs to Devon, and Lillie Langtry to Hampshire. The latter's association with this part of the world was the love-nest that was built for her at Bournemouth, and although this place is now part of modern Dorset, it has only been so since 1974 when the realignment of the county boundary moved it from Hampshire to Dorset. In Lillie's time it was definitely Hampshire.

Arabella Churchill would certainly have been "of Dorset" had not her father's impecunious state forced the family to move from Dorset to Ashe, near Axminster in Devon, shortly before her birth. He was Sir Winston Churchill, and it was the large fines imposed on him for his support of the Royalists in the

Civil War that caused his wife to move back to her family's estate at Ashe. Arabella was born there in 1649, her brother John (later the first Duke of Marlborough) in 1650, and her other brother Charles in 1656. By the age of sixteen Arabella was at Court as a Maid of Honour to the Duchess of York, and shortly afterwards started the ten year long affair with the Duke of York. Being born and bred in Devon, Arabella Churchill can therefore not be counted as a "Woman of Dorset".

UNEXPECTED ROYAL VISITORS

Imagine the scene at home. You are very hot and flushed, having just come from the kitchen where you have been inspecting the weekly bread-baking in progress. You are summoned to the front entrance. There you find the Queen, two Princesses and a large retinue on your door-step, asking to see over your home. You think it could never happen? Well that was the situation facing a Mrs Fookes of Wolverton, just north of Dorchester in October of the year 1804, when she received a visit from Queen Charlotte, wife of King George III.[m]

What went through her mind at that moment? Her husband was out somewhere on the estate: someone must be quickly sent to find him and summon him home. Apart from her two youngest children in the nursery, the only other member of the family at home was her eldest daughter: she must be summoned to greet the visitors. Were any rooms in disorder? Could a maid be sent to tidy them while she conducted her visitors in another direction first? All sorts of such thoughts must have been flashing through her mind as Mrs Fookes stepped forward to curtsey and greet the elderly Queen Charlotte and her two middle-aged daughters.

The tour of the house went off very well, the royal party being shown around by Mrs Fookes and her daughter. The Queen was most impressed by the Tudor carved-wood surrounds of doorways and fireplaces that are still a feature of the house today, but sadly most of the stained-glass windows containing the armorial bearings of generations of owners of the house had been recently removed - one of the features that the Queen had come especially to see. I expect that like most of us when showing visitors around our home, Mrs Fookes saw unexpected cobwebs that had materialized from nowhere, having not been there a short while before, and tried to avert her visitors' gaze from them.

Finally the tour was over and Mrs Fookes and her daughter entertained their royal visitors to refreshments in the Parlour, while the rest of the retinue was entertained in the adjacent dining-room. The two youngest members of the Fookes family - a boy of three and a baby of five months were brought in to be presented to the Queen by their proud mother. Mrs Fookes was almost immediately not quite so proud of her son for, upon entering the room, Master Robert Fookes took offence at seeing an old lady using his favourite seat as a foot-stool. He immediately ran across the Parlour, snatched it away from under the Queen's feet, took it into a corner and sat on it. Nothing would make him return the foot-stool and eventually another one had to be brought for the use of the Queen.

The baby on the other hand behaved beautifully; she lay contentedly in her mother's arms as she sat chatting to Her Majesty. Mrs Fookes was pleasantly surprised to find that the Queen was "just like an ordinary lady" and was happy to converse on all manner of domestic affairs. When it was discovered that the two of them had the same (very large) number of children, the elderly Queen displayed an unexpected sense of humour by remarking "I think we have both been useful subjects to His Majesty!".

Mrs Fookes must have been very relieved at this point by the arrival of her husband, who was duly presented to the royal party; but almost immediately she must have regretted the direction the conversation had taken. Queen Charlotte expressed her admiration for an article of furniture she had seen in an adjacent room in such a way that it was obviously a piece of "Royal blackmail". The furniture in question was one of Mrs Fookes' favourite possessions, a large octagonal table with a marble top and eight supporting legs carved out of mahogany in the shape of rampant lions. The Queen said it was just what she wanted for her ornamental (artificial) dairy at Frogmore. This ploy worked, as it was obviously intended to do, and Mrs Fookes lost her beloved table to Frogmore where it can still be seen.

The royal visit was not quite over, for they were now escorted outside to be shown around the gardens. Again Mrs Fookes' heart dropped when they reached the walled garden, and she saw how the large royal party rapidly stripped practically all of the remaining fruit ripening there in the autumnal sun. It had all been ready for preserving, and now the Fookes family were going to be short of desserts during the forthcoming winter and spring! To add insult to injury, Mrs Fookes was then asked by the Queen if some fruit could be packed for her to take to the King. Some newly-baked bread was also asked for and included. Mrs Fookes must have been greatly relieved that it was baking-day and there had been plenty of bread available for the refreshments. She must also have felt very proud that the Queen thought fit to congratulate her on the quality of the bread, and wished to take some for her husband.

There is a postscript to this story of Queen Charlotte's visit to Wolverton, involving the nursemaid, name unknown, who had brought in the baby to be presented to the Queen. Just prior to departure of the royal party, one of the ladies-in-waiting, Lady Matilda Winyard, asked Mrs Fookes how many female members of staff there were, and left a gold guinea for each of them; the male servants received nothing. The nursemaid used her guinea to buy a gown of fine flowered chintz, which she promptly named "The Queen's Dress". It was only worn on special occasions, including her wedding.

In view of the length of time spent in Dorset by Queen Charlotte and her family during the repeated visits of her husband George III, there are surprisingly few details of similar unexpected visits paid by them. But then most people didn't - or couldn't - write the stories down or, if they did, then the visit was disposed of in a few sentences. Such was the case with the diary kept by Mary Frampton.[5] Born in 1773, she was a young woman when George III paid his visits between 1789 and 1802, and was sixteen when the Royal Family paid an unexpected visit to her home in Dorchester in 1789. All she wrote of the visit in her *Journal* was the following:

> "We were sitting at work in my little room with Mrs Drax. I happened to look out, and actually saw the King and Princess Sophia with their attendants, at my garden gate. I screamed out, threw down everything about me, and flew out to them.
>
> Mr Damer [the butler?] met me, and told me the Queen and three of the Princesses and their suite were following.
>
> Mr D. helped to put the drawing room in order, and bespoke mutton chops. I ran through the house to meet them at the front door. The King called out 'Well run, Mrs Frampton.' They then proposed walking, and we all went through my fields to the Walks round great part of the town, and they seemed much pleased. After the repast, the female part went into all the bedrooms, and looked at everything everywhere."

These last two examples clearly demonstrate the differences in behaviour of royal visitors a mere two hundred years ago, compared with today. How different would have been records of royal visitors to Dorset in earlier centuries if someone had written down all the little details? They would have made extremely interesting reading, but sadly nobody recorded them!

7
DORSET WOMEN AND THE CIVIL WAR

INTRODUCTION

From the records it appears that very few women played a prominent part in the Civil War of the 17th Century between Cavaliers and Roundheads, either in Dorset or in England as a whole. This is quite naturally a reflection of those recording the events being more interested in the battles and politics of the event. But the lives of women were just as much affected by the conflict, although they didn't actually fight in the battles. For nearly every woman in Dorset must have had a husband, a son, or a father, who fought on one side or the other, often having no news of them for weeks or months on end. Loyalties were often divided, with a husband on one side and a brother on another - as in the case of Lady Digby - for example. The majority of these women had to stay at home, the richer ones running the estates in their husbands' absence usually with most of their servants away accompanying them - as did Lady Bankes: the poorer women were left struggling to make a living in the absence of the bread-winning male members of their families. Rumours were everywhere, and they never knew from one day to the next whether the sound of approaching hooves was a friend or foe, good news or bad. Some towns like Wareham and Blandford were first taken by one side and then the other. How the townswomen must have suffered at times like that!

But few such events involving women were recorded by historians, who didn't consider them of sufficient importance to be documented. Additionally, most records were written after Charles II had been restored to the throne in 1660; the writers were therefore on the winning side - the Royalists (Cavaliers) - and would therefore mention little of the lives, valour and other deeds of any women supporting the losing side - the Parliamentarians (Roundheads). If they did, then it was more likely to be biased and in a derogatory manner. For example, there are frequent mentions of the "brutal murder" of the Royalist-supporting Lady Strode of Parnham, but it is difficult to discover any details of the murder of the Roundhead-supporting Lady Sydenham of Wynford Eagle.

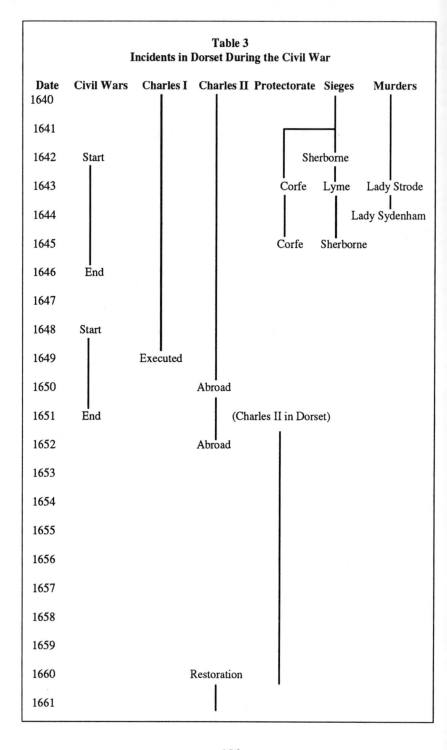

Table 3
Incidents in Dorset During the Civil War

Date	Civil Wars	Charles I	Charles II	Protectorate	Sieges	Murders
1640						
1641						
1642	Start				Sherborne	
1643				Corfe	Lyme	Lady Strode
1644						Lady Sydenham
1645				Corfe	Sherborne	
1646	End					
1647						
1648	Start					
1649		Executed				
1650			Abroad			
1651	End			(Charles II in Dorset)		
1652			Abroad			
1653						
1654						
1655						
1656						
1657						
1658						
1659						
1660			Restoration			
1661						

The two sides in the Civil War were not divided by class, for it was as much a religious war as a political one. On the political side it was a struggle between the King's determination to rule and keep his right to impose whatever taxes he wished. Parliament was equally determined that the people of the country should also share the right to govern. On the religious side the Royalists were loyal to the Episcopal form of Government (via Bishops), the Parliamentarians were mainly Puritans. Thus it was "High Church" versus "Low Church" as well. Probably many people didn't even know what the conflict was all about anyway, and just followed the example of their local Lord of the Manor.

What is normally described as *the* Civil War in England was actually two separate wars, and together they covered eighteen years in the middle of the 17th Century from 1642 to 1660. (Other Civil Wars in this country in the 12th and 15th Centuries are described elsewhere.) In this 17th Century one, the first war started when King Charles I raised his standard at Nottingham in August 1642, and ended in 1646 when he surrendered to the Scots and was handed over to the English (see Table 3). The second war broke out in 1648 - during which Charles I was brought to trial and executed - and ended at the Battle of Worcester in 1651. After this defeat many of the Royalists fled to the Continent, and it was at this time that King Charles II wandered around Dorset, vainly trying to get a ship to France. The Commonwealth/Protectorate continued under Oliver Cromwell and his son until the Restoration of Charles II in 1660.

Dorset had escaped relatively lightly during earlier wars and insurrections in England, but it suffered severely during this Civil War, even though no major battle was fought on its soil. Dorset's importance was two-fold: firstly, it formed a major link between the Royalist strongholds at Exeter and Oxford. This strategic position resulted in the repeated sieges of Sherborne Castle - where Lady Digby was a prominent figure. Its second important role was its forty-mile long Channel coastline with several ports that could be used for Royalist reinforcements and supplies from the Continent, particularly France. The sieges of Lyme and Corfe - where women played important parts - were direct consequences of this.

The involvement of Dorset women in the Civil War falls into two parts: those who were caught up with the fighting and sieges, all of which occurred in the first of the two wars; and those who were connected with the escape of Charles II from England to France in 1651, at the end of the second war.

SIEGES

WOMEN OF LYME REGIS

For many years afterwards, the six-week-long siege of Lyme Regis was commemmorated by an annual sermon, while the part played in it by the women of Lyme was commemmorated in 1645 by a poem written by the Puritan minister James Strong. The title of this poem on its own is fully informative of the part they played:

> "Joaneridos; or feminine valour: Eminently discovered in Western Women: As Well By defying the merciless Enemy at the face abroad, as by fighting against them in Garrison Townes; sometimes carrying Stones, anon tumbling of stones over the Workes on the Enemy, when they have been scaling them, some carrying Powder, others charging of Peeces [pieces = guns] to ease the Souldiers, constantly resolved for generality, not to think any one life deare, to maintain that Christian quarrell for the PARLIAMENT. Whereby, as they deserve Commendations in themselves, so are they proposed as examples unto others."

As soon as the Civil War broke out in August 1642, the Parliamentary leaders in Dorset rushed to secure the various ports along the coast, Lyme among them. Defensive earthworks were thrown up around the town. And none too soon, for in January 1643 news reached Lyme that Royalist forces were approaching. Preparations were carried out at fever-pitch, building up large stores of food and ammunition, for it was not known exactly when the enemy would arrive. On 21 April a large force under Prince Maurice the King's nephew finally arrived. Standing on the hill above Lyme and looking down on the town, the reader will see what the Royalist force saw (although the town was much smaller then) - a simple place to capture, or "a morning's work" as they are reported to have said.

Six weeks later, on 14 June, the siege was still in progress, barely credible in view of the fact that there were less than five hundred men in the town, facing a besieging force of over five thousand. But they hadn't counted on the women of Lyme, who played as great a part as their menfolk. As described in the above title to the poem, they manned the defences, fired muskets and cannon - one woman claimed to have fired sixteen muskets in one engagement (each firing taking at least one minute to reload). They brought stones to the earthen defence works and dropped them on Royalists attempting to climb up. They helped pull thatch off their houses in order to prevent them being put on fire by the enemy; they put out innumerable fires. And all this as well as performing the traditional female tasks of treating the sick and wounded, preparing meals, and caring for the frightened children.

Without doubt women played similar roles in all the sieges - Lady Bankes and her womenfolk at Corfe Castle for example (see later) - but there must have been something about the women of Lyme for them to be remembered so long afterwards, particularly as they were anti-Royalist, unlike Lady Bankes. It is probable that some of them were on a religious "high", for it is said that there were more than a dozen Puritan vicars in the town exhorting them to "fight God's fight". One young woman is recorded as having had her hand shot off and exclaiming "truly I am glad with all my heart that I had a hand to lose for Jesus Christ, for whose cause I am willing to lose not only my other hand, but my life also". Without doubt she must have been gripped by religious fervour to be able to say such words! Her words also reinforce the fact that she was fighting a religious war, rather than one against the King directly.

By the morning of the 15 June the siege of Lyme Regis was all over. The besieging Royalists had slipped away in the night. Amid all the joys of celebration and thanksgiving, one final act of the siege was performed by the townspeople on an old Irishwoman. She was a camp-follower of the Royalists - many of whom were Irishmen - who had not managed to get away with the rest of the forces - perhaps she had overslept through imbibing too much the night before. She was captured, paraded through the town and then hacked to death, her body being thrown into the sea. It was a very sad act at the end of six weeks of undoubted gallantry on the part of the inhabitants of Lyme, and particularly its womenfolk.

LADY BANKES AND THE SIEGE OF CORFE CASTLE

Lady Bankes first came to live in Corfe Castle and rear her children in 1634, after its purchase from Lady Elizabeth Hatton (see Chapter 8). She spent her time partly in Corfe, and partly in London where her husband was Attorney-General to Charles and was later to become Chief Justice. To a superstitious person - and they were certainly more superstitious in the 17th Century than now - a portent of what was to befall the peace of Corfe occurred in 1638 when the old raven at the Castle died. It was said[1] that he had been born before the birth of Christ. [An interesting parallel with the similar superstitious belief about the ravens at the Tower of London.]

On the outbreak of Civil War in 1642, Sir John hastily brought his family to Corfe Castle for safety, and quickly provisioned it in case of siege, before departing to Oxford to join the King. Most of the staff went with him, leaving only five male servants and female attendants there when the first siege came early the following year.

It was May Day 1641. In the Purbeck district this had always been celebrated with a stag hunt, and since there was no sign of the Civil War in this part of the country, Lady Bankes as Lady of the Manor decided to go ahead with the custom as usual. In Dorchester meanwhile, the Parliamentary Council for Dorset was fully aware that the stag hunt was going ahead and planned to take advantage of it to gain entry to the Castle by subterfuge. Someone informed Lady Bankes of the plan and she was fully prepared for the arrival of a party of fifty horsemen pretending to be strangers wishing to be shown over the Castle. The gates of Corfe Castle were firmly closed in their faces on her orders.

159

The Parliamentary Council next sent to demand the four small cannon sitting on the ramparts, the total heavy artillery possessed by the defenders. Lady Bankes refused to hand them over. A few days later a band of about fifty Roundheads arrived with a warrant *ordering* her to hand them over. Again she refused, and this time Lady Bankes and her servants managed to fire one of the cannon. The Roundheads hastily withdrew.

Now a siege began in earnest, but unlike the one at Lyme Regis the siege at Corfe Castle couldn't have been a very determined one, for the village folk were able to creep into the Castle to increase the number of defenders - preferring that to the occupation of the village by the Roundheads.

Within a short time provisions in the castle were running low, and Lady Bankes agreed to parley (talk) with the besiegers. Agreement was reached that if Lady Bankes gave up the cannon then she and her followers would be left in peace, still in possession of the Castle. [This apparently "gentlemanly" behaviour on the part of the besiegers, compared with those of Lyme, was probably a reflection of their being local people with local leaders who had probably had social intercourse with the Bankes family prior to the War. The attackers of Lyme on the other hand, were "foreigners", mainly Irishmen, under the command of Prince Maurice.] The cannon were handed over, and peace descended for a while, during which time Lady Bankes set about laying in as much food, weapons and gunpowder as she was able to obtain. Hearing that Royalist forces were approaching Blandford, she sent an urgent request for reinforcements to their leader Prince Maurice, the King's nephew. He could only spare a few trained soldiers under Captain Lawrence, a local man.

No sooner had Lawrence arrived than on 20 June 1643 the Roundheads were back in force for the start of what was to become a six week siege. Much artillery was used by the besiegers but it failed to make any impression on the strongly-built Castle, even when fired from the vantage-point of the top of the Church tower. Several direct assaults were made on the Castle, but they were repelled by Captain Lawrence and the men who defended the Lower Ward, while the Upper Ward was defended by Lady Bankes, her daughters and the womenfolk, who kept up a continual bombardment of small stones and buckets of hot cinders upon the men attempting to scale the walls.

Still the Castle held firm. The Roundheads departed in haste in August when they received news that Royalist forces were rapidly approaching to relieve the besieged Castle.

By the end of that year (1643) the Royalist forces were in the ascendancy almost everywhere, and all looked set for victory. Lady Bankes' husband paid a brief visit in the late summer of 1644: he was now fifty-five years old, and ageing rapidly from his travels about the country on the Assize Circuit in his role as Chief Justice (only in Royalist-held territories), as well as attending the King at Oxford and elsewhere. It was during that summer (1644) that the tide began to turn and the Parliamentary forces came into the ascendancy: by the end of the year all of Dorset had fallen to them apart from Corfe Castle.

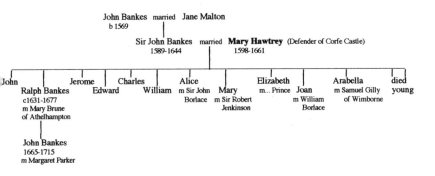

John Bankes married Jane Malton
b 1569

Sir John Bankes married **Mary Hawtrey** (Defender of Corfe Castle)
1589-1644   1598-1661

John | Jerome | Charles | Alice | | Elizabeth | | Arabella | died
Ralph Bankes | Edward | William | m Sir John Mary | m... Prince Joan | m Samuel Gilly | young
c1631-1677 | | | Borlace m Sir Robert | m William | of Wimborne
m Mary Brune | | | Jenkinson | Borlace
of Athelhampton

John Bankes
1665-1715
m Margaret Parker

Pedigree 7.1   Family of Lady Bankes of Corfe Castle

During the year since the previous siege, life had continued as normally as possible, but with large stocks of food and ammunition being laid up. At the end of 1644 Lady Bankes received the sad news that her husband had died in Oxford at the home of one of their daughters, Mary, and had been buried at Christ Church there.[2] (The two elder daughters of Lady Bankes, Alice and Mary, were both married and living in Oxford: Alice had married Sir John Borlace, and Mary's husband was Sir Robert Jenkinson, see accompanying pedigree, 7.1.) Late in 1644, shortly before he died, Sir John had been at the (Royalist) Exeter Assizes when the (Roundhead) Parliament in London impeached him of High Treason. Lady Bankes and all her children were declared "malignants" and all their property forfeited - including her widow's dower that should have come to her on her husband's death.

In January 1645 the expected siege came, and this time there were no Royalist forces to come to her aid. The Roundheads were led by Colonel Bingham, another local man. It was a ferocious siege - and defence - but all was over in less than a month. Corfe Castle fell on 27 February 1645. It was through no weakness on the part of Lady Bankes and her defenders, or strength on the part of the besiegers, but by the betrayal of one of the Royalists in the Castle garrison. He was a Colonel John Pitman who had obtained Lady Bankes' permission to go to Somerset to raise desperately-needed reinforcements. Instead, he went to Bingham and - in return for a safe conduct -

161

agreed to lead a party of a hundred Roundheads into the Castle disguised as the hoped-for Royalist reinforcements.

Out of respect for the gallant Lady Bankes and her defence of Corfe Castle for over two years, Colonel Bingham and the other Roundhead leaders took no reprisals against the defenders. Lady Bankes, her family and all their followers were allowed to leave in peace. As Lady Bankes rode out of the Castle, she deliberately had the keys of the Castle hidden on her person (they are still preserved today at Kingston Lacy). Since Saxon times keys were considered the most treasured possession of the lady of the house. Corfe Castle might be lost to her, but she was determined never to surrender the keys.

Corfe Castle was slighted, leaving the ruins we see today. Its contents were looted by the Roundheads, and many of its furnishings were dispersed among other manor houses of Dorset. After the Restoration, Lady Bankes' eldest son set about retrieving the family's lost possessions. The Binghams were made to hand over numerous looted items including tapestries from the Gallery and bedchamber, an ebony cabinet, gilt hangings of green leather and blue silk. Personal belongings, probably from Lady Bankes herself, were also retrieved; a crimson satin petticoat, a stomacher, sleeved linen with silver laces, and a sweet bag [pomander?]; also, a large bed without its feather mattress, a single velvet red chair and a suite of fine damask.

It is believed that Lady Bankes went to live at her father's home in Ruislip, Middlesex, after she was expelled from Corfe Castle. Although she had lost her right to a dower at the impeachment of her husband, this was eventually restored to her by Cromwell in 1647. The sequestration on the estates was also removed, but not before she had paid a fine of £455 for herself and £1,974 for her children, plus a settlement of £60 per annum for preachers.

Lady Bankes appears to have lived in relative peace for the rest of the Civil War, either on her estate at Kingston Lacy (eventually taken over by her eldest son Ralph), or at her family's home in Ruislip. The last years of her life were spent at Damory Court, Blandford. She died on 11 April 1661, having lived to see the Restoration of Charles II in the previous year, and her son Ralph knighted at Canterbury. Her death was completely unexpected, for in the morning of the day she died, she had attended the wedding of her son, Sir Ralph Bankes.

She was buried at St Martin's Church in Ruislip, Middlesex, where so many of her Hawtrey ancestors were buried. Her son erected a memorial tablet on the south wall of the chancel:

To the memory of
The Lady Mary Bankes, ye only
Daughter of Ralph Hawtrey of Ruislipp
in the County of Middx, Esquire
The wife and widow of the Honble Sr
John Bankes, Knight, Late Lord Chiefe
Justice of his late Majestyes Court of
Common Pleas, and of the Privy Councell

to His late Majesty King Charles the first
of Blessed Memory
who having had the honour to have borne with
a constancy & Courage above her sex, a
noble proporcion of the Late Calamities, and
the happiness to have outlived them so farr
as to have seene the restitution of the
Government, with great peace of mind
laid down her most desired life the 11th day
of April 1661.

She left 4 sonnes, 1. Sir Ralph, 2. Jerom,
3. Charles, 4. William (since dead without issue) & 6 daughters.

LADY DIGBY AND SHERBORNE CASTLE

Anyone gazing at the ruins of the Old Castle at Sherborne can only get a small inkling of the formidable, although very small, fortress that it must have presented at the height of its glory in the early 17th Century. Now it is just another heap of ruins. Like Corfe Castle it was slighted in the Civil War. The life of Corfe Castle was actively extended for over two years by the exertions of Lady Bankes in its defence; and Sherborne Castle too, had its life extended by a Dorset woman, but this time in quite a different manner.[i]

She was Lady Digby, married to George, Lord Digby, whose family had acquired Sherborne Castle from James I earlier that century. After the outbreak of the Civil War in 1642, Lady Digby remained in residence at the Castle when her husband went to support the King. While most of the gentry of the Dorset countryside were Royalists, the towns came out on the side of Parliament with the exceptions of Sherborne, Corfe Castle, Chideock Castle and the Isle of Portland. Sherborne was an important communication link between the Royalist strongholds at Oxford and Exeter, and with this in mind it was besieged by the Parliamentary forces in August 1642, soon after the war broke out.

Lady Digby remained living at the Castle while it was quickly garrisoned and fortified for the Royalists by the Marquis of Hertford. And none too soon, for almost immediately the Earl of Bedford arrived with a Parliamentary force. When he failed to take the Castle at the first attempt, he settled down to lay siege to it. In his pocket he had orders from Parliament that the Castle must be demolished because of its strategic importance - and that meant that most of the defenders would probably die with it. But William Russell, Earl of Bedford was in a great predicament, for Lady Digby was none other than his sister Ann. If he carried out his orders and attacked the Castle until it was demolished, then his sister would probably perish with it. In spite of this family division caused by the war, blood was thicker than water. Lady Digby therefore received a message from her brother, telling her of his orders to demolish the Castle, and asking her to leave it as soon as possible.

How well this indicates the splits that must have occurred in so many families during the Civil War, when a wife found herself married to someone who supported one side, while her own family supported the other side. Where did her loyalties lie? There was no doubt in Lady Digby's mind for, on receiving the message from her brother, she immediately rode out of the Castle to her brother's lodgings in the town of Sherborne, and told him in no uncertain terms that if he went ahead and carried out his orders, then he would find his sister's bones in the ruins. She then returned to the other Royalists within the Castle; which makes an interesting point that even in the middle of a siege, she was freely able to travel in and out of the Castle unharmed.

We are not told how much this statement from his sister played a part in the Earl of Bedford's decision, for in spite of the importance of his orders to destroy Sherborne Castle, the fact remains that he did not press the attack, merely kept up the siege. This proved effective for food soon became short within the Castle. On the 20 September 1642, after a siege of only a few weeks, an agreement was reached whereby Lady Digby, the Marquis of Hertford and all the other Royalists were permitted to ride out of Sherborne Castle unmolested and without being taken prisoner. What passed between sister and brother on this occasion is not recorded. Did she ride past him with her head held high, not giving a glance at the brother who was about to destroy her home? Shortly afterwards her brother changed sides and became a staunch Royalist. Did his sister ever forgive him?

As it turned out, the Castle was not destroyed on that occasion, merely occupied by the Parliamentary forces for a few months before it was retaken by the Royalists. Did Lady Digby then return to her former home? Was she there when King Charles I paid a visit in 1644 and reviewed his troops in the park? Was she there the following year, 1645, when Sherborne was again besieged by Parliamentary forces under Fairfax and Cromwell? This time the Castle was soon taken, and on 15 August 1645, the order was given for it to be slighted, forming the ruins seen today.

Lady Digby faded away in history after her memorable defiance at the first siege (she subsequently died in the mid-1690's, and was buried at Chenies in Buckinghamshire), but at least she contributed to the history of Sherborne by helping to preserve its Castle for another three years. Her "invisibility" in history, however, is even more marked by the fact that few of the records refer to her by her Christian name. She is variously described as "the wife of George, Lord Digby" or as "sister of the Duke of Bedford", but never given the courtesy of a name for herself! [I finally traced her name as Ann, courtesy of the archivist to the Duke of Bedford.]

SUFFERING FOR THEIR CAUSE

Two Dorset Ladies of the Manor were both assassinated during the Civil War: one was Lady Strode of Parnham, a supporter of the Royalist cause; the other, Lady Sydenham of Wynford Eagle, was very much committed to the Parliamentary cause. Little detail is available of how either of the actual deeds was committed.

LADY STRODE

Virtually none of the reference books on Dorset mentions Ann Strode of Parnham near Beaminster who was murdered by Parliamentarians in the Great Hall of her home, and it was certainly difficult to find information concerning the event.[al] A relative of her husband's by the name of Richard Strode gives a little more information about the incident when he wrote:[a]

> [At the time when Cromwell] "had totally routed the enemy in the West, one of his soldiers with his sword casually killed the said Sir John's wife in the same place [Parnham] which she so unlawfully kept against [Sir Richard] by colour of the same fraudulent deed for her son, who about the same time also fled into another place and was taken prisoner by Parliament for his malignancy".

This appears to add more confusion, for it somewhat ambiguously suggests that Lady Strode may have been killed not bcause she supported the Royalists, but because of some dispute about a deed. To understand what this was all about it is necessary to look at the background of this woman.[3] Lady Strode had been born Ann Wyndham, of the all-powerful Royalist-supporting Wyndham family of Orchard in Somerset (see accompanying pedigree 7.2). She had married a man old enough to be her father - her husband Sir John Strode (1561-1642) was born only three years after her father. The dates of her birth and marriage are uncertain, but her eldest son was born in 1624, suggesting a marriage only a year or so before that, and a date of birth between about 1600 and 1606.

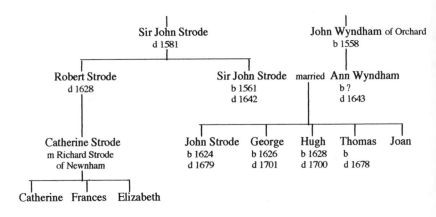

```
          Sir John Strode                    John Wyndham of Orchard
             d 1581                                b 1558
    ┌─────────────┴─────────────┐                    │
Robert Strode              Sir John Strode  married  Ann Wyndham
   d 1628                      b 1561                    b ?
                               d 1642                    d 1643
     │                            └──────────┬──────────┘
Catherine Strode         ┌──────────┬────────┼──────────┬────────┐
m Richard Strode     John Strode  George    Hugh     Thomas    Joan
  of Newnham            b 1624    b 1626    b 1628      b
                        d 1679    d 1701    d 1700    d 1678
┌───────┬─────────┐
Catherine Frances Elizabeth
```

Pedigree 7.2   Family of Lady Strode of Parnham

Her husband was the younger son and had inherited Chantmarle on the death of his father in 1581, while his elder brother Sir Robert Strode had inherited Parnham. Robert Strode married his only daughter Catherine to a kinsman Sir Richard Strode of Newnham in return for £2,000, on the condition that Parnham should go to a son of the marriage. However, there were no sons of the marriage when she died young, leaving only three daughters, Catherine, Frances and Elizabeth. Shortly before his death in 1628, Sir Robert Strode changed his mind about the inheritance of Parnham, and drew up the subsequently controversial deed whereby it should go instead to his brother Sir John Strode, Ann Wyndham's husband: the latter therefore took possession.

A massive amount of litigation ensued between the "dispossessed" Sir Richard Strode and his uncle-in-law Sir John Strode. The latter was a successful lawyer, and managed to keep possession of Parnham until his death in 1642, aged eighty-one, just after the outbreak of the Civil War. During these fourteen years of litigation, Sir Richard had been unceasing in his attempts to obtain possession of Parnham, but the court action came to an end with the outbreak of the Civil War. However, while Ann and her husband were staunch Royalists, Sir Richard was a Parliamentarian. In the first year of the Long Parliament (1642-1650), he therefore had Sir John ordered by Warrant to produce the "fraudulent" deed before Parliament (the deed that reputedly gave him the right to inherit Parnham). This Sir John refused to do, but "chose rather to die than give obedience thereunto": he died (naturally) later the same year.

166

This then, was the situation in relation to Parnham when Lady Ann Strode met her end. She was a Royalist, and she had held on to Parnham on her husband's death (supported by her Wyndham relatives), in deliberate defiance of an Order from Parliament. Additionally, a few months earlier her eldest son, the eighteen year old John Strode, had taken up arms on the Royalist side: he had been captured and was even then being held prisoner at Taunton.

No detailed record appears to exist of what occurred in the Great Hall at Parnham when Lady Strode died. Was it merely that a Parliamentary soldier 'casually killed her"[a] by chance, because of her support of the Royalists? Or was he perhaps one of a deputation who had been sent to take possession of Parnham on behalf of Sir Richard Strode, and Lady Strode was maintaining that he would only take it "over her dead body" when he took her literally at her word? It is possible that she was driven beyond endurance by the death of her husband, the capture of her son, her defence of her possession of Parnham, and now the invasion of her home by the "enemy" soldiers; so much so that *she* attacked the soldier and he only acted in self defence?

LADY SYDENHAM OF WYNFORD EAGLE

The reverse incident - the murder of a Parliament-supporting Dorset woman by a Royalist soldier - doesn't get a single mention in any of the reference books, and it has proved very difficult to track down any details of the event.[4,5] She was Lady Sydenham of Wynford Eagle, near Maiden Newton, murdered in her home in August 1644.

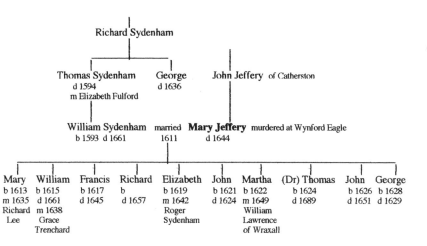

Pedigree 7.3   Family of Lady Sydenham of Wynford Eagle

167

Mary Jeffery was probably born in about 1593, the daughter of John Jeffery of Catherston (see accompanying pedigree 7.3). In 1611 she married William Sydenham whose family had owned Wynford Eagle for over a hundred years. (His father had died before he was one year old, and he had inherited Wynford Eagle on his grandfather's death in 1607 at about the age of fourteen.) Mary and William were to have ten children, and must have taken great pride in their five lusty sons who reached manhood.

All this was to change with the outbreak of the Civil War in 1642. Mary's husband and five sons were very prominent on the Parliamentary side. Her husband William became a Captain in the Parliamentary army, while her eldest son, William junior, became a Colonel, and was later to hold high office in London under Cromwell. Three of her sons were to die for the Parliamentary cause during the Civil War, another one was to die "a broken man" the year after the Restoration, while the fifth son was to become the most eminent physician of his age.[4,5] But Mary was to know nothing of the fate of her five sons, for she was dead before any of them, murdered by a Royalist soldier.

In August 1644 Dorchester was being successfully held for Parliament against a Royalist attack, with three of the Sydenham sons probably involved in the defence. At some time during or shortly after this event a group of Royalist soldiers went to Wynford Eagle, and there Lady Sydenham was killed by a Major Williams. It has not been possible to trace any further details as to why, how or when it happened. The Sydenhams had their revenge shortly afterwards when one of the sons - probably Francis - killed Major Williams in battle.

Two Dorset women who died for the respective sides in the Civil War, both killed in their own homes, but scarcely a mention of them anywhere.

WANDERINGS OF CHARLES II IN DORSET

All reference books on Dorset elaborate fully on the wanderings of the young King Charles II through Dorset during his efforts to escape to France after the Royalist defeat at Worcester in 1651. Surprisingly, the total duration of these wanderings amounted to less than three days. [Some might argue that he spent nearer three weeks, but the rest of that time was spent in hiding at Trent near Yeovil, then in Somerset.] On Monday 22 September Charles and his party left Trent for Charmouth, intending to stay there only a few hours before embarking on a ship for France. But the plan went wrong and the rest of the night was spent in Charmouth: the party then travelled *via* Bridport to Broadwindsor, where a second night was spent. They then returned to Trent and an eventual escape to France.

Several women were involved in Charles' journeyings through Dorset, some directly and others indirectly: not all their names have been recorded. The most prominent was Juliana Coningsby, the niece by marriage of Colonel Wyndham, the owner of Trent. Throughout Charles' travels in Dorset - and subsequently - she rode pillion behind the King, who was acting as her servant. The intention was that anyone who saw them - and particularly Parliamentary soldiers - would be so attracted by her beauty that they would fail to pay any attention to her "servant". (This plan had already worked as far as Trent, with Jane Lane playing the same role as Juliana.) After the Restoration Charles did not forget all those who had helped him, and Juliana Coningsby received a pension of £200 a year.

Whereas Juliana was only too aware of the identity of Charles, the two other Dorset women with whom he came into *direct* contact were unaware until long after the event. They were the landladies of the two inns where Charles and his party stayed the night. The first was Mistress Margaret Wade, landlady of the Queen's Arms at Charmouth where Charles had only intended staying a few hours prior to his embarkation for France. Juliana and the King were playing the part of star-crossed lovers, trying to escape from her uncle and guardian by eloping to France where they could be married. They were accompanied by friends who were supposed to be aiding their "elopement" - Lord Wilmot, Charles' aide and close friend, Colonel Wyndham of Trent, plus one (genuine) servant. The twenty-six-year-old King could not help but flirt with the middle-aged Mistress Wade. This led her to keep a strict eye on the "lovers" for, as she told them, she kept a respectable house and she was not standing for any misbehaviour under her roof before the eloping couple were married!

What should have been a few hours stay at the Queen's Arms turned into an overnight stay when the escape plan went wrong - due to the intervention of another Dorset female, Mrs Limbry (see later). By dawn, most of the party were on the road for their journey back to Trent. Lord Wilmot was delayed because one of his horse's shoes needed replacing. The ostler at the inn had already had his suspicions aroused by the overnight visitors, and had gone to consult with the local parson, a very zealous Puritan minister by the name of Bartholomew Westley (or Wesley, great-grandfather of John and Charles Wesley, the founders of Methodism). Mr Westley was at his prolonged morning prayers and could not be disturbed. The ostler returned to the Queens Arms and took Wilmot's horse to be shoed. The blacksmith, by name Hammett, also had his suspicions aroused when he recognised that one of the horse-shoes came from Worcestershire - the scene of the last battle - and was even more suspicious when he learnt more about the visitors from the ostler. Hammett in turn went to consult with Mr Westley (who had now finished his prolonged prayers) and the two were soon on their way back to the Queen's Arms where the following conversation is said to have occurred:

"Why, how now Margaret? So you are a maid of honour?"
"What mean you, Mr Westley?"
"Why, Charles Stuart lay last night at your inn, and kissed you on his departure [he had!], so now you can't but be a maid of honour!"

169

"Strangers certainly lay in my house last night. I know not who they were, nor would demean myself to pry into what is no concern of mine."

"Was there not a tall, dark man amongst them?"

"And what if there were?"

"Woman, that was none other than Charles Stuart!"

"So it was the King that lay in my house was it? You scurvy, ill-conditioned rogue! You'll go about to bring me and my house into trouble, will you? But let me tell you this, Mr Westley: if I thought it was the King, I should think better of my lips all the days of my life! And so, Master Parson, get you out, or I'll get those that shall kick you out!"

The parson and the blacksmith hastily departed and repaired to the nearest Justice of the Peace, a Mr Butler; but he didn't believe them - or didn't want to - and took no action. The ostler meanwhile had walked the few miles to Lyme where he eventually told his story to Mr Macey, a Captain of a Parliamentary troop, and was finally believed. Macey soon led his troop out onto the Bridport road in pursuit of the King, who had several hours' start.

Snatching a hasty meal at Bridport - which was full of Parliamentary troops - Charles, Juliana and the rest of the party met up again with Wilmot and continued on their journey to Trent. Fearing that they might be pursued, they turned off the main Dorchester road, and eventually after travelling along numerous byroads and cross-country, they arrived at Broadwindsor. The host at the George Inn (now a private house) was Rhys Jones, a former and trusty servant of Colonel Wyndham who was accompanying Charles. It was here that two more women played a part in his travels, one providing a humorous interlude for the King, and the other unknowingly playing a major part in preserving the King's safety while he was staying overnight at the George.

During their travels in Dorset, Lord Wilmot had several times been mistakenly greeted by passers-by as Sir Bullen Reymes of Waddon in Devon, who by coincidence was Colonel Wyndham's brother-in-law. It was therefore decided that when they reached the George Inn, Colonel Wyndham should introduce Wilmot as Reymes to Rhys Jones, the host at the inn. But this had a totally unforeseen consequence, for many years earlier the wife of Rhys Jones had been a mistress of the real Sir Bullen Reymes! She was also mistaken in Wilmot's identity, for she also "recognised" him as her former lover (without her husband's knowledge, of course) and appeared more than anxious to renew their acquaintance - to the great delight of his "servant", the King!

Mistress Jones was therefore the third of the Dorset women who came into direct contact with the King, but that very same evening another female came upon the scene who played a very large part in ensuring the King's safety that night. Who she was, where she came from, and what happened to her, are not recorded. What we do know is that she went into labour that night at the George Inn, and gave birth to a baby son.

No sooner had the King settled to his supper in the safety of the attics of the George Inn, than the Parish Constable brought a troop of forty Parliamentary soldiers to be quartered for the night at the self-same inn. They were *en route* for embarkation to the Channel Isles. The landlord and his wife certainly ensured that the ale flowed freely that night, so that the drunken soldiers would not be interested in exploring the rest of the inn. But soon a young woman's screams more than made up for their noise, when one of the camp-followers went into labour.

In a very short time this news reached the ears of the Parish Constable and he, together with other officials of the parish and many local folk, arrived hot-foot to investigate, particularly with a desire to identify the father. In those days, an illegitimate child with no known father became a financial burden to the parish in which it was born. If the mother wasn't married - or quickly made so - or if the father was not identified, then it was quite common for the Parish officials to take the mother-to-be, even in the midst of labour, and eject her out of their parish so that the cost of the baby's upbringing should fall on the neighbouring parish instead.

When they discovered that she wasn't married and wasn't prepared to name the father - or couldn't - their efforts to effect her removal was the signal for a fight to break out between the now somewhat inebriated soldiers and the local men. The fighting continued for a considerable time - interspersed with further drinking - until one by one the contestants sank to the floor into the oblivion of sleep.

Amidst all this din, Charles and his party slept peacefully in their attic, completely undisturbed by the otherwise pre-occupied soldiers. In the morning they were easily able to depart before a soul was stirring, apart from the inn-keeper and his wife; the latter was determined to take an affectionate farewell of her former lover "Sir Bullen Reymes". And so Charles, Juliana and the others finally made their way back to Trent after their adventurous three days roaming around Dorset.

And what of that other Dorset woman, Mrs Limbry of Charmouth, plus her two daughters, who had been indirectly involved in Charles' visit, and was the means of preventing his departure for France? Mrs Limbry was the wife of Stephen Limbry, a sea-captain and owner of a 30-ton ship that traded between West Dorset and France: he was due to sail for St Malo on Monday 22 September. Unknown to his wife he had been approached the previous Monday about transporting some fugitive Royalists to France: he almost certainly didn't know till long afterwards the true identity of one of them. The Limbrys, together with two grown-up daughters, lived in a cottage at Charmouth as a tenant of a Mr Ellesdon, a squire living a few miles away. While Charles was still at Trent, Colonel Wyndham had approached his friend Ellesdon, who in turn had contacted Limbry, and agreement was reached that the latter would take the fugitives to France for the sum of £60.

Limbry kept the secret of his extra "cargo" from his wife until a few hours before he was due to sail, when he returned home to collect some fresh linen for the journey. But the escape plan had not allowed for Mrs Limbry. On that Monday, 22 September, she had gone from Charmouth to the Fair at Lyme Regis. There she had heard, read, or more probably had read to her, the proclamation of 10 September offering a reward for the capture of Charles - the same proclamation that was probably responsible for arousing the suspicions of the blacksmith, Hammet.

> ".....Take notice of him to be a tall man above two yards high, his hair a deep brown near to black, and has been, as we hear, cut off since the destruction of his army at Worcester, so that it is not very long..... Whoever shall apprehend the person of the said Charles Stuart and shall bring him or cause him to be brought to the Council of State, shall have given and bestowed on him or them as a Reward for such service, the sum of One Thousand Pounds."

When Mrs Limbry heard of her husband's intended trip that night, she put two and two together and guessed who his passengers were to be. She and her two daughters locked Limbry in his bedroom, having first taken and hidden his trousers - presumably his only pair! A contemporary account[6] describes it thus:

> "Therefore, with prayers, tears, and almost offering violence to him, she endeavours against it; at length she thumbed with such out-cries, as she would like to gather all her neighbours about their ears, therefore being overcome by her importunity, he remained at home and commits himself to be governed by his wife."

And so Stephen Limbry was unable to keep his appointment that night to take Charles to France. It is interesting that none of the records tell us of the exact reason for Mrs Limbry locking up her husband. Was she a Puritan who had no wish to be involved with aiding Royalists, even though she could not bring herself to give them away to the authorities? Was she so in love with her husband that she didn't want him to put his life at risk? Even had he made a successful trip to France, did she fear that the truth might come out afterwards? Or was it her own life for which she feared, should her husband's deed be discovered? It is curious that no-one appears to have questioned her - or her daughters - after the Restoration, when everyone from the King downwards was busy writing memoirs of their exploits at this time. And what was Mistress Jones' reaction when she discovered that she had mistakenly flirted with "Sir Bullen Reymes" in the presence of the King at Broadwindsor?

A final female who had cause to remember Charles' wanderings through Dorset was an unnamed young lady in the home of Sir Hugh Wyndham of Pilsdon Manor: he was an uncle of the Colonel Wyndham of Trent who accompanied Charles on his Dorset travels. Apparently, when the soldiers set off in pursuit of Charles and his party from Lyme Regis and Charmouth, they followed him along the Dorchester road. It may be remembered that Charles soon turned off this road, going northwards to Broadwindsor. When the soldiers failed to find Charles in Dorchester, they retraced their steps and began searching all likely houses where he might have hidden instead. One of these houses was Pilsdon Manor. According to a contemporary record,[6]

"they most accurately look into all the chests and corners of the house, and violently apprehending the whole family, they suspect a young gentlewoman of exceedingly great beauty and rare endowments, as if she had been the King disguised: neither did they discharge her of this suspicion before they had tried by undoubted experiment to determine of what sex she was."

Poor unnamed girl! How could they possibly have mistaken her for Charles - he was over six feet tall! There is no record that she later received any compensation from the King after the Restoration for being molested in this way, on his behalf.

173

8
DORSET WOMEN AND MARRIAGE

INTRODUCTION

It would be possible to fill a book purely with the background to the subject of marriage from the woman's point of view, and how it has changed down the centuries: instead a collection of stories to do with marriage are presented in random order. Surprisingly, the one thing that has remained practically unchanged from Saxon times, if not earlier, is the marriage vow. Then it was: "I take thee, ——, to be my wedded husband, to have and to hold, from this day forward, for better, for worse, for richer, for poorer, in sickness, and health, to be bonny and buxom in bed and at board, till death do us part, and thereto I plight thee my troth".

On the other hand, what has dramatically changed is the manner of terminating a marriage. Before the 7th Century it was possible for a man to put away his wife "if she was barren, fetid, silly, passionate, rude, a glutton, a drunkard, quarrelsome, and abrasive".[17] It was in the 7th Century that a general council of the English Church tried to reconcile the pagan and Christian views of marriage. They forbade incest [commonly a son marrying his widowed step-mother for reasons of inheritance] and the abandonment of wives for reasons other than adultery; they allowed a woman to remarry after one year if her husband had been condemned to penal slavery; a man could remarry after the same period if his wife, 'despising him' had left him; both men and women were allowed to remarry after five years if their spouse had been carried off 'into hopeless captivity'.[17] In a coastal county like Dorset, that latter clause must have been used many times in consequence of the innumerable raids made upon its inhabitants from the sea.

But one thing that set many Dorset girls on the road to matrimony was the long climb up to St Catherine's Chapel, that dominant landmark at Abbotsbury. St Catherine is the patron saint of spinsters (also of clergy, nurses, students, wheelrights, millers, spinners - and hilltops!).[18] After making an offering to the Saint, the girls would place their hands and one knee into "wishing holes" in the doorway, and say the following prayer (in the corresponding Dorset dialect):

> "St Catherine, St Catherine, oh lend me thine aid,
> And grant that I niver may die an wold maid.
> A husband, St Catherine,
> A good one, St Catherine;
> But arn-a-one better than
> Narn-a-one, St Catherine.
> Sweet St Catherine,
> A husband St Catherine,
> Handsome St Catherine,
> Rich St Catherine,
> Soon, St Catherine."[19]

MABEL FITZHAMON OF CRANBOURNE

Cranborne Chase,[21] that great hunting ground of former times, was to provide a major attraction in the betrothals of two Norman ladies, Mabel Fitzhamon and her grand-daughter Adelicia Fitzroy. But whereas the betrothal of Mabel led to an apparently happy but very traumatic marriage, that of Adelicia was a complete disaster, for she was literally "married for her money" - and property.

Cranborne Chase, together with the monastery at Cranborne (later moved to Tewkesbury) were given by William the Conqueror to his wife, Matilda. She endowed them on her son William Rufus, who in turn gave them to his faithful soldier and favourite, Robert Fitzhamon (or Fitzhamo, Fitzhaymes), who already had the overlordship of much of the West Country, Glamorgan, and the Welsh Marches, and was known as Lord of Gloucester. After the death of William Rufus, Robert Fitzhamon gave his allegiance to the new King, Henry I, and died in his service in 1109. He was married to Sybil Montgomery, daughter of the Earl of Shrewsbury, and they had four daughters, but no son (see accompanying pedigree 8.1). Two of the daughters were already in a religious life (see Chapter 2), and one had married the Count of Brittany. All Robert Fitzhamon's lands and titles therefore came to his other daughter, the sixteen-year-old Mabel.[1,2]

Because the lands of Cranborne and Gloucester were held of the King, it meant that Henry I automatically became Mabel's guardian with the right to give her in marriage to whomsoever he wished. (If Mabel refused his choice, or went ahead and married someone without the King's permission, then her lands were automatically forfeited.) Henry I's choice fell on Robert, the eldest of his more that twenty illegitimate children, who was the son of a Frenchwoman, Sybil Corbet, daughter of Robert, a burgess of Caen. Mabel's great wealth, plus being the owner of the great hunting grounds of Cranborne, certainly made her a "good catch", a very suitable match for Henry I's much-loved son Robert.

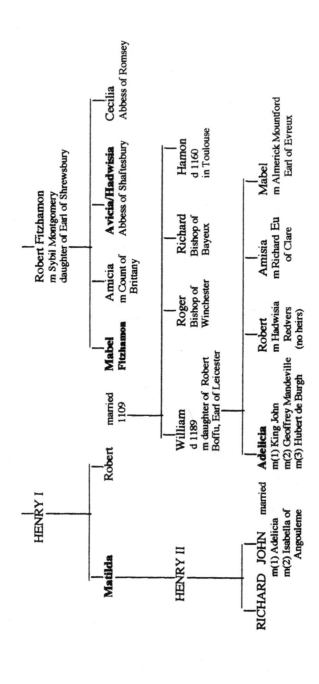

Pedigree 8.1 Families of Mabel Fitzhamon and Adelicia of Cranborne

Mabel was only sixteen years of age - as was Robert - but she certainly had a will of her own, for to everyone's surprise she turned down the King's offer. I suspect that there was more to it than this, in view of what is reputed to be the conversation she had with the King. She was fully aware that her lands would be forfeit if she declined to marry the King's son, and therefore suggests that she fully planned to marry Robert but determined to make the most of the situation, probably egged-on by Robert himself. The following is the report of this conversation reputed to have taken place between Mabel and her prospective father-in-law.[n]

"When the King made the proposal that she should marry his son, she was against it and long withstood it, and when the king solicited her, she at last answers like a good and courteous maiden - 'Sire,' said she, 'I see plainly that your heart is set on me more for the sake of my inheritance than of myself; having such an inheritance as I have, it would be dishonourable to me to have a lord who had not two names. My father's name was Sir Robert le Fitz Hayme, and that inheritance ought not to be any man's that was not of his rank; therefore, for God's love, let me have no man for a husband who has not two names whereby he may be known.' 'Damsel' quoth the King, 'though sayest well in this case; thy father's name was Robert le Fitz Hayme, and I will take care that my son shall have one as fair, for his name shall be Sir Robert Fitz le Roy [son of the King]. 'Sir,' said the maiden, 'that is a fair name and of great repute as long as he shall live, but what shall his son be called, or any other of his descendants? Unless care be taken of that also, they may soon come to have no name!' The King perceived that the maiden said nothing unreasonable, and knowing that Gloucester was the chief part of her heritage, 'Damsel' saith he 'thy lord shall have a fair unobjectionable name for himself and his heirs; his name shall be Robert, Earl of Gloucester, and he and his heirs shall be Earls of Gloucester.' 'Sir,' quoth the maiden, 'then I like this well. On these terms I agree to all, and my goods are his.'

In 1109 Mabel Fitzhamon went ahead and married Robert, the new Earl of Gloucester, and more or less fades out of the pages of history. It is known that she had at least four sons and three daughters (see previous pedigree 8.1): two of her sons became bishops, one became a soldier, and the eldest, William, succeeded to the titles. William Fitzhamon had only one son who died with no heirs, and for the second time in three generations, the manor of Cranborne was again the inheritance of a female, Mabel's grand-daughter Adelicia.

But while Mabel fades out of the picture, there is a large amount recorded of the exploits of her husband, for he was the self-same Robert of Gloucester who, as half-brother to the Empress Matilda, daughter of King Henry I, led her forces during the conflict between her and her cousin Stephen for the English throne (see Chapter 6).

ADELICIA OF CRANBORNE, COUNTESS OF GLOUCESTER

When Mabel Fitzhamon's son William of Gloucester died in 1189, he left three surviving daughters. Since two of them were already married (see previous pedigree 8.1) everything came to the third one, who was styled Adelicia, Countess of Gloucester. As had been the case with her grandmother Mabel, the King had the full right to give this new heiress in marriage to whomsoever he wished, since he had automatically become her guardian on the death of her father.

The king in this case was Henry II (1154-1189), son of Matilda, and for much of his life he had sought to give his youngest son, John (later King John), lands of his own in England. Shortly before Henry's death this new heiress came within his grasp, and he quickly arranged for John to marry her. Since the grandparents of Adelicia and John were half-brother and sister (both offspring of Henry I, see previous pedigree 8.1), this close relationship made the Church strongly against the marriage on grounds of consanguinity. The marriage was postponed for a few months while the necessary dispensation was obtained.

When the marriage finally went ahead a few months later, Henry II had died and Richard Lionheart (John's elder brother) had come to the throne. He gave the married pair an income of £1,000 a year, as well as conferring the titles of Duchies of Cornwall, Devon and Somerset on them after his coronation. (Many of the Cranborne lands still form part of the Duchy of Cornwall.)

It is a shame that unlike her grandmother's, we have no knowledge of the courtship - if any - of Adelicia and John. It was to be a strange marriage for never once did Adelicia appear in public as John's wife. It therefore appears that she was purely used as a pawn for John to get hold of her lands at a time when he had no possessions of his own in England. Also, John could not fail to have known of the superb hunting grounds of Cranborne Chase, and have been aware that all would come to Adelicia on her father's death. Knowing what we do of John's character, there is a sneaking suspicion that Adelicia's father may not have come to an entirely "natural" end!

In 1191, less than two years after his marriage to Adelicia, John was contemplating marriage with a French princess - without having considered divorcing Adelicia first! It fell through, but Adelicia and John were divorced in 1199 (the year John came to the throne) when, strictly against the law of the times, John held on to all of the possessions that Adelicia had brought to the marriage, including Cranborne. John kept Adelicia a State prisoner for the next fourteen years until 1213 when he sold her to Geoffrey Mandeville (or Manders), Earl of Essex, for 20,000 marks (about £6,500).

Adelicia's second husband died two years later, and John promptly married her off again; this time it was to one of his henchmen, Hubert de Burgh. She was his second wife and the marriage took place only a few days before her own death. (Was she "disposed"of?) Hubert de Burgh was an unpleasant favourite of King John, and it was he who ten years later told Ela of Canford the false story of her husband's death, and subsequently murdered him at Old Sarum (see Chapter 1).

Cranborne remained with the sovereign for many centuries until it was finally granted by James I to the Earl of Salisbury, by whose family a portion of it is held to this day.

PENELOPE DARCY OF WOLVERTON

Four centuries after Mabel of Cranborne was able to have some say about her prospective husband, another sixteen-year-old heiress in Dorset was also able to make the decision for herself, literally over and over again. She was Penelope, second daughter of Lord Darcy of Chirk, Viscount Colchester and Earl Rivers. She was also heiress to the estates of her mother Mary, daughter of Sir Thomas Kitson of Hengrave. Penelope Darcy was therefore a very rich young lady, but instead of having the problem of whether or not to accept a suitor, she had the problem of choosing between three of them.

It is said that the following episode took place in about 1625 at Wolverton, just north of Dorchester, at the home of Sir George Trenchard, one of the suitors.ᵐ He had spent much time in London at the Court of James I, and was noted for his horsemanship. The three suitors - the others being Sir John Gage and Sir William Harvey - together with Penelope's father had been great friends at Court, but when it came to competing for Penelope's hand, they decided to settle it once and for all by jousting with lances and by archery target shooting.

When Penelope found out what they had planned, she forbade them to do so, for fear of injuring each other. She then said she would keep them in suspense no longer and had made her decision. She proceeded to tell them that if only they would be patient she would be a wife to each of them in turn - and actually fulfilled her promise.

Firstly she married the fifty-year-old Sir George Trenchard of Wolverton soon afterwards. Within the year he was dead and she married the middle-aged Sir John Gage. A few years later she was widowed for the second time and was able to marry the youngest of her three original suitors, Sir William Harvey.

Was it pure chance that Penelope married them in the "right" order and so fulfilled her promise? Was she a good judge of how long each of them was likely to last?

JOAN BASTARD

The Bastard family of Blandford will for ever be famous as the architects of the new town built after the disastrous fire of 1731. But there is an amusing anecdote about one of their female ancestors over a century and a half earlier.^j

Joan Bastard was the wife of Thomas Bastard, a well-to-do blacksmith in the town of Blandford. According to his will, proved in 1570, he owned three houses in the town, and he left one to each of his three sons. Sadly his wife Joan received no property, so it is hoped that she owned something in her own right as part of the dowry she had brought to the marriage. Her husband did condescend to leave her a feather bed and some household implements, but only on the condition that she remained unmarried - and chaste! She must have been into her forties at the time of her husband's death, for her eldest son was already twenty-six years of age!

All sorts of speculations flash into one's mind as to why her husband put in this stipulation. Had Joan been unfaithful to him during their married life? Was this his way of punishing her? And what a difficult task he had set his son! How on earth was it possible for him to keep an eye on his mother's chastity? I have been unable to find any record of Joan's remarriage, so presumably she settled for the feather bed - on her own!

CHARLOTTE FIELDING

In 1735 a newly-married young woman, Charlotte Fielding, came to take up residence in her new home, a small Manor House at East Stour between Sherborne and Shaftesbury. She had grown up as Charlotte Cradock of Salisbury, one of the great beauties of the City. It is therefore not surprising that a 28-year-old visitor fell in love with her at first sight, and they were married shortly afterwards. Charlotte brought a settlement of £1,500 to the marriage, and with the money they planned to live in Dorset as "County" people, keeping open house for their neighbours, and running a pack of hounds and a stud of horses.

Their plans came to fruition and they settled into their comfortable lifestyle, becoming very popular with their neighbours. Unfortunately they had not budgeted for their living costs very well, and withing a year the Fieldings were stony-broke, the estate was sold, and the penniless young couple had left Dorset and moved to London. [Nothing now remains of the Rectory where they lived:

it was demolished and Church Farm built on its site. There is one concrete reminder of this family's connection with East Stour in that a street is named "Fielding Close" after them.]

Being penniless was nothing new to the young husband. He was Henry Fielding the dramatist (best remembered for his novel *Tom Jones*). Born in Somerset in 1707 and brought up at the Rectory in East Stour (his grandfather was Archdeacon of Dorset), he was educated at home and at Eton. Although destined for the legal profession, he soon found himself short of funds and at the age of twenty he turned to play-writing to provide himself with additional income. He had become moderately successful by the time he met Charlotte and determined to exchange his extravagant London life-style for a quiet country life with his wife at East Stour. But his spend-thrift ways didn't change, and in the spring of 1736 with an empty purse, Charlotte faced a squalid life in London with her husband and their baby daughter Amelia.

Poor Charlotte. For the next four years she struggled to keep the home going while her husband resumed his legal studies, supporting the family with a meagre income from writing. Her only solace was a young Dorset woman who had come to them as a maid when they lived in the grand style at East Stour. Henry was called to the Bar in 1740, but was totally unsuccessful as a lawyer. The struggle was too much for Charlotte and by 1742 she had become seriously ill. She died the following year after barely seven years of marriage. No doubt her great beauty that had first attracted Henry had all disappeared under the strain.

That the young couple loved each other is shown by the fact that Charlotte stayed with Henry through all the adversity and hardships, and also by the biography of her that he faithfully portrayed as the heroine of his book, *Amelia,* published in 1751.

The maid, Mary Macdaniel from Dorset, who had stayed with her young mistress through all the good times and the bad, remained to serve Henry and his daughter after Charlotte's death. She was a great comfort to him, being the only person who could talk to him about his beloved wife. More for the sake of propriety as well as for companionship, Mary Macdaniel and Henry Fielding were married in 1746. But Henry's health was already in decline and he gradually deteriorated until in 1754, he, Mary, and Amelia - the daughter born at East Stour in 1736 - set out in search of warmer climes. Henry Fielding died in Lisbon in 1754 at the age of forty-seven. The faithful Mary returned to her native Dorset, still caring for Charlotte's daughter, but not in the life-style to which Amelia had been born.

But that is not the end, or rather the beginning of Henry Fielding's connection with women of Dorset. As mentioned earlier, he is best-known for his novel *Tom Jones*, made into the roistering 20th Century film of the same name. The heroine of *Tom Jones* is Sophia Weston, and it is claimed that Fielding based this character on that of his first love, a Dorset girl by the name of Sara Andrews.

SARA ANDREWS OF LYME REGIS

Sara Andrews was born in 1710 in Lyme Regis where her father was a rich merchant and owned much property. She was his only child, and on his early death, she became a very rich heiress at the age of fifteen. She was made a Ward of Court and placed in the guardianship of her uncle, Andrew Tucker of Lyme Regis, in whose home at Tudor House she lived with his family. It has been suggested that her guardian had an eye on a betrothal between his son John and his extremely wealthy ward Sara, in the not-too-distant future.[3,4]

But Sara had another distant relative, and he also came a-courting of the rich heiress. He was the eighteen-year-old Henry Fielding (or Feilding, as his name was then spelt), just finished with his schooling at Eton and apparently simply enjoying a life of leisure before commencing the law career that had been planned for him. He came to Lyme in the summer of 1725, perhaps for a holiday, but more likely to visit his distant cousin and win her as a wife - with one eye on her fortune. He was accompanied by several friends and a servant by the name of Joseph Lewis. Apart from Fielding's wooing of Sara, he no doubt showed his high spirits and indulged in drinking and possibly brawling.

On 2 September Fielding brought a charge of assault against Joseph Channon, a servant of the town miller, James Daniel, claiming that he had been struck several times in the face and body in an unprovoked attack. Unfortunately, the sequel to this charge has not been preserved, so the full story of the event will never be known. There is a suggestion that the attack may have been at the instigation of Sara's guardian Andrew Tucker, or his son John, neither of whom would have taken kindly to Fielding's attention to Sara.

Still Henry persisted in his courtship of Sara, and it is probable that she concurred in this against the wishes of her guardian, for Fielding was still in Lyme two months later when matters came to a head. On Sunday 14 November Sara Andrews left Tudor House in the company of Andrew Tucker and his family to walk the short distance to Church. An attempt to abduct Sara was made by Henry Fielding with the aid of his servant. They were foiled - probably literally foiled by a sword in those days!

The same day Andrew Tucker laid a charge against Fielding and his servant before the Mayor of Lyme, in his role as a Justice of the Peace. The charge was surprisingly not to restrain Fielding from attempting another abduction, but for the threat of attack by Fielding upon his (Tucker's) person. The servant, Joseph Lewis, was soon apprehended but Fielding eluded capture by the Constables.

Andrew Tucker had obviously reached the end of his tether, for not only was Fielding a probable rival with his own son for the hand of Sara and had threatened violence against them, but Tucker was in a difficult position in relation to his guardianship of Sara. If the attempted abduction had been successful and the pair had married, then he would most likely have faced imprisonment by the Lord Chamberlain for, as a Ward of Court, Sara needed its permission for her marriage.

Henry Fielding had departed from Lyme by the next day, despairing of winning Sara's hand in the circumstances, but not before he had put up a handwritten poster ridiculing Andrew and John Tucker in a prominent position in Lyme stating: "This is to give notice to all the World that Andrew Tucker and his Son John Tucker are Clowns, and Cowards. Witness my hand, Henry Feilding". The original of this poster amazingly survived.[4]

And what became of Sara Andrews? After the Fielding abduction incident she was sent away to Devon and the care of a new guardian, another uncle, Ambrose Rhodes. Soon she had married this guardian's son, also Ambrose Rhodes. She lived to the age of seventy-three, dying in 1783, thirty-eight years after Fielding's death.

Henry Fielding therefore had three Dorset loves in his life. His first love, Sara Andrews, was immortalized as Sophia Weston in *Tom Jones*, published the year after his wife's death. The memory of his wife Charlotte Cradock was perpetuated as *Amelia*, published six years after her death. Mary Macdaniel, the ever-faithful maid and second wife, was apparently never honoured in any of his novels, but had the distinction of being with him at his death and subsequently caring for his only child.

MOLLY PADDOCK née GILES

Why did a Dorset woman, Molly Paddock, give her wedding ring to a dying woman so that it might be buried in her coffin? If I say that the reason was the hope that a long-standing mystery might be solved, then it adds another enigma. But that is exactly the reason for this unusual action, an attempt to discover the whereabouts of a long-lost husband. The story came from Molly Paddock of Lytchett Matravers herself who, as an elderly woman, kept a shop in the village of Lytchett Matravers at the beginning of this century.[5]

The young Molly Giles lived at Kingston, near Corfe Castle, with her farmer father. [Yes, Farmer Giles!] She had grown into a beautiful seventeen-year-old girl, much admired by the young men of the neighbourhood. In the late afternoon of a summer's day, she was lingering by the gate that gave onto the grassy track running past the farm. The road was rarely used by strangers, usually only by local people going to and from work. It was for the purpose of having a word with one of her sweethearts that she lingered there. He didn't arrive and Molly was just about to return to her neglected duties in the farmhouse when she saw a young man approaching in the distance. It was no

183

one she recognised, but as he drew nearer she could see that he was a very presentable young man.

As he came up to her he removed his hat, gave her a courteous bow and enquired in a very gentlemanly voice if there was a bed to be had at the farm-house. Molly suggested that he had a word with her father who was working in the nearby paddock. Her ploy worked, for when she accompanied the young man to where her father was working, he was offered a few days work with the hay-making then in progress, and was told he could sleep in the barn. One thing puzzled Molly though, and that was although the young man had first spoken in a cultured voice to her, he now spoke in a very rough voice to her father. Molly put this puzzle on one side as she heard her father ask the young man his name. He replied "Thomas," and then added after a little pause, "Thomas, er, Paddock".

The young man worked so well that when hay-making was over, Farmer Giles asked him if he would like to stay on working for him for a small wage. Thomas Paddock was happy to accept, and became a permanent resident at the Giles farmhouse. Molly was still intrigued at the change in manner between when she had first seen him and the character he had adopted since. She felt sure that he was really a gentleman and day-dreamed about where he had come from - he always avoided answering the question. She concluded that there must be some romantic story attached: perhaps he was the son of an important house who had quarrelled with his father and flung out of the house vowing never to set foot in it again.

The air of mystery about Thomas Paddock added to his attraction for her, and soon there was no doubt that her feelings were reciprocated. But the virtuous Molly resisted all his advances at seduction, until he realised that there was only one way to win her, marriage. Thomas asked Farmer Giles for Molly's hand in marriage, and although he refused initially, he relented in the face of Molly's pleadings.

And so Molly Giles and Thomas Paddock were married in the Parish Church of Kingston. When it came to signing the Register, Molly was extremely surprised when her new husband told the vicar that he couldn't write, and his name was indicated by a cross (as may be seen to this day), for she knew that Thomas could write perfectly well.

The young couple, apparently very much in love, settled happily into their new life in a little cottage on the farm given to them by her father. The next few months were idyllic as far as Molly was concerned, and soon her happiness was complete when she found she was pregnant. Money was a little tight, especially with another mouth to feed in the not-too-distant future; Molly's father could not afford to pay Thomas any more money. Molly therefore understood perfectly when one day her husband told her that he had heard of some well-paid work that was available a few miles away at Lytchett, and he was going over to see if he could be employed there.

Molly packed some food for him and waved goodbye as he set off down the grassy track and round the corner at the end. That was the last that

184

Molly saw of Thomas. Although searches were made high and low for many miles around, he had vanished as mysteriously as he had appeared less than a year earlier.

Molly was heart-broken. She stayed on alone at the cottage, always hoping that the next day would bring Thomas back, but to no avail. The baby was born in due course, a little girl, but she survived only a few hours. Molly had lost her husband, now she had lost her daughter, and a short while later her father died, leaving her completely alone in the world. To add to her misfortunes, it was then found that her father had been in debt, leaving Molly penniless as well as homeless.

A family in the village took her in to look after a very sick, elderly parent. When he died, she did the same again, and then again, until she found a vocation in nursing. For the rest of her active life she moved from house to house, living in to care for anyone who needed her services. In this way she came to be living in Lytchett Matravers as a very elderly woman.

Molly never married again, for she never felt herself to be a widow, and lived in hopes that some day Thomas would come back again to her. Money was still tight at the end of her life, and in the village she turned one of her rooms into a village shop, selling everything from groceries to materials and all manner of household goods. It was in the shop one day that she told her life story to the sister of the lady who afterwards wrote her story down.[5] Molly added the anecdote concerning the wedding ring mentioned at the beginning, which had occurred a few years earlier.

She had been nursing one of her last patients, a very sick old woman named Mrs Perks, who was close to death. Talking to the old woman about her life and the disappearance of her husband, Molly suddenly pulled off her wedding ring and put it on one of the dying woman's fingers, saying: "There, do'ee now take my wedding ring with 'ee and let it be buried in your coffin, and if ye come acrost Thomas, tell him I sent it". And so this was done, and old Mrs Perks was buried with two wedding rings on her fingers. There is no record of whether a ghostly Thomas ever received it in the after-life.

Poor Molly, for so many years she had gone through life not knowing whether she was a widow or still married. Who was Thomas Paddock? Was he indeed - as Molly believed - the son of some great house, and did he return there to become reconciled to his family, and perhaps settle down to a new "wife" and family? Did he ever give a thought to Molly? Was his real name Thomas? It probably wasn't Paddock for, as Molly believed, it was almost certainly suggested to him by the paddock in which they were standing when Molly's father asked his name. Poor faithful Molly.

Or has Thomas been completely misjudged? Did he come to a sticky end on that day he set out to find work at Lytchett, fully planning to return or send for her? Does his skeleton lie somewhere in the Isle of Purbeck, undisturbed to this day?

BESSIE SURTEES

In telling the story of the elopement of Bessie Surtees in his book *Highways and Byways in Dorset,* Treves[n] has done a great injustice to Bessie in order to make a more romantic-sounding story. His version is:

> "In the older Church in the village of Kingston near Corfe there are memorials to John, first Earl of Eldon and his wife Elizabeth, Countess of Eldon. These very high-sounding titles cover the remains of two very simple folk - John Scott a poor lad who made his way in the world, and Bessie Surtees, his humble sweetheart. The romance of the lives of these two is of an old-fashioned type. John Scott was born in Love Lane, Newcastle, in June 1751, of "obscure but respectable parents". When he was 21 years old and still very poor he ran away with Bessie Surtees and married her. At the time this rash act nearly ruined him, but it proved in the end to be a fortunate step, for his lifelong and pathetic devotion to his "Bessie" atoned for the many defects in his character. He took to the law, and by his stupendous abilities raised himself to the position of Lord Chancellor. Thus Bessie's needy lover became an Earl, and left behind him a fortune of over half a million pounds. He purchased the estate of Kingston where, at the age of 87, he died, and side by side in the now empty church, the daring lad and his trusting Bessie rest together."

The above quotation certainly tells a romantic story of the poor young couple eloping to be married against their parents' wishes; and then although he achieved high office through hard work the Earl of Eldon still retained his love for his humble, ill-educated "Bessie". The truth tells a different story.[w] "Bessie" certainly wasn't poor: she was the daughter of a banker wealthy enough to give her a dowry of £1,000 after the couple were reconciled to their parents after their elopement. (His parents were also wealthy enough to match this with another £1,000.) Coming from such a home it is extremely unlikely that Bessie was either "humble" or poorly-educated. The true facts about their background are as follows.

John Scott, born 4 June 1751, was the second son of a respectable Newcastle merchant trading in coal. He eventually followed his elder brother to Oxford University - indicating that his family may have been "obscure" when viewed from London, but it certainly couldn't have been "poor". He was awarded his Bachelor's degree in 1770 at the age of eighteen, and continued on a fellowship at the university. On 18 November 1772 he eloped with his childhood sweetheart, Miss Elizabeth Surtees, daughter of Aubone Surtees (or Auberon or Surties), a banker of Newcastle. In doing so he forfeited his fellowship. After being reconciled to both sets of parents - and receiving the

£2,000 - it was agreed that Bessie's husband would take up Holy Orders, providing that a vacancy occurred during his year of grace at Oxford. When no such vacancy occurred, it was decided that he would enter the legal profession, and the couple moved to London.

Most biographies (of men) wax lyrical about how they achieved their fame, but completely ignore any part played by their wife. Such is the case with John Scott: thus we are told that "he showed great devotion to his studies, rising at 4 a.m., having abstemious meals, and working to late hours, cooling his head with a wet towel to avert drowsiness". [While not wishing to detract from his achievements, what part did his wife play in all this?] In 1776 he was called to the Bar, and in 1780 his legal career took off. At the age of 32 he became an MP, at the age of 37 he became Solicitor-General, followed by Attorney-General, and Chief Justice of the Court of Common Pleas in 1799 at which time he took his seat in the House of Lords as Baron Eldon. He took the office of Lord Chancellor in 1801 when he was aged 49, from which he finally retired in 1827 with the title of Viscount Encombe and Earl of Eldon. He died in 1838 at the age of eighty-six. There is one amusing anecdote dating from his time in London[6] describing how the Lord Chancellor was observed stealing into *The George*, a coffee house in the Haymarket, for a pint of wine. Apparently Lady Eldon did not permit him to enjoy it in peace at home.

During all this lengthy career of her husband, Treves - as in the above quotation - would have us believe that Bessie remained his "humble sweetheart" to whom he had a "lifelong and pathetic devotion". It is difficult to believe that while the couple advanced socially to a very high position, Bessie - the daughter of a banker - was left completely behind in intellect, social graces, etc., as proposed by Treves.

CATHERINE PRIOR

Catherine Prior was brought up in London at the height of the rejoicings accompanying the Restoration of Charles II (1660). Her father was a vintner, and kept the *Rummer Tavern*, a very popular haunt of the wits of the day. His daughter showed early signs of great beauty and by the time she was into her teens, her father Arthur Prior feared for the safety of his daughter's virtue in the immoral, licentious London of the day. In order to keep her safe, he had the idea of sending her to live with his brother who some years earlier had left London to live in Wareham in Dorset.[d]

The arrival of this beauty in the provincial town of Wareham caused quite a sensation and she was described as a "blazing star". However it was not long before one of her suitors from London - a Mr Grey of Yorkshire - found out where her father had hidden her away and came in hot pursuit of her. As she eloped with her lover in his coach and six, it was the end of a very brief stay for Catherine in Dorset, for they were bound for his native Yorkshire.[22]

Only a short while before Catherine Prior's elopement, we have a good piece of evidence that elopements were so well established that they caused little or no comment. It may be remembered that in 1651 Charles II was wandering through Dorset in his attempts to escape to France after the Battle of Worcester (see Chapter 7). At one point he used the guise of pretending to be a lover escaping with his sweetheart from the wrath of her guardian who wished to prevent her marrying. At the Charmouth Inn when Charles and his female companion played the part of these lovers trying to escape to France to be married, they caused no adverse comment, and indeed the landlady at the Inn "smiled sweetly upon them".

If elopement had not been an established and widely practised procedure, then it is impossible to believe that they would have even pretended to be doing such a thing, especially in the middle of a Civil War!

CLOTILDE LAWRENCE

Almost certainly born after the execution of Louis XVI in 1792, Clot(h)ilde Clairet grew up in the newly-established French Republic, living at Germain-en-Laye, ten miles north-west of Paris. She saw Napoleon Bonaparte reach his peak, fall, and be exiled on Elba. After a brief reappearance of the monarchy, she witnessed the triumphal return of Napoleon for his glorious "Hundred Days" in 1815, before his defeat at Waterloo and final exile to St Helena. She must have been very frightened at what the future was going to hold when the Allied Armies arrived for the Occupation of Paris. But somewhere amidst all this turmoil she managed to meet, fall in love with, and marry a soldier from Dorset, a Sergeant in the 40th Foot.[7in]

Clotilde was in fact not her real name: she had been baptized Marie Louise Clairet. At the time of Napoleon's rise to power, his first wife's name was Marie Louise also. Napoleon issued a decree that no-one else should have the same name, and hence Marie Louise Clairet became Clotilde Clairet. Now in 1815, she was about to become the wife of Sergeant Lawrence. She was the daughter of a gardener, and sold most of his produce on a stall outside the barracks where William was living, together with other items like tobacco and spirits. Lawrence fell in love with her from the first time he went to buy something at her stall, and was soon spending all his spare time there, "thus forming an attachment which I never afterwards repented". He quickly made up his mind to marry her, and obtained the necessary permission from his Colonel - who thought Clotilde might be useful for teaching the troops French.

Soon after their one-day honeymoon, the Regiment was ordered to Scotland. It was an infantry regiment: the soldiers walked everywhere, and so did the wives. First to Calais, and then by "rickety water-tubs of colliers" to Leith, near Edinburgh. At least that was what was planned, but Clotilde's first introduction to the country that was to be her new home was washing clothes in Bridlington, Yorkshire. The journey from Calais to Leith should have taken three days but lasted over seven weeks: adverse winds and then storms sent the ships first to Bridlington - where they were allowed ashore during the day and Clotilde and the other wives were welcomed into private homes to do their washing - and then to North Shields. After arrival at Leith there was a three-day march to Glasgow, where they remained for three weeks.

Then came Clotilde's first introduction to Dorset, when William had a six week furlough. But the journey here in those days was very different from the few hours of today! Two days walk to Leith, covering thirty miles in the first day; ship to London at a cost of £2-10s; walk to the western outskirts of London where they were able to pick up a "road-wagon"; a day on this rumbling cart to Salisbury for two shillings; a day's walk - seven miles before breakfast - from Salisbury to Blandford; and then the following morning the last eight miles to Briant's Piddle (now Puddle) to William Lawrence's home and the family he hadn't seen for over sixteen years since he had run away from his apprenticeship to enlist in the army.

They could only spend eighteen days in Dorset before it was time to return. This time William and Clotilde planned to walk to Bristol and there take ship for Glasgow. The first part went well but they arrived at Bristol to find no ship available. At Clotilde's suggestion they walked all the way to Glasgow and arrived back at the barracks with one day to spare. At an outside estimate, that meant walking at least *thirty* miles every day! The only outcome was that Clotilde suffered frost-bite for a week.

Soon after their return to Glasgow, Lawrence's regiment in common with other regiments post-Waterloo was being drastically reduced. First the old and sick were "demobbed", then more were chosen by lot. William was one. After another voyage to London and a discharge at Chelsea Hospital, William was a civilian again. With a pension of nine-pence a day, the happy pair returned to his native Dorset. He chose to live in the village of Studland, where he had originally been apprenticed, and became a farm labourer to supplement his pension.

Within nine months he was back in the army. This time he was recalled to the "Third Veteran Battalion" a form of Reservist Regiment, and sent to Ireland to guard against smuggling - mainly tobacco. Clotilde went with him, and thoroughly enjoyed her year in Ireland. In June 1821 it was back to Plymouth and a second and final discharge from the army. The couple walked back to Studland to resume their civilian life. After trying several different trades, they ran the local inn there for over thirty years until her death in 1853. Her husband survived for another sixteen years. Both lie quietly in Studland Churchyard.

Clotilde's husband, William Lawrence had been born in 1791, one of the seven children of a farmer reduced to being a farm labourer. He received no education as he was required to work from an early age, first as a bird-scarer (2d a day), then as a plough-boy (6d a day), before being apprenticed, from which he ran away to join the army. He served in South America, the whole of the Peninsular War (being seriously injured at one point), finishing at Waterloo and the Occupation of Paris. In later life, after his beloved Clotilde had died, the story of his life was written down - he was illiterate - and there we can read about his beloved wife and her life in gentle Dorset, after the traumas of her early life in Paris, and all those miles of walking while William was still in the army.[7]

ANN HUTCHINS

Every one who has made any study of the history of Dorset cannot fail to have consulted the monumental work by John Hutchins, first published in 1774, the result of over forty years' labour. Few will realise that if it hadn't been for his wife - usually only referred to as "Mrs" Hutchins - this work would never have seen the light of day.

"Mrs" Hutchins was born Ann Stephens, the daughter of the rector of Pimperne, Rev Thomas Stephens.[8] She in turn only had one daughter, Anna Maria, who married John Bellas of the East India Company, and it was the latter who was responsible for bringing out the second edition of Hutchins' book. Ann's husband John Hutchins (1698-1773) first started collecting material for his book when he was curate at Milton Abbas: it was continued while he was successively vicar at Swyre (1729-33), Bingham's Melcombe (1733-44) and Holy Trinity, Wareham (1744-73). Through those dates we can therefore learn where Ann spent most of her life.

On Sunday 25 July 1762, John Hutchins was away at Bridport when the disastrous fire started that was going to destroy most of Wareham. The weather had been hot and dry for several weeks past, and there was a south-westerly breeze blowing when, at about 3 o'clock in the afternoon, a servant at The Bull's Head in the centre of Wareham threw some turf ashes onto a dung-hill. The ashes had not been fully quenched, and when combined with the dryness everywhere, the breeze, and the prevalence of thatched roofs, a fire soon sprang up that was almost immediately out of control.

It is said that the rectory was the fourth house to catch fire, so it didn't leave Ann Hutchins much time to save herself, let alone many of her belongings. Nevertheless, she is reported to have saved nearly a quarter of their possessions, including all her husband's notes and papers in connection with his proposed book, and carried them to safety. Judging by the large amount of material eventually published, it wasn't a case of snatching up one pile of notes and running, but meant saving piles and piles of papers and manuscripts, correspondence and probably many illustrations as well. Could she have carried them all herself? (She was an elderly lady, remember.) If she had to organize several people to help her, then this must certainly have required great presence of mind and authority to achieve such a thing in the middle of the terrible fire when the house must have been starting to burn about her, and burning thatch was flying everywhere.

But where did Ann Hutchins put all these piles of papers for safety? Did she have a pony and trap that could be used, or had her husband used their only conveyance to go to Bridport? She couldn't leave them in the garden for there was burning debris flying around. So what *did* she do with them all? Did it require many trips into the burning house to retrieve everything? How did she know which of the papers were the right ones to save in what must have been a very overcrowded study? (Her husband later regretted that none of his sermons had been saved!) Or had Ann Hutchins been actively involved in helping her husband with his work over the years: if so, then it would explain how the right ones were saved?

Imagine her emotions when she was re-united with her husband. He must have rushed back on hearing of the fire, not knowing whether his wife was alive or dead. He would see the ruins of Wareham and fear the worst. Imagine his great relief when he found that she was safe, but then imagine that scene when she was able to present him with his life's work, unscathed by the fire, when he must have thought it was among the ashes of the rectory.

It certainly required great strength of mind on the part of Ann Hutchins to rescue those papers of her husband's, when there must have been so many personal possessions that she longed to save instead. It certainly showed great devotion to put her husband's work first. During all those years when he had been invoved in collecting the material for his history of Dorset, did she never begrudge the time and money he had spent? Did she never once say to herself that she wished that it could "all go up in smoke" - and at last she had her chance!

We are told nothing of her reason for rescuing the papers, it being assumed that she did it for altruistic reasons. Perhaps I can be a little cynical and say that there might have been an ulterior motive - but I am probably doing her a great injustice. When John Hutchins died in 1773, nine years after the fire, he had made no financial provision for his wife - all his money had gone into his researches. The only exception was the future income from sales of his book, just being printed for the first time as he died. At the time of the fire, was Ann Hutchins aware that the future book was her "pension fund"? Was she mercenary enough to be aware that if she didn't save her husband's thirty years of notes and writings, then her future financial security was literally about to go up in smoke?

Although she probably did her heroic deed for purely altruistic reasons, there remains the sneaking suspicion that it may have been another purpose that motivated her. It is to be hoped not! As it turned out, she certainly

191

had need of that "pension fund" for she survived her husband by more than twenty years.

AGATHA TRUSSEBUT

In his book, *The Marches of Wessex*,[d] Darton gives this snippet of information gleaned from the State Papers, concerning Agatha Trussebut. (What a marvellous surname!)

> 11 July, at Corfe. Know that we [King John] received at Corfe on Tuesday, the Translation of St Benedict, in the 18th year of our reign [1216], from Agatha Trussebut, wife of William de Albeny, and her chaplain William, 500 marks for the ransom of the said William de Albeny.

Darton is using this as an example of King John's visits to Dorset, and his only other comment about the incident is "poor Agatha; and poor tenants of Agatha and William". Just one little incident, but what insight it can give into various features of the life of the times - but unfortunately leaving many unanswered questions. Thus was it usual for a wife to be known by her own name? If not, why was Agatha so addressed? How did her husband come to be imprisoned at Corfe? What agonies must Agatha have gone through knowing that if she did not raise the ransom, then her husband would be killed? Even if she did come up with the ransom, was she able to trust King John to release her husband? What was the background to the story?

Agatha's husband was the grandson of Adelicia of Louvaine the widow of King Henry I, by her second marriage to William d'Albini (or Albiney, Albeny, etc.) The only clue to her husband's age is that his father was one of Adelicia's seven children born between her marriage in 1138 and her death in 1151. It is therefore likely that Agatha's husband William d'Albeney was at least in his thirties and probably into his forties by the time of this incident in 1216. He was one of the Barons who rebelled against King John, and in September 1215, soon after the signing of *Magna Carta* he was sent to Rochester Castle shortly before it was besieged by King John and his foreign mercenary troops. Owing to lack of provisions and ammunition William was forced to surrender two months later. The infuriated King wished to kill all the defenders, including Agatha's husband, but was persuaded to keep the knights for ransom, while all "other ranks" were slain. Agatha's husband was sent as a prisoner to Corfe Castle to await his fate. [Did he meet the Scottish princesses and Eleanor there? - see Chapter 6.]

What was Agatha doing all this time? Did her husband keep her informed of what he was doing during his long involvement in the Rebellion against King John? Did she know that he was besieged at Rochester Castle in a hopeless position, and was she resigned to the worst? Then came the news - he was a prisoner, his life dependent on whether she could raise the ransom. Her relief at his safety must have been virtually outweighed by her despair at being able to raise such a large sum.

How *did* wives gather together a ransom in those days? They couldn't just go to the bank and draw out the money. It had to be raised in actual cash. Did they carry large amounts of money around with them wherever they went? Her husband's continued fighting against King John in the previous few years must have been a great drain on their resources. Did Agatha go round members of her family trying to borrow as much as she could? Did she sell - or pawn - her jewels and other valuables? Or did she have to penalise the tenants on their estates, as suggested by Darton?

It would appear that Agatha had great difficulty in raising the ransom, for in the above quotation she arrived at Corfe with 500 marks, but the total ransom for the release of her husband was 6,000 marks.[23] Was this all she could raise immediately, and did she bring it along to show good-will, a part-payment to keep her husband alive until she was able to raise the rest of the money? (She obviously had difficulty in raising this further amount, for her husband wasn't released until after the death of King John the following year.)

The actual arrival of Agatha at Corfe is interesting in several respects. It specifically mentions that Agatha and her chaplain brought the money themselves. Presumably they would have had some kind of armed escort, but it nevertheless indicates that even in those terrible times of the reign of King John, it was still possible for a woman to travel unmolested, with many aware that she would probably be carrying a large sum of money for the ransom. She brought the money herself, either hoping to see her husband or, as is more likely, because there was no trusted servant left to bring it, since most of the able-bodied servants would probably have been with her husband at Rochester Castle and hence among the "other ranks" slain there. Was Agatha running the estate almost single-handed then?

As was said earlier, a small incident in the State Records, but further consideration shows that there are many aspects of those times revealed in it. As a post-script, Agatha's husband survived for another twenty years, dying in 1236. The date of Agatha's death, like that of her birth, are unrecorded.

ALICE ESCHELLING

The following entry also occurs in the State Papers in the time of King John,[n] concerning the Manor of Shillingstone in Dorset.

> "Alice, wife of John Eschelling owed 15 marks
> that her land might be in peace and in the King's
> protection, and that her lord might not pass over the sea
> with horses and arms."

The author has puzzled over the ambiguity with respect to "over the sea". Does it mean that Alice Eschelling was a loving wife who was willing to pay money to keep her husband this side of the Channel? Alternatively, does it mean that Alice was paying money to King John to keep her husband on the other side of the Channel, away from her? What do you think?

At first sight it would appear to be the former - Alice wishing to prevent her husband from going away to France to fight. But then why was Alice paying it and not her husband? She was also paying "that her land might be in peace". Who had she been having trouble with? Her husband? Again, it is "*her* land"; why not her husband's land?

Sadly, the author has been unable to trace anything further of these events to satisfy her curiosity as to exactly what this Dorset woman was up to in the 13th Century!

LADY ELIZABETH HATTON

Such a prominent landmark as Corfe Castle (at least before its demolition in 1645) could not fail to be mentioned over and over again in this book - from the Anglo-Saxon Elfrida to Lady Bankes its last owner. For most of its life it was in Royal hands and had quite a stormy history, being besieged many times. But this stormy history enacted around the outside of the Castle was nothing to the stormy life that went on within its walls during the life-time of its penultimate owner, Lady Elizabeth Hatton. It is amusing that while this lady has come down to us as Lady Hatton, this was her correct name for only a year or so of her more than sixty years; and even during that period she could have been known as Lady Elizabeth Newport.^{finx}

She was born Elizabeth Cecil in about the year 1580, the fourth daughter of Thomas Cecil, Earl of Exeter, eldest son and eventual heir to William Cecil, first Lord Burghley (or Burleigh). In the mid-1590's she married William Hatton who was a widower with one infant daughter, Frances Hatton. He had been born William Newport, but had recently changed his name to Hatton at the request of his uncle Sir Christopher Hatton (Lord Chancellor to Queen Elizabeth I) whose heir he was. Corfe Castle was one of the many gifts showered on Sir Christopher Hatton by the Queen, and on his death in 1591, it had passed to this nephew, the son of his sister Dorothy.

At the time of their marriage, William Hatton had settled Corfe on his new wife, and so his death shortly afterwards in 1597 left Lady Elizabeth Hatton in full possession, a beautiful and wealthy young widow. She also inherited the whole of the Isle of Purbeck, and Hatton House in London. As well as her wealth and beauty, which alone made her a good catch, she had another great attraction - her political connections. Her grandfather, William Cecil (who was to die the following year, 1598) had been a close adviser of Queen Elizabeth (1558-1603) for over forty years, acting in a capacity that today would be equated with Prime Minister. Already following in his footsteps was Elizabeth's uncle, Robert Cecil, Earl of Salisbury (1563-1612), while her father, Thomas, was a proven military commander.

When such political connections were added to her youth, beauty and wealth, it is not surprising that there should be a queue of suitors for the hand of the widowed Elizabeth Hatton. Head of the queue was Francis Bacon, but the disfavour he had shown to the Cecils counted strongly against him. The twenty-year-old Elizabeth chose - or rather had chosen for her - the forty-seven-year-old Edward Coke, with the encouragement of her grandfather, and they were married in 1598, less than a year after she had been widowed.

Edward Coke had himself become a widower only a few months before, after sixteen years of happy and contented marriage to a member of the Paston family (at least on his side it had been happy, for his meek wife remained at home in Norfolk, quietly producing a baby annually). What a different life he was to lead with this new wife in a marriage that was to last over thirty-six years (most of it lived separately). She was of a fiery temperament, given to a life of pleasure: she frequently took part in Court masques, and was complimented in verses by Ben Jonson. She spent her time between London and Corfe, entertaining lavishly at both. Her husband on the other hand was committed to his political life. He was Chief Justice, described as "a narrow-minded and bitter-tempered man, but very highly-respected as a lawyer and with a reverence for the law that overrode every other instinct".[x] He was also the father of seven sons and three daughters by his first wife, none older than fifteen at the time of his second marriage. Lady Elizabeth had two daughters in the first couple of years of her marriage to Coke, Elizabeth and Frances, and her stepdaughter Frances Hatton was also made her Ward.

Lady Elizabeth and Coke were totally unsuited to each other in every possible way, and their public rows became notorious, even taking place at the table of the Privy Council. She was twenty at the time of their marriage, didn't want to marry him, and had no respect for this second husband. In particular, she appears to have been a woman ahead of her times, for she was a strong believer in the emancipation of women. What especially enraged her was that on her marriage, all her property and wealth immediately became the possession of her husband, and she had no further rights in its management and disposal. (As it happened she was right to be enraged about it, for her husband negotiated many nefarious deals with it.) Coke "sold" Frances Hatton in marriage for £4000 against Lady Elizabeth's wishes, and he and his sons by his first marriage - one was known as "fighting Clement" - broke down the doors of her residence in order to get at the unwilling Frances. Lady Hatton always refused to use her husband's name, Lady Cook as she spelt it. ["Cook" is the way the name was, and still is, pronounced in that branch of the Coke family.]

Lady Elizabeth was a great friend of the Queen, Anne of Denmark. She was always involved in intrigues and affairs, and apart from her former suitor, Francis Bacon, her name was linked with the unfortunate Earl of Essex, and also Gondomar, the Spanish Ambassador. It is to Lady Elizabeth's husband that the saying "an Englishman's house is his castle" is attributed, and one wonders how much she was responsible for its origin!

Queen Elizabeth I died in 1603 and the accession of James I made a great difference to the career of Lady Elizabeth's husband as he struggled to keep his integrity and independence as a judge in the changed circumstances: finally he was out of favour. In 1617, at the age of sixty-six he tried to win his way back into favour with the one tool at his disposal, Frances, his second daughter by Lady Elizabeth. (Their first daughter was already married by this time, and died soon after.) He tried to marry the fourteen-year-old Frances Coke to Sir John Villiers, brother of Lord Buckingham. Lady Elizabeth was completely against the match, as was Frances herself. The latter "voluntarily and deliberately protested that, of all men living, she would not have him".[X]

With mother and daughter of one mind, they escaped from Coke's house and Frances was hidden at the home of a friend. Determined not to be thwarted in his plans and having found out where she was hidden, Coke came riding there with several of his sons by his first marriage - including "fighting Clement". They battered down several doors and eventually found Frances and her mother hiding in a closet. To the sound of Lady Elizabeth's yells and screams, they took the unwilling Frances away from her mother. A short while later Coke informed Buckingham that his daughter was very much in love with Villiers and wished to marry him, and there was good evidence that Frances had been repeatedly beaten by her father to make her "willing". Negotiations were very quickly completed and the marriage was rushed through at Michaelmas 1617 before Lady Elizabeth could intervene again, she being imprisoned on a trumped-up charge at this time.

Mother and daughter were right in their summing-up of the character of Villiers, for in 1620, after being elevated to the peerage as Viscount Purbeck, he deserted his young wife and fled to the Continent to continue his profligate life. Before long the young Lady Purbeck followed in her mother's footsteps and her adulterous affairs soon brought her to the punishment of doing penance in a white sheet at the Savoy Church in London. Frances declined to perform this public penance and escaped back to Corfe and her mother, there to continue in their reckless and extravagant life-styles.

The turbulent and stormy lives of mother and daughter continued for many years, to the great amusement of Dorset people when they occurred at Corfe and its neighbourhood. The death of Coke in 1634 at the age of eighty put a damper on this Dorset part of their life, for there was insufficient income to keep up both the Dorset and London establishments. Corfe was sold to Sir John Bankes in the same year as Coke died, and it was with Bankes' wife that the active part of the life of the Castle came to an end in the Civil War (see Chapter 7). Lady Hatton returned to her London home for good (it now forms part of Hatton Garden) where she still lived a riotous life until her death on 31 December 1645, having apparently lost the will to live after the death six months earlier of her beloved daughter Frances.[9]

One interesting point is that if Lady Hatton had not sold Corfe Castle to Sir John Bankes, then it might still today be the magnificent edifice that it then was. For it was destroyed by Roundheads in the Civil War after being held by the Royalist-supporting Lady Bankes: Lady Hatton was a Roundhead-supporter.

BESS THROCKMORTON

Elizabeth "Bess" Throckmorton (or Throgmorton) was an attendant (a "maid-of-honour") at the Court of Queen Elizabeth I when she was seduced by, and subsequently secretly married to, Sir Walter Raleigh (or Ralegh) at the end of 1591 or the beginning of 1592.[10,11,pjx] He was about thirty-seven years of age by this time (born circa 1554), and she was twenty-six (baptized 16 April 1565). He had been at Court since 1580 and had become a great favourite of the Queen who was highly offended when she learned of his seduction of Bess - principally because she did not like to think of sharing the favours of one of her favourites with anyone else. She promptly had Sir Walter and his new wife thrown into the Tower. He was soon released but Bess remained there till the end of the year. Although her husband was soon restored to royal favour, Bess never returned to Court: it was soon afterwards that they came to live in Sherborne.

Poor Bess did not see much of her husband in the next few years, for he went off on two expeditions to South America before being restored fully to the Queen's favour at Court in 1597. The death of Elizabeth I in 1603 and the accession of James I was Sir Walter's downfall: he was tried for High Treason, convicted and condemned to death, reprieved, and imprisoned in the Tower again from 1603 to 1616. Because of his great popularity, his imprisonment was less severe than meted out to others: he could receive his friends, take exercise on the battlements, and from 1605 he was joined (voluntarily) by Bess.

Following an abortive attempt to find "El Dorado" in 1617, he was finally executed on 29 October 1618. Bess Throckmorton survived her husband for another twenty-nine years, dying in 1647 at the age of eighty-two. That she and her husband had a great love for each other is shown by two facts, one gruesome and one loving. During the years of Raleigh's imprisonment in the Tower from 1603 to 1605, she was rarely able to visit him, but he wrote her many letters, some of which have survived. One of these is particularly touching: it was written on the eve of what he thought would be his execution in December 1603, and he is giving her advice about what must inevitably happen to a rich widow in those days - a re-marriage.

"... When I am gone noe doubt you shall be sought by many, for the world thinks that I was very rich. But take heed of the pretence of man ..... I spake not this (God knoweth) to dissuade you from marriage, for it will bee best for you: both in respect of the world and of God. As for me, I am noe more yours, nor you mine. ..."

Bess didn't remarry when her husband was finally executed in 1618, and made her feelings for him perfectly plain by the fact that wherever she went during her widowhood she carried the embalmed head of her husband with her in a red leather bag. Normally the head of a traitor was placed on a spike and hung up high at the Tower of London for everyone to see until it rotted away, but out of respect to the much-loved Sir Walter Raleigh, it is said that the executioner smuggled his head to Bess Throckmorton who was waiting nearby in a coach.

As a postscript to this gruesome anecdote, there are currently two Churches which claim to have the head of Sir Walter Raleigh buried within their precincts.[12] One is the Church at West Horsley in Surrey which claims that the head was buried 'under the floor, to the left of the organ' in the grave of Bess and Walter's grandchildren. The other Church is St Margaret's, Westminster which claims that the head was buried in the grave of their son Carew Raleigh (died 1666), and the same Church also claims that the body of Sir Walter himself was secretly buried there also. Whether this was carried out is uncertain, for at the time of his death Bess had other ideas about the disposal of her husband's body, as shown by a letter written by her on 30th October 1618 and addressed to "My Best Brother, Sir Nicholas Carew,[24] at Beddington". With its quaint spelling it states

"I desiar, good brother, that you will be pleased to let me berri the worthi boddi of my nobell hosban, Sir Walter Raleigh, in your churche at Beddington, wher I

desiar to be berred. The Lordes have geven me his did
boddi, though they denied me his life. This nit hee shall
bee brought you with two or three of my men. Let me
here presently. God hold me in my wittes.

E.R."

ELIZABETH JESTY

Ann Notley, Mary Reade and Abigail Brown were three 18th Century
Dorset women associated with one of the major medical events of the 20th
Century, and yet their names are unknown in connection with it. If the
name of Elizabeth Jesty is added, then some might recognise that they were
involved in the eradication from the face of the Earth of the dread disease
of smallpox. Edward Jenner is renowned as the "father of smallpox
vaccination", and perhaps rightly so, for he dedicated his life, money and
reputation to spreading the use of vaccination from the first time he used it
on a boy called James Phipps in 1796, at Berkeley in Gloucestershire. But
over twenty years earlier, in 1774 at Yetminster in Dorset, a farmer's wife
by the name of Elizabeth Jesty, together with her two sons, had been
vaccinated by her husband.[13dx]

In 1774 thirty-three year-old Elizabeth Jesty was living in
Yetminster with her husband Benjamin, their two sons Robert and
Benjamin aged three and two, and a baby also called Elizabeth. The family
were looking forward to the birth of another baby later in the year. The
highly infectious disease of smallpox was raging in the area in the spring
and summer of that year, and Benjamin feared for his wife and young
family. He himself had had smallpox as a child, and was therefore
immune. In common with many country people he was fully aware of the
age-old tradition that those who had earlier caught the mild disease of
cowpox did not catch the usually fatal disease of smallpox.

This was particularly brought home to him by the presence in his
farmhouse of the two maids, Ann Notley and Mary Reade. Both these girls
had previously had cowpox, and both had recently nursed members of their
families who had caught smallpox in the present epidemic; they had come
through unscathed. It was almost certainly these two girls who decided
Benjamin in his resolve to perform what later came to be described as a
vaccination.[25] His reasoning must have been that if dairymaids who
caught cowpox *accidentally* were immune to smallpox, then someone who
caught cowpox *deliberately* should be equally immune.

Hearing of an outbreak of cowpox on the farm of a Mr Elford at
nearby Chetnole, Benjamin quickly took Elizabeth and her two sons there -
presumably the baby Elizabeth was considered too young. There, out in the

199

field, Benjamin took some infected pus from the udder of a cow and, with the point of a stocking needle (knitting or darning is not specified) he scratched Elizabeth's arm just below the elbow and inserted the pus. The first authenticated vaccination had taken place. He then repeated the procedure with his two sons.

During the next few days the mild disease of cowpox ran its normal course in the two young boys, and they were soon fully recovered and running around as normal. But poor Elizabeth Jesty became very ill - she was well into a pregnancy, remember. She ran a high fever and her arm became very inflamed. Her husband called in the local doctor to treat her fever, and needless to say he was a little put out when Benjamin revealed what he had done! Fortunately the fever subsided and Elizabeth recovered fully; so much so that she lived for another fifty years.

Having recovered from her illness, poor Elizabeth now became an object of derision to her neighbours. For as word got round of what Benjamin had done to her, the neighbours were fully expecting that she and the boys would turn into cows, or at the very least would grow horns. Benjamin in his turn was "hooted at, reviled and pelted whenever he attended markets in the neighbourhood. He remained undaunted and never failed from this cause to attend to his duties".

How long this scorn lasted is not known, neither is it known how many further vaccinations were performed in the area - people who were vaccinated probably kept very quiet about it in view of the derision the Jestys had received. It must be presumed that Benjamin carried on with them, for in later years there is a clearly documented record of one of them. In 1797 the Jesty family moved to Worth Matravers in the Isle of Purbeck, and it is in the Church of this Parish that there is a tablet in memory of a Mary Brown which states that her mother Abigail Brown was vaccinated by Benjamin Jesty; the same inscription is also on the gravestone in the Churchyard.

It is perhaps understandable that the Jestys are not known to the world in general in connection with smallpox vaccination, compared with Edward Jenner. The latter was a doctor, had influential friends in the medical world in London, and devoted time and much money to developing and refining the technique of vaccination. Jesty on the other hand was a country farmer, and had the news of his vaccination procedure reached the medical world in the decades before Jenner came into his own, then it would almost certainly have been written off as an "old wives tale".

Jenner himself never accepted that he had been pre-empted by Jesty; this was partly professional pride (or was it arrogance?), but mainly Jenner's desire to be recognized as the discoverer of vaccination in order to secure a large financial reward from Parliament. (Jenner got the money, Jesty got nothing.) The full story of this "rivalry" can be read in the booklet *The First Vaccinator* by Marjorie Wallace.[13]

On the other hand, the Jestys freely admitted that they were probably not the first with vaccination, as indicated on their gravestone.

These graves lying just behind the Parish Church in Worth Matravers, gently shaded by a large yew tree, clearly state that Jesty was "the first person (known) that introduced the Cow Pox by inoculation". They were thus respecting the fact that the widely-known immunity against smallpox given by cowpox may well have inspired other anonymous people to perform the same procedure as Benjamin. Nevertheless, Elizabeth Jesty of Dorset can certainly claim to be the first *recorded* person to have been vaccinated.

DOROTHY HASTINGS née WILLOUGHBY

When we visit an old house or read about it, we can envisage what the building must have looked like formerly, perhaps in Elizabethan or Georgian times. But that still leaves only an empty shell, for even with furniture it is still lacking that one essential ingredient that literally brings it to life - people. We can never really envisage what the interiors of these houses were like when they were bustling hives of activity, families growing up, new generations appearing, and all those little stories and anecdotes that form part of everyone's life. What did the rooms really look like when everyday things were scattered about?

We are very fortunate in having just such a description of the interior of a Dorset Manor House - Woodlands - in the middle of the 17th Century, probably written about the time of the Civil War.[14cn] Unfortunately, while we have the description, the house itself is no more. On the other hand, it is to be hoped that the interior of this house was not typical of those times, for, as Treves[n] says about the lady of the house, "if she was a lady of dainty tastes, she probably avoided both the Parlour and the Great Hall". The lady in question was Dorothy Hastings, née Willoughby, and the house had been in Dorothy's family for many generations, passing only by marriage (see accompanying pedigree 8.2). Dorothy Willoughby was the heiress of her father, and had married Henry Hastings in about 1587. He was the second son of the Earl of Huntingdon, and became lord of the manor of Woodlands on his marriage with Dorothy. The air at Woodlands must have suited them both, for Dorothy was nearly seventy when she died in 1638, while her husband went on to be ninety-nine at his death in 1650. While the air at Woodlands may have contributed to his longevity, it could well have been Henry Hastings' way of life that had something to do with it, as this description shows. One can only wonder at how Dorothy put up with these living conditions in a marriage that lasted fifty years.

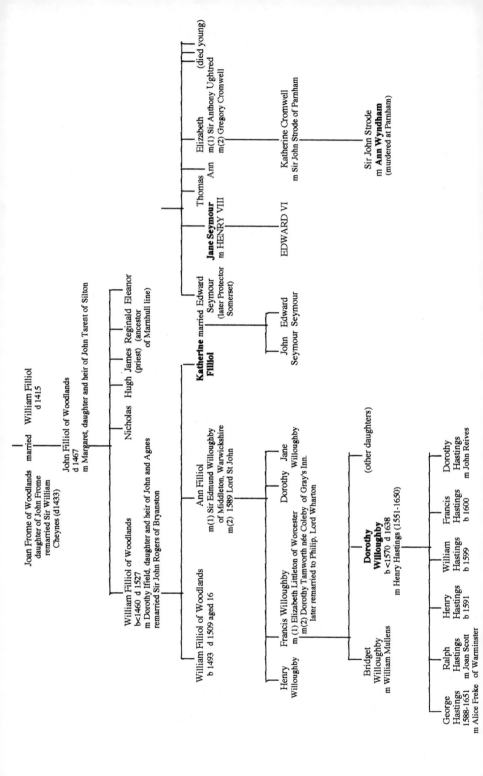

Joan Frome of Woodlands   married   William Filliol
daughter of John Frome   d 1415
remarried Sir William
Cheynes (d1433)

John Filliol of Woodlands
d 1467
m Margaret, daughter and heir of John Tarent of Silton

Nicholas   Hugh   James   Reginald   Eleanor
                        (priest)   (ancestor
                                       of Marnhull line)

William Filliol of Woodlands
b<1460 d 1527
m Dorothy Ifield, daughter and heir of John and Agnes
remarried Sir John Rogers of Bryanston

Ann Filliol
m(1) Sir Edmund Willoughby
of Middleton, Warwickshire
m(2) 1589 Lord St John

Katherine married   Edward
Filliol   Seymour
                               (later Protector
                               Somerset)

Thomas   Ann

Elizabeth   (died young)
m(1) Sir Anthony Ughtred
m(2) Gregory Cromwell

Jane Seymour
m HENRY VIII

Katherine Cromwell
m Sir John Strode of Parnham

EDWARD VI

John   Edward
Seymour Seymour

Sir John Strode
m **Ann Wyndham**
(murdered at Parnham)

William Filliol of Woodlands
b 1493   d 1509 aged 16

Francis Willoughby
m (1) Elizabeth Littleton of Worcester
m(2) Dorothy Tamworth née Coleby of Gray's Inn.
later remarried to Philip, Lord Wharton

Dorothy   Jane
           Willoughby

Henry
Willoughby

**Dorothy
Willoughby**
b <1570 d 1638
m Henry Hastings (1551-1650)

(other daughters)

Bridget
Willoughby
m William Mullens

George   Ralph   Henry   William   Francis   Dorothy
Hastings   Hastings   Hastings   Hastings   Hastings   Hastings
1588-1651   m Joan Scott   b 1591   b 1599   b 1600   m John Reives
m Alice Freke   of Warminster

It is usually claimed that this description was written by Sir Anthony Ashley Cooper in 1638, the year of Dorothy's death: the last few sentences however, indicates that they at least were written after Henry's death. Although the article was written specifically about Henry Hastings, it gives a very good idea of what Dorothy had to put up with. What would Dorothy's version have been like?

"In the year 1638 lived Mr Hastings, by his quality son, brother and uncle to the Earls of Huntingdon. He was, peradventure, an original in our age, or rather a copy of our ancient Nobility in hunting, not in warlike times. He was low [short], very strong, and very active, of a reddish flaxen hair; his clothes always green cloth, and never worth, when new, five pounds. His house was perfectly of the old fashion, in the midst of a large park, well stocked with deer; and near the house, rabbits for his kitchen; many fish ponds; great stores of wood and timber; a bowling-green in it; long, but narrow, full of high ridges, it being never levelled since it was ploughed; they used round sand bowles; and it had a banqueting house like a stand, a large one built in a tree. He kept all manner of sport-hounds, that ran buck, fox, hare, otter, and badger; and hawks, long and short-winged. He had all sorts of nets for fish. He had a walk in the New Forest and the Manor of ChristChurch; this last supplied him with red deer, sea and river-fish; and, indeed, all his neighbours' grounds and royalties were free to him who bestowed all his time on these sports, but [except] what he borrowed to caress his neighbours' wives and daughters, there being not a woman in all his walks, of the degree of a yeoman's wife, or under, and under the age of forty, but it was her own fault if he was not acquainted with her. This made him very popular; always speaking kindly to the husband, brother or father, who was to boot very welcome to his house. Whenever he came there, he found beef, pudding and small beer, in great plenty; the house not so neatly kept as to shame him or his dirty shoes; the great hall strewed with marrow-bones, full of hawks, perches, hounds, spaniels, and terriers; the upper side of the hall hung with fox-skins, of this or the last year's killing; here and there a pole-cat intermixed; gamekeeper's and hunter's poles in great abundance. The parlour was a large room, as properly furnished. On a great hearth, paved with brick, lay some terriers, and the choicest hounds and spaniels. Seldom but two of the great chairs had litters of cats in them, which were not to be disturbed: he having always three or four attending him at dinner; and a little white stick, of fourteen inches long, lying by his trencher [dinner plate], that he might defend such meat as he had no mind to part with for them. The windows, which were very large, served for places to lay his arrows, cross-bows, and stone-bows, and such like accoutrements; the corners of the room full of the best chosen hunting and hawking poles; his oyster table at the lower end, which was of constant use, for he never failed to eat oysters all seasons, both dinner and supper: the neighbouring town of Poole supplied him with them.

The upper part of the room had two tables and a desk, and on the one side of which there was a Church Bible, and on the other side the Book of Martyrs: on the tables were hawks' hoods, bells and such-like; two or three old hats, with their crowns thrust in, so as to hold ten or a dozen eggs, which were of the pheasant kind of poultry; these he took much care of, and fed himself. Tables, dice, cards, and boxes, were not wanting. In the hole of the desk were stores of tobacco-pipes that had been used. On one side of this end of the room was the door of a closet, wherein stood the strong beer and the wine, which never came from thence but in single glasses, that being the rule of the house exactly observed; for he never exceeded in drink, or permitted it. On the other side was the door of the old chapel, not used for devotion; the pulpit, as the safest place [from the dogs], was never wanting of a cold chine of beef, venison pasty, gammon of bacon, or great apple pye, with thick crust, extremely baked. His table cost him not much, though it was good to eat at it. His sports provided all but beef or mutton, except Fridays, when he had the best of salt-fish, as well as eating other fish he could get; and this was the day his neighbours of best quality visited him. He never wanted a London pudding, and always sung in eating it, "With my pert eyes thereina" - (my *part lies* therein)". He drank a glass or two of wine at meals; very often put syrup of gilly-flowers [wall-flowers] in his sack, and always holding a pint of small beer, which he often stirred with rosemary.

He was well-natured but soon angry, calling his servants bastards and cuckoldry knaves, in one of which he often spoke the truth to his own knowledge, and sometimes in both, though of the same man. He lived to be an hundred, and never lost his eye-sight, but always

wrote and read without spectacles, and got on horse-back
without help. Until past fourscore, he rode to the death of
the stag as well as any."

So now we know what the interior of one 17th Century Manor
House looked like when everyday articles were strewn around. The fact
that Ashley Cooper took the trouble to record it, suggests that it was far
from typical of its time, as was the owner himself. What did Dorothy think
of it all? Did she have her own room elsewhere in the house where
everything was to her own tastes, and where she could entertain her own
friends? Or was she a "hunting, shooting and fishing" type herself, and
thoroughly enjoyed joining in? At least her husband wasn't a heavy
drinker! Did Dorothy ever enter the Great Hall or Parlour and shudder at
the sight within, perhaps remembering what it had been like in her
childhood, or had her father been similarly inclined? At least Dorothy must
have pleased her husband in bringing five healthy sons into the world (see
previous pedigree 8.2)!

ALICE DE LACY

If the present-day media *papparazzi* had been around at the beginning of
the 14th Century, what a field-day they would have had following the
fortunes and antics of Alice de Lacy of Kingston Lacy. Her great-
grandfather, John de Lacy, had been one of the Barons chosen to ensure the
observance of Magna Carta and its successor, the Charter of King Henry
III. This latter King had rewarded John de Lacy with the manor of
Kingston (Lacy) in 1229, followed three years later by creating him Earl of
Lincoln. In 1257 Alice's father had married Margaret Longespée, great-
grand-daughter and heiress of Ela of Canford and Countess of Salisbury
(see pedigree 1.1 in Chapter 1). On the death of Alice's father in 1311, she
was therefore left as the sole heiress of vast estates - including Canford and
Kingston Lacy - which also carried the titles of the Earldoms of Lincoln
and Salisbury.
    In 1294, seventeen years before she came into her inheritance,
Alice de Lacy had married Thomas, Earl of Lancaster and Earl of Derby, a
grandson of Henry III and first cousin to King Edward II. On the death of
her father, Alice's husband was therefore the possessor of the four
earldoms of Lincoln, Salisbury, Warwick and Derby, as well as becoming
the new owner of Canford. These titles, combined with his Royal blood,
served to establish him at the head of the English baronage, and his
struggles with his homosexual cousin, King Edward II, elevated him to
supreme power in the Kingdom.
    While it is possible to read much of the public life of the Earl of
Lancaster - his popularity with the people and his poor leadership qualities

in connection with the barons' opposition to the King - little is recorded of his private life with his wife. And this must have been a stormy relationship, for in 1317, after twenty-three years of marriage, she was kidnapped to get her away from her husband. The instigator of this action was John de Warenne, Earl of Surrey, but records disagree about the nature of the event. While some give the impression that Warenne stole her away from Canford for romantic reasons,[i] others state that with the full agreement of the King, Warenne deputed a knight to go to Canford to rescue Alice from her husband and escort her in her flight from him.[15] [It has not been possible to determine whether or not Alice became the mistress of the Earl of Surrey.]

Then out of the blue appeared a man named Richard Martin - described as a hunchback - who took legal action against Alice, claiming that at the time of her marriage to the Earl of Lancaster, Alice was already married to him. He therefore asserted that as Alice's rightful husband, it was he and not the Earl of Lancaster who should have received the titles of Earls of Salisbury and Lincoln. Consternation! Alice promptly returned to her "husband" the Earl of Lancaster in order to defend the case, which appears to have gone in her favour, although there still remains a doubt that Richard Martin may well have been her true first husband. Whether Alice remained with her "husband" is uncertain, but the remainder of his life was short-lived: the Earl of Lancaster rebelled against the King once more, was taken prisoner, and executed less than three years later in 1322.

Undeterred by these events of her married life, Alice went on to marry twice more, and outlived all her husbands - including Richard Martin. She lived to be almost seventy, dying in 1348, and in spite of all her husbands, she died childless. The large estates she had inherited from her father had already been forfeited to the Crown in 1322 on the execution of her "husband", the Earl of Lancaster. Edward II promptly gave them to Alice's "kidnapper", the Earl of Surrey, for "his life", and he therefore became the new Lord of Canford - whether Alice was also there is not disclosed.

After the brutal murder of Edward II in 1327, his widow Queen Isabella and her son, the new King Edward III, returned to England from France. Accompanying the Queen in her travels had been a lady by the name of Joan, and in the same year, 1327, this Joan appears as Warenne's wife when her name was also added to the grant of Canford "for her life". As has happened frequently in its history, Canford was once again in the hands of a female when Joan became its owner after the death of her husband in 1344 until her own in 1361.

After Joan de Warenne's death Kingston Lacy (and Canford) reverted to the Crown where it remained for another 300 years - it was the birth-place of Margaret Beaufort in 1441 (see Chapter 2) - until it reappears in this book after it had been sold in 1636 to the Attorney-General of Charles I, Sir John Bankes. It subsequently became one of the homes of his widow, Lady Bankes after her gallant defence of Corfe Castle.

THE TWO (OR THREE) MRS LAWRENCES
OF WRAXALL

There certainly appears to have been a great difference in the married lives of two wives of William Lawrence - at least as seen from his point of view.[fil] (He was born at Wraxall, near Rampisham in 1611, and became a lawyer of note in the Civil War.) Elizabeth, the first of these two wives, died in 1672, and as well as a memorial brass to her in the church at Wraxall, his inscription to her which was on the former tombstone, describes how highly he obviously thought of her - and perhaps of himself too:

> Goodness in heaven gave a birth
> In her to goodness here on earth,
> And having time long with her blest
> Took her to heaven there to rest,
> Goodness on earth doth now in mourning go
> Because he hath no patience here below.

However, at some time within the next ten years another Mrs Lawrence appeared on the scene, for in 1682 at the age of seventy, he wrote a treatise on marriage on account of this second wife. What her name was, where she was from, and when they were married, are not recorded, but every reference takes great delight in describing her as "a red-haired buxom woman".[26] Such a description leaves the reader with the idea that she was a very plump red-haired woman with a temper. Perhaps she was, but it seems unfair to describe her thus, and not to indicate what her husband was like as well - a short, tubby, bow-legged, disagreeable, pernickety old man, perhaps!

It would appear that some dispute arose between them, said to be on the subject of her dishonesty to him (although of course we only hear his side of the story!). The consequence of this was that he took up his pen and wrote a treatise on marriage entitled "A Vindication of Marriage by the Moral Law of God". It has not been possible to trace a copy of this treatise, and discover the full nature of its contents.

While trying to trace details of these two wives of William Lawrence, the author came upon what appears to be yet another wife, who would have been his first. She was Martha Sydenham of Wynford Eagle. (Her father and five brothers were very much involved on the Parliamentary side in the Civil War, as was William Lawrence, and her mother was murdered by Royalists at their home in 1644 - see Chapter 7.)

In 1649 Martha Sydenham married *a* William Lawrence of Wraxall, but whether or not it was *this* one is unknown - it could have been a cousin for example.

William Lawrence would therefore have been in a good position to write a treatise on marriage if he had indeed been married three times: firstly Martha Sydenham in 1649 - William was already thirty-eight by this time so there was plenty of time for him to have had at least one more wife before this; secondly, to Elizabeth (above) who died in 1672; thirdly, the anonymous "buxom" woman.

FRANCES MEAUTYS

Frances Meautys must have thought she was a very fortunate young woman when she married Henry Howard and came to live at Lulworth in Dorset. Frances and her brother Hercules had been brought up as Wards of Queen Elizabeth I, to whom she had become a lady-in-waiting, and it was at Court that she met the young Henry Howard.j He was heir to his father Thomas, first Viscount Howard of Bindon, a member of the powerful Howard family to whom the Queen's mother, Ann Boleyn, had belonged.

Frances Howard was soon disillusioned in her married life. Her husband treated her with great disrespect almost from the beginning of their marriage, and in spite of the birth of a daughter, Douglas, his behaviour became worse and worse. It soon became obvious that her husband was not just violent towards her, but his strange behaviour generally soon deteriorated into bouts of total insanity.j At times he dressed like the lowliest of peasants, while at other times he dressed over-lavishly even for the costume of those Elizabethan times. He didn't just receive smuggled goods from the very active smuggling fraternity of the area, but spent mch time consorting and carousing with them, and probably joined them on some of their nefarious deeds.

Frances and her young daughter were deserted by Henry in favour of a mistress, and they were intermittently cared for by her father- and mother-in-law at Bindon. Gossip about his treatment of wife and daughter and also the rift between him and his father was known at Court, but virtually no action was taken until 1580. This was only after Henry Howard had assaulted the Sheriffs of Dorset and Hampshire. He was then summoned to appear before the Privy Council to answer for this attack, and also for his treatment of his wife. He was sentenced to a month in Marshalsea Prison, after which time he apologised to the Privy Council, and also promised that this time he would keep former promises made to them in respect of his behaviour towards his wife.

Needless to say he did not keep these promises. Four years later in 1584, Frances planned to marry her daughter Douglas to Arthur Gorges in order to get her away from the terrible home life. Henry Howard was strongly against the marriage, but Frances managed to get it to go ahead in secret, and Douglas was taken away from the clutches of her father by her new husband. Henry Howard was furious when he found out how he had been tricked and attacked his wife very severely. Queen Elizabeth at last decided to intervene personally and take Frances, her former lady-in-waiting, away from her husband. She sent a letter to Henry ordering him to free his wife, but strangely she sent this letter via Frances' brother, the very weak, ineffectual and inappropriately-named Hercules Meautys. He was accompanied by the then Sheriff of Dorset, John Strangways, and it is from this latter person that we have a detailed account of the overnight visit of the Queen's Messenger, written as a report to the Privy Council. I can do no better than quote from Lloyd's version of this:[j]

> "In the Great Hall of Bindon sat the Lord Viscount [Henry's father had died in 1582] supported by Henry Rogers and Thomas Ayres, and by his bitter-tongued brother Thomas Howard. When Strangways approached with the bowing Meautys, Bindon summoned these men to act as witnesses. He was at the top of his form that day. "Brother Meautys, why can'st thou not tell thy tale without shaking thy head and ruff?" he asked. Then he said he would only believe the Queen's letter, and not what Meautys had to say. Whereupon, not unnaturally, Master Meautys left the rest of his message unsaid.
>
> They went to supper, and Bindon attacked his lady 'in terms of dishonour', saying that she had been brought up in a dissembling house. 'In Her Majesty's Court', protested the scandalized Meautys, whereupon Bindon 'lifted his leg and let fly behind'. This was taken as an implied insult to the Queen.
>
> Worse was to come; 'He waded so far in fury that he would have stricken Master Meautys with one of his crutches', saying he would make small regard to send away his lady, for 'she was a filthy and porky whore', but it was to his great grief to part with his daughter.
>
> They retired to bed, but surely not to sleep. Next day the storm still raged, Bindon attacking Strangways and calling him a knave for attempting to make known the Queen's message, wishing the pox and plague to take both him and the Lady Howard. Strangways reported to the Privy Council that there were other unseemly and choleric speeches 'too tedious to relate and almost impossible to remember'. He was scandalized when Bindon ordered 'the veriest jade out of the stable' to convey his lady away 'in a manner quite unfitting to her station'.

Before the party left for Melbury [Strangways' home] there was a final convulsion, Bindon calling Meautys a 'porky knave', threatening to thrust him through with the pike of his crutch, 'and so great mischief must surely have ensued', had not Strangways and another stepped in between them and prevented the murder."

Henry Howard, second Viscount Howard of Bindon was certainly not a nice character for Frances to have had as a husband, but now she was legally away from him, under the protection of the Queen again as her Ward - even if she did have to leave on the poorest horse in the stable! What happened to Frances in the next few years is not known, but it must have been a great relief to her when her husband died in 1590. Sadly for Frances though, her only child Douglas Gorges also died in the same year.

Since there was no male heir, the estates of the second Lord Bindon came to his young grand-daughter, Ambrosia Gorges, the only daughter of Douglas and Arthur Gorges. The title however, could not come to Ambrosia because she was female: it was inherited by Henry's brother, the 'bitter-tongued' Thomas. But he had inherited a hollow title, for there was no money or land to go with it, apart from the Manor of Waterston which had already been settled on him by his father, the first Lord Bindon. This gave rise to a new problem in the Howard family, this time between Thomas Howard and the infant Ambrosia.

AMBROSIA GORGES

The new third Viscount Howard of Bindon appears to have inherited much of the family vindictiveness, for immediately on inheriting the title in 1590 he challenged the right of his great-niece, the infant Ambrosia, to succeed to the Bindon lands, claiming that she was a changeling. He argued that his niece Douglas Gorges née Howard had been of such a physique that it would have been impossible for her to have had a child, and hence that there was no way that Ambrosia could be the legitimate heiress.

A Commission was therefore set up at Dorchester to hear witnesses on both sides of the argument. Frances Howard appeared as one of these witnesses, but surprisingly she was giving evidence *against* her own grand-daughter and in favour of her brother-in-law. Fortunately for her, Douglas was dead and hence not able to hear the detailed discussions about every feature of her anatomy concerned in child-bearing aired in public. The case dragged on for over a year and was finally terminated when Queen Elizabeth intervened to claim the wardship of the infant Ambrosia after her father Arthur Gorges complicated the issue by remarrying.

Who looked after poor little Ambrosia for the next few years is not recorded. Sadly she died in 1600 at the age of nine, but not before her great-uncle Thomas had been imprisoned for spreading slanders about her. But at last, after Ambrosia's death, Thomas, third Lord Bindon was able to inherit the Bindon estates to go with the title he had inherited from his brother ten years earlier. When he died in 1611 with no heir, there ended the saga of the short-lived family of Howard of Bindon. This branch of the Howard family had only lasted for four generations, and in three of those generations, the female members had suffered from their men-folk.

CATHERINE FILLIOL

By only a few years one Dorset woman missed out on being the wife of one of the most powerful men in 16th Century England, and also being a hostess entertaining her King at her Dorset home. She was Catherine (or Katherine) Filliol, born at Woodlands in about 1500.

After the death of their only brother William in 1509 at the age of sixteen, Catherine and her sister Ann became co-heirs of their father William Filliol (he eventually died in 1527). No doubt it was Catherine's being a co-heiress that attracted the attentions of the young Edward Seymour, eldest son of Sir John Seymour of nearby Savernake in Wiltshire, for she was described as being "no great beauty". They were married in about 1520 and had two sons, John and Edward.[11m]

Edward spent much time at the Court of Henry VIII, and reference to his family tree indicates how successful were the intrigues carried on there by Edward and his father. For his eldest sister was none other than Jane Seymour, the third of Henry's wives (married 1536), and mother of his only son, later Edward VI. Edward Seymour became a close confidant of the King and was later to become Protector Somerset, Regent for his infant nephew.

But Catherine was not to share in any of these high offices achieved by her husband, for in about 1532 he sent her home to Woodlands in disgrace, and it was here that she died during the reign of Jane Seymour's predecessor, Ann Boleyn (1533-36). At least Edward considered it was in disgrace, for we will never hear Catherine Filliol's side of the story. She was described as being very much of a flirt, and her husband became convinced (or wanted to be convinced) of her unfaithfulness: he even went so far as to renounce his paternity of their two sons. Immediately after Catherine's death he married a second time and again had two sons, the first of which he also confusingly called Edward. In later years he settled all Catherine's lands on his children by this second marriage, totally ignoring his rightful heirs by Catherine. However, all issue of this second lot of sons died out within a few generations, and it was the descendants of Catherine's second son Edward, who eventually inherited their rightful properties in Dorset.

PAMELA DIGBY-CHURCHILL-HAYWARD-HARRIMAN

When a baby girl was born in Dorset in 1920, no-one could possibly have foreseen the future that life held - and still holds - for her.[16] Married three times, once to the son of a man about to become one of the most famous in the world; known to most of the leading politicians, statesmen and ambassadors of the last fifty years in the Western world - and some of the Eastern world too; organiser of very sought-after salons and soirées in London, Paris and Washington; and in 1993 she was appointed the American Ambassador to France, and is still being wooed by many of the leading figures of the day. And all this happened because of a visit to a girl-friend's flat where she serendipitously answered the phone.

She was born Pamela Beryl Digby, the first of the four children of the 11th Lord Digby. Her place of birth was Minterne Magna, a house that had been in her family for generations, and is now the home of her brother, the 12th Lord Digby. She was educated privately, and then at the behest of her mother, gained a qualification in Domestic Science. After a year or so at a finishing school on the Continent, she returned to London in 1938 for The Season, was presented at Court, and obtained a job as a translator in the Foreign Office. It was in these early years in London that she is reported as saying that she felt a "real country bumpkin" amongst all the smart, elegant and confident females she encountered

In September 1939 she happened to be at a friend's flat when the telephone rang, and as her friend was absent, she answered it - and changed her life. The caller was a twenty-eight-year-old army officer with a weekend pass, who was ringing to ask her friend out for dinner: Pamela Digby went instead. The young officer was Randolph, son of Winston Churchill. Two weeks later they were engaged, and they married in the October.

The following spring Winston Churchill was called in to become Prime Minister and he invited the now-pregnant Pamela to live at 10 Downing Street. The worst of the blitz was spent in the air-raid shelter in the cellars beneath Downing Street. Her son - now Winston Churchill MP - was born in autumn 1940 at Chequers, the Prime Minister's country residence.

The marriage had not been successful from the start, and although they weren't divorced until 1947, it had irretrievably broken down soon after their son was born. With the aid of Lord Beaverbrook she obtained employment at the Ministry of Supply, and it was through the same connection that the twenty-one-year-old Pamela met the forty-nine-year-old American, Averill Harriman, with whom she was soon having an affair.

Harriman was a special liaison officer for the U.S. President, Franklin Roosevelt. His stay in London was curtailed late in 1941 when America entered the War after Pearl Harbor.

Soon Pamela was involved with Ed. Murrow, the American broadcaster famous for his live roof-top broadcasts from the midst of London during the blitz. Probably at Winston Churchill's instigation, she held *salons* in war-time London, aimed especially at Americans. She entertained General Eisenhower and General Marshall (of later Marshall Plan fame) as well as English people like Anthony Eden, Hugh Gaitskell and Edith Sitwell.

Soon after the War the divorced Pamela Digby-Churchill and her son moved to Paris, where her *salons* became famous in political, literary and "rich people's" circles. Among her many admirers were several of the Rothschild family, Porfirio Rubirosa, Ali Khan, Stavros Niarchos, Aristotle Onassis, and Frank Sinatra. Other names who attended her Paris *salons* were the Duke and Duchess of Windsor, Nancy Mitford, Cecil Beaton and the Duff Coopers. She had a five-year love-affair with Gianni Agnelli, the Fiat heir.

It has been said that Pamela Digby-Churchill showed great devotion to those whom she loved. During her affair with Agnelli, for example, she converted to Roman Catholicism, and also spoke English with an Italian accent. Elie de Rothschild had an obsession with antiques: during their romance she became an expert in that field.

From 1955 she was spending more and more time in America, and in 1960 the forty year old Pamela married for the second time, to a theatrical producer named Leyland Hayward. She now became an expert on Broadway, and again she was holding *salons* but this time most of those who came were from the world of theatre and the arts. Their ten year marriage was said to have been very happy, but only four months after his death she remet her war-time lover Averill Harriman, now a widower. They were married in 1971. Averill Harriman was seventy-nine by then, having had a very successful career, serving every Democratic President since Roosevelt. He had also been a one-time presidential candidate himself and Governor of New York, combining it all with a career in banking. He introduced her to the world of the Democratic party - Harry Truman, L.B. Johnson and the Kennedy clan. She was very involved in the unsuccessful Presidential Campaign for Muskie in 1972, and the successful one for Jimmy Carter in 1976.

By 1980 Averill Harriman's health was failing, and it is said that it was at this time he encouraged his wife to prepare to replace him in his active political career. By the time of his death in 1986 she was backing a losing party, for the Democrats were out in the cold as first Reagan and then Bush won.

Now into her sixties, Pamela Digby-Churchill-Hayward-Harriman entered into the next phase of her life - organising a political action committee for the election of a Democratic President - known as

PAMPAC. It organised meetings, people and fund-raising. She became the social centre of the Democratic party, but she was also asked for her advice on foreign policy. She had travelled widely with her late husband, visiting Russia and talking personally with Andropov and the Gorbachovs. She also had knowledge of European affairs, contacts with many influential people and, of course, her knowledge of Britain.

She backed Dukakis and Gore in their unsuccessful attempts to gain the White House in 1988, but it was at one of the meetings that she picked out a rising star in a young man called Bill Clinton; she is credited with introducing him to the Democratic "Establishment" and giving him much support in his successful campaign to become President. So much so that it was claimed that after Hilary Clinton, Pamela Harriman was the second most powerful woman in the United States. It was rumoured that she was offered - and declined - the post of Ambassador to Britain, but then in the summer of 1993 she became the U.S. Ambassador to France. Her fluency in the language and her knowledge of the country from her several decades of residence there made her a very suitable choice. Looking at least twenty years younger than her real age, she has now started on her new career at the U.S. Embassy in Paris, will almost certainly continue giving her *salons,* and remains a very influential hostess. Not bad for the "country bumpkin" of a Dorset girl.

9

A MISCELLANY OF
DORSET WOMEN

INTRODUCTION

Finally, the following is a heterogenous collection of stories of Dorset women. Some are amusing, as in the case of Nanny Gill and her runaway horse; some are sad, like the inquest on Elizabeth Taylor; others, like the first one on Christian names, demonstrate how great has been the change down the centuries in particular aspects of the lives of women.

DORSET WOMEN'S NAMES IN THE 14th CENTURY

In the 14th Century a third of all Dorset women were named either Alice or Maud, and 85% of them shared only ten Christian names between them. These interesting figures come from an analysis of the Dorset Lay Subsidy Roll of 1312.[4] This Roll lists everyone in the County who owned enough property to pay tax, and the amount for which they were assessed. Out of a total of 7,621 people on the Roll, 536 are women. This fact in itself is interesting, for it demonstrates that one person in every thirteen was a woman in charge of her own affairs - a surprisingly high number.

This Roll does not include the names of all women living in Dorset in 1312, for it only listed those females who owned land or property *in their own right:* thus widows were included, but dependent wives and daughters were excluded (all their property would come under their husband's or father's names, to whom it "belonged"!) Surprisingly, from the values of their goods most of these property-owning women belonged to the lower-middle or peasant classes and not, as might be expected, to the upper classes. The simple explanation is that rich heiresses and widows were unlikely to remain in the unmarried state for long, for there would be many suitors clamouring for their hands with an eye on their riches (there are certainly many examples in this book!); after marriage or remarriage their property would appear on the Roll under their husband's name.

Table 4: Christian Names of C14th. Women Land-owners in Dorset

No.	Frequency	Name	Latin	Origin	Notes
1	81	Alice		GA	
2	75	Maud	Matilda	GM	
3	55	Agnes		G	
4	47	Christian	Christi(a)na	L	Christian
5	44	Joan	Johana	H	St John (male)
6	41	Edith		AS	
7	24	Isabel		FH	French for Elizabeth
8	22	Em(m)	Emma	GM	
9	14	Margery	Margeria	FG	Derivative from Margaret
10	9	Amice	Amicia	Fvar	Amy = Amie (friend)
1	9	Margaret	Margaret(a)	G	
12	6	Sybil	Sibilla	G	
1	5	Gillian	Juliana	L	
14	4	Clarice	Claricia	FL	
15	3	Eleanor	Alianora/Elianora	FG	Derivative of Helen
16	3	Isot	Isola/Isolda	GM	
17	3	Beatrice		L	
18	3	Cecil	Cecilia	L	
19	3	Felice	Felicia	L	
20	3	Gunnild		ON	
21	3	Katherine	Katerina	G	
22	2	Avice		GM	
23	2	Elizabeth		H	
24	2	Hawis(e)	Hawisia	GM	
25	2	Helen/Ellen	Elena	G	
26	2	Lucy/Luce	Lucia	L	
27	2	Parnel/Per(o)ne	Petronilla	L	
28	2	Susan	Susanna	H	
29	2	Wymarcha			Celtic or Breton origin
30	1	Alana		Norman	
31	1	Annabel	Anibilia	L	
32	1	Anastasia		G	
33	1	Anne	Anna	H	
34	1	Denise	Dyonisia	L	St Dennis (male)
35	1	Florence	Florencia	L	
36	1	Gunnota		ON	Scand. via Norse
37	1	Gyanna		ON	
38	1	Mabe	Mabilia	L	
39	1	Nic(h)ol	Nichola	G	St Nicholas (male)
40	1	Phillip	Phillipa	G	St Phillip (male)
41	1	Rose	Rosa	GM	
42	1	Sabin	Sabina	L	
43	1	Scolastica		G	1st Abbess, sister of Benedict
44	1	Thomas	Thomasi(n)a	H	St Thomas (male)
45	2	Vincent	Vincentia	L	St Vincent (male)

Frequency = frequency of occurrence in list of 477 names. Name = believed form of name in daily use. Latin = manner in which name actually occurs in Roll. Origin = presumed origin of name. L = Latin. G = Greek. H = Hebrew. GM = Germanic. ON = Old Norse. FL, FG, FH = French derivatives of names borrowed from Latin, Greek and Hebrew.

Of these 536 women's names on the Roll however, some are the same person appearing more than once, since they owned property in different parts of the County. The total number of *different* females is thus reduced to 477. All these 477 women only share 45 different names between them, and a third of the names only appear once. These names together with their frequency of occurrence and origins, are listed in Table 4. It may or may not be a surprise to learn that all but two of these names had been introduced into this country by the Normans. The only two exceptions are the Anglo-Saxon Edith and the Celtic Wymarcka.

One frustrating thing about the Roll is that the names are all listed in Latin. This leaves considerable doubt as to what the owner was called in everyday life. Thus one might expect Alicia to be the Latinized version of Alice, but it could equally be Alison - as was called Chaucer's 'Wife of Bath'. Even more complicated is the fact that a woman may have been known by a pet name or a shortened version of her name, the proper name being used in legal documents only. Even today there are many examples of this; thus the author has a friend named Eluned who is always known as Lynne: similarly, Helens are known as Nelly, and Elizabeths as Betty. One has only to think of the variations of Margaret - Madge, Maggie, Meg, Maisie, Peg, and Peggy; or of Elizabeth - Bess, Bessie, Beth, Betty, Elisa, Elise, Elsie, Elsa, Eliza, Liz, Lizzie, Lisbeth, and Lisa, etc., to realise that it is impossible for us ever to know the answer to the question of what these 14th Century women were actually called in everyday life.

Occasionally there is some comparison with contemporary documents that were written in English. One feature revealed in this way is that names in the list such as Phillipa were only so in Latin; in English they were Philip. This use of Philip as a girl's name still survived in Dorset into the 17th Century, for in the Church at Bloxworth is a memorial to Dame Philip Trenchard née Speke, died 1694. The use of the masculine form in the 14th Century probably extended to other names such as Vincent(ia), Denis(e), and Thomas(ia) or Thomas(ina). [It was only with the Gothic revival of Victorian times that there was a reversion to Latinized forms of the names, and Joanna, Juliana, Philipa etc., became popular.]

During the 11-13th Centuries there had been a revolution in the names given to girls (and boys) consequent on the Norman Conquest. Virtually all Anglo-Saxon and Celtic names had disappeared - Edith and Wymarcka being the only exceptions in this Roll. This had occurred through all levels of Society and not, as might be expected, merely among the direct descendants of the Norman invaders - principally the upper class. Many of the Anglo-Saxon names would have disappeared through intermarriage, but almost certainly the disappearance was more attributable to those of Anglo-Saxon stock not wishing to be recognisable as such through their names and hence treated as second-class citizens.

It wasn't just a question of new names coming over with the Norman Conquest, but a new way of forming the names. Many of the Anglo-Saxon names mentioned elsewhere in this book were typical of their

217

times, a compounded word that had a definite meaning. Thus *aethel* or *ethel* meant "noble birth", and *flaed* or *fleda* and *gyth* or *geda* meant "war" and "beauty" respectively: hence Ethelfleda and Ethelgeda. Not infrequently, these Anglo-Saxon names were formed by a permutation of the names of the parents: thus Alfred and Edith might name their daughter Aldith.

All this was wiped away with the arrival of the Normans. They either passed the same name on in their families (remember Ela of Canford in Chapter 1), or gave names in honour of friends or famous people - either of the times (Queen Matilda, for example) or not infrequently, of Classical times (Sybil, Helen, and Florence).

Another revolution in name-giving had also occurred between the time of the Conquest and this 14th Century Dorset Roll, and that was due to the increased influence of the Church. The power of the Church became very strong in Norman and Plantagenet times, and it had been trying to influence parents to choose either Biblical or Saints' names for their children. The effectiveness of this influence can be seen by the preponderance of such names in the Roll - Christianna, Elizabeth, and Scolastica (the latter was the first Abbess, sister of Benedict).

If we examine the derivations of these forty-five names (Table 4), it can be seen that the majority are ultimately of Greek, Latin or Hebrew origin, although some show slight variations or are derivatives. Seven names are of Germanic, and two of Old Norse origins: it is likely that these names migrated with the earlier settling of the Normans (Northmen) in Normandy, and after surviving there, later migrated across the Channel after 1066. The two non-Norman names, Edith and Wymarcka, have already been mentioned.

It is of interest to note some of the names that are *not* included, although they might have been expected. Thus there is no Mary (or Marie or Maria), but possibly like the boy's name, Jesus, it was considered too sacred to be used. None of the local Dorset Saints names are used - Wita, Judith, Walbuga, etc., - but these were, of course, Anglo-Saxon names. Others not appearing, although popular in Classical times, were those related to the months - Avril (April), May, June, Julia, and Augusta.

A comparison of these Dorset names with contemporary records in other parts of the country reveals the surprising fact that those which were most commonly used here, were also so elsewhere. Thus two of the top three names in Dorset, Alice, and Agnes, were in the same position in other parts of the country also (see Table 5).

This 14th Century Roll doesn't tell us anything at all about the lives of these females living in Dorset in 1332, but it indicates that every single one of these 477 women actually existed, owned property in their own right (and were hence unmarried), and were living scattered around this County.

Table 5: Comparison of Most Popular C14th Names in Different Parts of England

	Dorset 1332	Worcs 1327	Suffolk 1327	Essex (nd)	London 1319	West Riding 1379
1	Alice	Alice	Alice	Joan	Alice	Joan
2	Maud	Agnes	Agnes	Alice	Agnes	Alice
3	Agnes	Maud	Maud	Agnes	Margaret	Agnes
4	Christi(a)na	Isabel	Margaret		Margery	
5	Joan	Margery	Joan		Christi(a)na	
6	Edith	Christi(a)na	Christi(a)na		Maud	
7	Isabel	Petronilla	Isabel		Isabel	
8	Em(ma)	Juliana				
9	Margery	Edith				
10	Amice					

MRS PIGON AND THE DORCAS SOCIETY

Charitable works by and for women take many forms. One of the lesser-known ones is the Dorcas Society, very active in the 19th Century and into the early part of the 20th Century. Its principal aim was to help women during their confinements, and there were strict rules for both the "givers" (subscribers) and the "receivers". There was obviously a very active Dorcas Society in the combined parishes of Weymouth, Melcombe Regis and Wyke Regis, for among the records in the Dorset Record office[1] are some notes written in 1883 by the wife of the departing rector of Wyke Regis, Mrs C.L. Pigon, for her successor, Mrs England, which refer to this Society. Although the notes refer primarily to the Dorcas Society, there are some additional notes about several old and poor women in the Parish who were evidently on a regular visiting list. A printed set of the rules of the Dorcas Society were enclosed:

1. The funds of the Society are applied to the relief of poor respectable married women of the Parishes of Weymouth, Melcombe Regis and Wyke Regis.
2. Every subscriber of 5s-0d is entitled to one Card of recommendation, of 10s-0d to two, and so on in proportion.
3. No woman is entitled to a Card till she has lived six months at least in the Town.
4. No woman is entitled to a Card for her first child.
5. Each Card must be produced at least one month before the Pack is required.
6. Each woman to bring the Card herself, if possible, to the Treasurer as soon as possible, for signature.
7. Each Pack must be returned clean and tidy at the end of the month.

Mrs Pigon lists eleven subscribers, two at 5s-0d, two at 10s-0d, and seven at £1, providing for an annual sum of £8-10s-0d. In theory then, each year over two hundred women could be provided with one of these packs to help her at the time of her confinement. Each pack consisted of bed-linen, night gowns and baby linen. Also, at the time a Card was issued, the applicant was given a Ticket for a bucket of coal and 4s-0d in money. If the pack was returned in good condition and within the month, a piece of flannel and a piece of print material were given to the new mother.

Many a poor woman must have been grateful for the benefit of one of these Packs at such a time of great need - there was no free National Health Service in those days - but it is curious that the birth of the first child was excluded. Additionally, there were regular work groups or "sewing parties" at the rectory for the "ladies" to sew the garments included in the Packs.

As stated earlier, Mrs Pigon went on to give details of some of the "worthy" old people of the Parish who were on the visiting list. Two examples are:

"Widow Mawson: A woman always in feeble health, has had many troubles and is very grateful for sympathy. A very affectionate heart and has much of her comfort for many years on friendship from the Rectory. Has one son living with her who has been a great trial, but is improving since taking the Temperance Pledge, and has now for several months kept it."

"Widow Burridge: A very needy but industrious woman as a laundress. Suffers always in her leg, but never complains. A Dissenter by habit, but I think seldom able to go to any worship. She has now at home, owing to delicate health, a very nice daughter, Emma Burridge, who had been a most efficient servant (a friend) to Mrs Newman [also on the visiting list], but gave it up owing to her health. She is often useful as a Nurse in confinements or sickness - a nice-minded young woman - she is better now and very anxious to get into service, the more so as the steam from her Mother's washing tries her so much. She would like a house maid's place and if her health continued better, she would be a useful house servant, but she is not fit for hard work."

Reading Mrs Pigon's notes, she emerges as a very pleasant person, not condescending in any way about the poor in the Parish. One can only hope that her successor was also so inclined! The background information was more than sufficient for the incoming rector's wife to break the ice on her first visits, and must have been very helpful. Mrs Pigon's notes concluded with a list of tradesmen and odd-job men that she could recommend for a variety of services, giving quite a lot of detail about each. It is notable that there is no mention of any that she *doesn't* recommend, leaving Mrs England to find those out for herself.

MARIE STOPES

Two prominent buildings on the Isle of Portland belonged to one of the greatest reformers of this century, certainly in the eyes of women.[1] She was Marie Stopes (1880-1955) who is perhaps best known for being the first person to open a birth-control clinic in this country. It was, however, the publication in 1918 of two of her books, *Married Love* and *Wise Parenthood*, which perhaps did more to contribute to the decrease in the high rates of infant and mother mortalities.[2]

Marie Carmichael Stopes was not a medical doctor, but after an education at Edinburgh, Munich and London Universities, she joined the scientific staff at the University of Manchester in 1904. Three years later she spent nearly eighteen months in Japan, collecting fossils. After various affairs, she was married briefly to a Canadian botanist, R.Gates, from 1911 to 1916, but the marriage ended in divorce on the grounds of non-consummation. In 1918 she married H.V. Roe - a second marriage that was also unsuccessful - and it was the same year that her two books were published.

It is not certain when in the early 1920's Marie Stopes acquired her two Portland properties, both notable landmarks today. Her second home was the old lighthouse at Portland Bill, now used as a bird observatory; the earlier one was a 17th Century thatched cottage in Easton. The latter was given to the Island as a Museum and is perhaps better known from its use as a setting in Hardy's *Well-Beloved*. It is, of course, "Avice's Cottage, Easton, Portland".

Occasionally there are references to Marie Stopes keeping a love-nest on Portland,[5] and there was much gossip at the time about male visitors to the old lighthouse. If true, then she was in good company, for just a little way along the coast was another love nest, that of her great friend Bertrand Russell at Lulworth. She died in 1958 at the age of seventy-eight and her ashes were scattered from a high rock over her beloved Portland Bill.

THE SKIMMINGTON LADY

"They seek her here, they seek her there,
Those soldiers seek her everywhere.
Is she in heaven? - Is she in hell?
That demned elusive Lady S."

With great apologies to Baroness Orczy, that paraphrase admirably describes the search for the mysterious Lady Skimmington of the 17th Century. Everyone knew of the Skimmington Lady and her doings in the Gillingham area around the year 1628, but no-one would admit to having actually seen her. The authorities, in particular, wished to find her, for she was the ring-leader in the revolts against the enclosure of the Royal Forest of Gillingham in the years 1626-30.[3]

They never did find Lady Skimmington for the simple reason that she didn't exist, as was revealed long afterwards. This fictitious name was used as a figure-head to provide a focus of leadership. This united the various groups of individual rioters, giving them an organisation and control over feelings that may well have led to actions that would otherwise have damaged their cause.

How long did the authorities spend searching for her? It must have been a very successful ploy to have a mythical leader like this, for exactly the same thing happened in the same area two centuries later when "Captain Swing" was again a mythical leader of rioters. Truly a case of "women first"!

ADELA CURTIS

Although it is only a little over thirty years since the death of Adela Curtis of Burton Bradstock, few people will ever have heard of her.[5] And yet within her life-time she helped thousands of people, and was a very visible presence to all passers-by on the coast-road between Bridport and Abbotsbury. Adela first came to Dorset at the age in life when most people come to find somewhere to retire. Within a short time she had purchased land and built a house that was to be the start of a thirty-year project for a group of people to live "the good life". But this was to be "the good life" with a difference. It is described in the 1930 brochure thus:

> "In 1921 a Bible student [Adela Curtis] bought
> 17 acres of derelict farmland on the Dorset sea-coast
> which for 50 years had produced nothing but gorse,
> brambles and couch grass, rabbits, weasels, stoats,
> snakes, foxes, badgers, and wild birds. The pioneer's

purpose was to prove on a small scale that England could not only be self-supporting in food, clothing, fuel, housing and all other necessities that could provide for a far larger, healthier and happier home population than she had ever imagined possible *if* she could learn the law of the Lord of the Land. The Bible was taken as the source of the inspiration on every subject and the results were so good that a little colony of wooden cottages with 1/4 acre fruit and vegetable gardens gradually grew up."

Who was Adela Curtis and why did she start this project so late in life? Her association with Dorset did not start until she was fifty-seven and in poor health, but surprisingly it was to last for another thirty-nine years until her death in 1960 at the age of ninety-six. Perhaps a large degree of the success of this settlement at Burton Bradstock was because it was not her first such project, but the third: the other two had been in London and Berkshire. This third one in Dorset was the most successful, and many came from the earlier project. Starting late in life was nothing new to Adela Curtis, for she was into her forties before she started her public life.

Adela Marion Curtis was born in 1864 in Japan where her father built hotels, and she had rather a chaotic upbringing as her father made, and lost, two fortunes. She made several journeys home to England, and it was on one of these visits that she had her first religious experience at the age of five when, on being taken to an adult baptism service, she had a great awareness of the presence of God. Her early life in the East had exposed her to Eastern religions, and although she remained a confirmed Christian throughout her life, she was very much influenced by these religions of the East and especially their mysticism. She was also very interested in spiritual psychology, coming under the influence of Dr James Porter Mills of Chicago, a patient and student of Sigmund Freud. It was believed by many that she had a long affair with this Dr Mills, although for most of her life she remained celibate.

Before the end of the 19th Century she had settled in London in reasonably comfortable circumstances. She was well-educated, speaking French, German, and Classical languages, and was well-versed in Ancient Greek drama and literature. She attended lectures in London by the "thinkers" of the day, and met them socially: many became lifelong friends and visited her at Burton Bradstock. At the beginning of this century she entered public life, giving lectures herself, and in 1904 published the first two of her more than fifty books. She also set up her first Spiritual Centre in Kensington, followed by the second one in Berkshire; this latter was the forerunner of the one in Dorset. It was a large house set in 100 acres called *The Order of Silence*, a self-sufficiency farm and children's school where "silence is observed three times a day at morning, noon and evening, and the rest of the day is spent in study, and in practising and teaching various arts, crafts and science necessary for the maintenance and welfare of the body".

By 1921 Adela was suffering exhaustion and her health was giving way under the major work-load she had set herself. Apart from running the two Spiritual Centres, she was writing books, pamphlets, and articles; she had launched a magazine, and had opened three craft shops in Kensington. These latter sold books, dresses, hand-woven articles, pictures, statuettes, and also had a vegetarian restaurant - half a century before they came into fashion. Most of the stock for the shops and the restaurant came from her self-sufficiency settlement.

And so Adela Curtis came to recuperate at Burton Bradstock, her first visit to Dorset. She stayed with two nieces, Phyllis and Eve, who had recently returned from New Zealand. Two years later she had purchased 17 acres of waste land between Burton Bradstock and Swyre from the Pitt-Rivers estate. A seven-bedroomed house was designed and built there; fifteen wooden "cottages", each with a quarter acre of land were constructed, and her new settlement was ready to open. During its existence it was variously known as:

St Bride's Farm,
The Bible Students' Colony,
Anchorite Cellowship,
The Household Fellowship,
The Community of Christian Contemplatives,
The Christian Contemplative Charity.

Local people referred to it as "Whiteladies", because of the creamy-white robes and veils worn by its mainly female occupants: indeed Adela Curtis had herself from her earliest days in London wore long flowing white robes. She always had a commanding presence and was very noticeable; she was 5'-6' tall, with black hair, hazel eyes and a beautiful face; she was slim when young, plump when older; she had a Welsh lilt to her voice - inherited from her Welsh mother - which added to her eloquent speech, whether to an audience of many, or of one.

In 1935 a chapel seating a hundred people was added to the new settlement, and it is a measure of the respect in which the local people held Adela Curtis and her community, that over two hundred of them attended the dedication service, some having contributed to its building costs.

And so the Bible Colony that was to flourish for over thirty years was set up against her doctor's advice. Even when this stretch of coast-line was occupied by the military in the Second World War, the Colony still continued its (relatively undisturbed) life of self-sufficiency. The residents - mainly wealthy spinsters - lived in spartan and very disciplined conditions. "There were seven periods of worship a day, starting at 5 a.m. Water came from the sky, not the mains; coal, coke, gas and electricity, sewers and cess-pools were forbidden. The "sisters" were summoned to Adela by a bell. The summons was variously for devotion, spiritual guidance and instruction, Bible study, and even for disciplining and chastisement - she was not above raising an umbrella to strike her elderly, seventy-year-old students.

Adela Curtis ruled her Bible Colony at Burton Bradstock in an authoritarian and dictatorial manner: every decision concerning it had to come from her. It is therefore not surprising that it did not long survive her death in 1960 at the age of ninety-six. Many of the other residents had grown old with her, and once their strong-willed leader had died, the Colony soon died too.

It is impossible to give a single label to Adela Curtis, as she was a woman of many parts. One article describes her thus:[5]

"[She was] a Christian, vegetarian, teetotaller, English patriot, Dorset devotee, pioneer of self-sufficiency. She was a spiritual director, spiritual healer and founder of three spiritual centres. She was a Bible scholar, school-teacher, economist, and ecologist. She was an organic farmer, vegetable gardener, fruit-grower and bee-keeper. She was a weaver, shoe-maker and clothing-manufacturer. She was a dietician, hygienist, and sewage expert. She was an author, publisher and book-seller. Above all she was an instructive contemplative who practised a most practical mysticism. She developed a holistic system of meditation and health."

Quite an achievement for one woman of Dorset!

LISA BROWN OF BRIDPORT

In 1990 Lisa Brown of Bridport achieved what should have given her a place in the *Guinness Book of Records*.[6] At the age of seventeen she became the youngest person ever to qualify as a Funeral Director, when she gained the appropriate diploma from the National Association of Funeral Directors. [A few years earlier, Dorset also had the oldest active Funeral Director - but he was a man. Starting at the age of fourteen, he was still going strong in Weymouth at the age of eighty-five in 1983.[9]]

JESSIE BROOKS OF TRENT

In December 1974 Jessie Brooks of Trent retired from service in the village primary school. She was presented with a testimonial which read:[7]

Jess Brooks has worked at Trent School for over twenty-three years - a total of 6,900 days. Over these years Jess has washed 469,000 plates. If piled one on top of another they would make a pile 13,650 metres high - as high as the Matterhorn. If placed end to end these plates would stretch from Trent to Gloucester - a distance of 70 miles. She has washed 690,000 knives, forks and spoons - 28 tons in all. Vegetable dishes washed total 172,500. To this must be added 234,000 glasses. All these items added together total 1,560,000 - and not one broken or lost. In fact, almost as many as the thanks she richly deserves for her twenty-three years of perfect and faithful service to Trent School.

NANNY GILL

Nanny Gill of Abbotsbury was so proud of herself. She may be a mere fisher-woman, but as she set out for the market at Dorchester she felt on top of the world.[8] Or rather on top of a large black horse. It was a great improvement on her last broken-down old hack, which had finally given up its ghost a few weeks earlier. Now she had this strong healthy horse beneath her, destined for many years of good service. And even better from her point of view, it could carry at least twice as many of her fish-pots as her previous horse. That meant twice as much profit for each trip to market. Who knows, she day-dreamed to herself, she might be able to buy a second horse with even more profit!

This horse had certainly been a good buy! She had bought it at Dorchester Market for a very good price. It was an ex-army horse. Good breeding, built for strength: but then had come the day when it was past its peak for military service and it was labelled a cast-off, although perfectly fit and healthy for lighter duties like carrying her and her fish-pots. There were a lot of these horses coming up for sale these days, for the army was in residence again as it was each year when King George III and his family came to pay one of their annual visits to Weymouth.

Over 10,000 soldiers were said to be here this year, mused Nanny Gill as her horse jogged along, most of them up on Bincombe Down. All those lusty young men, come for their annual camp and army exercises. And it wasn't just the daytime exercises they came for either! Why, if she was forty years younger, she would give them a run for their money! She'd always had an eye for a soldier in his red uniform, mounted on their beautifully-groomed horses. She sighed. What wouldn't I give to be young again and off with one of those gallant soldier-boys?

By this time Nanny Gill was nearing Maiden Castle, and her old eyes lit up with a sparkle as she saw lines and lines of those red-coats she had just been day-dreaming about. What were they up to? She rode closer and joined a group of onlookers. In the far distance she saw a small group of horse-men in uniform with one on his own in front. It was the King! He had come to review his troops. The Market can wait, thought Nanny Gill, I'm going to watch this! She sat there on her horse as the soldiers performed their manoeuvres, and her heart thrilled. Most of them were now close to her and she could see the handsome men individually. Now they were all lined up in their rows in front of her, facing towards the King. The trumpeter sounded the "Charge" and with a great thundering of hooves the mass of soldiers set off at full gallop.

No-one had told Nanny Gill's horse that he was no longer in the army! True to his military training he set off at a full gallop when he heard the sound of the trumpet! Poor Nanny Gill! Although she was taken completely by surprise, she somehow managed to hold on to the reins and keep on the horse. But that was all she could do. Regardless of her tugging and yells, the horse just kept on with its "Charge", straight down the field with Nanny Gill's red cloak not too indistinguishable from the red uniform of the soldiers. But soon they realised that all was not well in the ranks. They could hear the high-pitched yells from Nanny, and the clattering of her mackerel pots at the horse's sides as fish went flying in all directions. On went the horse, straight past the King and his entourage, who were at first speechless and then almost doubled up with laughter when they realised what was happening.

Not until they reached the far end did Nanny Gill's horse come to a gentle stop, shaking his head as if to say "Didn't I do well?", and expecting a pat from his rider. What he *did* hear is not printable here! Summoning as much dignity as was possible, Nanny Gill gathered in her reins and off she went to Dorchester Market with the few remaining fish. No doubt the story would reach the Market before long and she would be the butt of many jokes before the day was out. But with a wry smile she thought to herself, "At least I've been with the soldiers once more!"

DOREEN OF BEAMINSTER

In a collection of poems entitled *Songs of Beaminster* published in 1931,[10] there is one written about an anonymous barmaid entitled *Fair Doreen*. As well as not giving her a surname, it also doesn't say which of the numerous pubs of Beaminster was the one where she worked. On the other hand, when you see just how atrocious this poetry is, then perhaps for her sake it is as well that she remained anonymous! The poet in question was H. Cooper Pugh, and he describes himself as "London's saddest poet"!

I can find no greater pleasure
Than to sip my glass at leisure,
Listening to the footsteps of Doreen
    Sweeter than the liquid in my glass,
    For the fingers of the fair lass
Have polished it and made it bright and clean.

I have long since ceased to worry,
Though my dogs both fight and scurry,
And urge on me the closing hour and home;
    I love virtue when I see it,
    Though I know not how to woo it,
And like my dogs, I love a marrow bone.

I can always drink her cider,
For I love it and I love her,
Who could not drink the cider of Doreen;
    Kiss her fingerprints on the glass,
    Talk of hay crops and cows and grass
Then bid a last good-night to fair Doreen.

ELIZABETH TAYLOR

No details of the life of *this* Elizabeth Taylor remain, except for the manner of her death in March 1759. It was a particularly unpleasant way to die, as was revealed in this report of the *post mortem* inquest held the following day, 9 March.[11] The coroner, Mr Filliter, was paid one pound for conducting it. His report is quoted verbatim.

"An inquisition indented taken at Ower within the Parish of Corfe Castle in the Isle of Purbeck and County of Dorset, the ninth day of March in the Year of Our Lord One Thousand Seven Hundred and Fifty Nine before me William Filliter, Gentleman, one of His Majesty's coroners for the said County on view of the Body of Elizabeth Taylor there lying dead. On the oath of John Bishop, Richard Greenham, David Hibbs, George Osmond, Samuel Welch, Thomas Domany, John Briggs, John Brown, Edward Spear, John Hockley, John North, George Stockley, William Ingram, Simon Brown, and Shadrach Stockley, good and lawful men of Corfe Castle aforesaid, sworn and charged to enquire how and in what Manner the said Elizabeth Taylor came to her death Who do say on their oath that between the Hours of eight and nine in the Evening of the Eighth Day of March instant as the said Elizabeth Taylor was Crossing the Inlet or arm of the Sea Between the town of Poole and the said Isle of Purbeck from Poole aforesaid in a boat called the Ower Passage Boat, the said boat by the violence of the Wind and the Weather was driven aground on a certain Tract of Studland near the South West end of the Isle of Brownsea within the Parish of Studland in the said county of Dorset and filled with water, And the said Elizabeth Taylor Endeavouring to Walk across such a Mud Land from the said Boat to the Shore Stuck therein and was the same night there Suffocated or Drowned and so the said Jurors on their oath say that the said Elizabeth Taylor in manner and form aforesaid and by the aforesaid accident came to her death. In Witness whereof as well as the said Coroner as the Jurors aforesaid to this Inquisition interchangably have set our Seals this Day and Year first above written."

This report was followed by the signatures of the twelve jurors, two of them marking their names with a cross. We shall never know what took Elizabeth Taylor across those stormy waters, late at night. What agonies must she have gone through as she struggled to get through that mud to safety. The actual evidence given at the Inquest is not available, so we will never know why the ferry-man set out in what was obviously bad weather. Was it a rowing boat, or did the ferry have a small sail? It must be presumed that the ferry-man survived as there is no corresponding inquest into his death. Did he try to help Elizabeth, or was he only concerned with saving himself? Did he accompany Elizabeth Taylor in her struggle across the mud flats or was he able to swim to safety?

THE LADY OF LYDLINCH

There was a traditional legend connected with the foundress of the delightful little Church at West Parley that had been carried down the centuries, and which apparently found surprising confirmation last century.[13] This legend referred to "the Ladye of Lydlinch", who endowed the Church in Norman times with its glebe lands and the tythes of nearby Dudsbury Farm and of Knowle Farm in Woodlands.

This unnamed lady was said to have grown up in West Parley which she loved dearly, but was forced to live in Lydlinch in the north of Dorset, probably as a result of marriage. But before this time it was reported that she had the Church at West Parley rebuilt by Saxon workmen re-using stones from an earlier Saxon Church, and it was then that she gave it its endowments. The legend went on to say that before she died in Lydlinch, she asked her retainers to promise that they would bury her heart in the Church at West Parley, as it was there that her heart had lain in life.

During renovations last century, at a depth of three feet below the surface of the church, was found an earthenware urn about fifteen inches in both height and diameter, covered by a flat stone. The contents were of an organic nature and had the consistency of finely-sifted earth, suggestive of an interment and not a cremation. Experts dated the urn to about 1100. Tradition said that the heart of the Lady of Lydlinch had been buried at West Parley, and here was an urn of the right date, containing what could well have been the remains of a heart, Q.E.D.[21]

The urn has been transferred to a glazed recess in the outer wall of the Church, behind the altar, for all to see. For safety, the urn now stands on top of the flat stone which originally covered it.

DOROTHY WORDSWORTH

It is the Lake District that claims Wordsworth as *its* poet, and quite rightly so, for it was there that practically all of his poetry was written, and where he was born and died. But practically no-one is aware that it was only during a two year stay in Dorset that Wordsworth found himself as a poet, and even less so is it realised that this was all due to a female - his sister Dorothy.[12] If this hadn't happened in Dorset, then there would probably have been no poet for the Lake District to claim!

It was in the autumn of 1795 that the twenty-five-year-old William Wordsworth and his sister Dorothy arrived at Racedown to set up their first adult home together. William Wordsworth was at the lowest ebb of his whole life, and was in the middle of a deep spiritual and moral crisis. It was the care he received from Dorothy during their time in Dorset that brought him out of his melancholia, restored his physical and mental health, and gave him the confidence to develop his innate poetic abilities. She gave him love and sympathy, she consoled and inspired him. He arrived in Dorset in utter despair, and left a completely changed man, and although he was not to die for another fifty-three years, his greatest poetry was to be written in the next ten years.

The reasons for his melancholia were three-fold; no money, no profession, and an illegitimate daughter who, through no fault of his own, he was unable to see, and for whom he could accept no responsibility. Between 1790 and 1793 he had paid several visits to France at a time when the French Revolution was in its infancy, before the later horrors. He was caught up in the idealism of the Revolution, and would very much have liked to have played an active part. While in France he had fallen in love with a girl by the name of Annette Vallon, and in December 1792 she gave birth to their daughter. Three months later England was at war with France and Wordsworth was back in England with no news of his daughter and her mother. Money was a great problem for the Wordsworths. Their mother died in 1778 when William was eight, and his father died five years later, leaving the orphaned children penniless in practice, but not in theory. He had been owed much money by his employer Lord Lowther, who refused to pay anything to the children on their father's death. (It was to be another eighteen years before the son of Lord Lowther paid what was due to them, on the death of his father.) Dorothy lived with one uncle while William went to Cambridge at the behest of another. He graduated in 1791, untrained for any profession. After his final return from France he published his first poems in 1793, followed by more in 1794, but these fell by the wayside. He wandered aimlessly, separated from his daughter and the girl he loved, penniless and living off friends, until an old school-friend offered him a job in Bristol as companion to his brother who was dying of tuberculosis. When the young man died, he left William a legacy of £900. Then another friend by the name of John Pinney, a Bristol merchant, offered to lend his house at Racedown, furnished and rent-free.

And so for the first time in his young life, William Wordsworth had somewhere to live, and some money of his own - in fact he and Dorothy lived on this money for the next nine years. But he was a broken man, described at that time as "disillusioned, poor, aimless and uncertain of himself".[12] "What is to become of me, I know not," he had written to a friend at the time in 1795. He had not reckoned on Dorothy's care. She recognised that his previous aimless way of life had not been conducive to the mental activity necessary for his literary abilities. She ensured that they lived a very quiet life in Dorset, walking for two hours every morning, growing their own vegetables, cutting wood for their fires and other domestic activities. Plus much reading, discussion and meditation. It worked wonders, and Dorothy brought William out of his depression and freed him of the remorse and guilt that had so darkened his soul. At last he was able to write again, and we all know how much he went on to achieve - thanks to Dorothy and Dorset.

WITCHES OF DORSET

When trouble or misfortune strike us, it is part of human nature to find someone else to blame, even when a little thought would clearly show that we are the cause of our own undoing. Nowadays we usually blame the local Council, the Government or the Common Market, but in times past the cause was usually attributed to witchcraft - the local witch had cast her "evil eye" over a person, and from that day on his or her afflictions began.[14,18] A "cure" for this "overlooking" was to draw blood from the suspected witch without her knowledge, and usually with the aid of a needle. Such a belief still persisted in Dorset at the end of the last century, as described in a letter to *The London Times* in June 1883 from a Dorset vicar, Rev R.F. Meredith of Halstock.[14]

Witches can be divided into two kinds - "black" witches and "white" witches. The white witches - the harmless ones - are better described as "cunning" (wise) women, who are full of old folk knowledge of herbal cures and remedies, and frequently have the gift of foretelling the future. Such a white witch was Mother Herne who lived for over eighty years in an isolated cottage on Milborne Down. She only died in the 1930's, and a visit to her has been well-recorded at first hand.[14] This author describes the interior of the low-ceilinged, smoke-filled cottage, with bunches of herbs hanging all around, and a great steaming cauldron over the open fire, stirred by Mother Herne with a cat perched on her shoulder. Surely a staged setting - a scene set to create the right atmosphere? Every detail of the future foretold for the author - she and her sister had gone to "cross Mother Herne's palm with silver" - was remembered in detail, and everything turned out as predicted.

The fame of this white witch, Mother Herne, in effecting cures both of humans and animals, was spread over a wide distance, and she was quite prepared to travel to a client if they were not well enough to visit her - by train if necessary. Several horse-carriages were often to be seen outside her cottage as their occupants patiently waited their turn to go and consult her. She was visited by all classes of people, from gentry down to the poor local girl who had "got herself into trouble": Mother Herne refused to help these girls by doing anything illegal, but then drinking a herbal concoction could hardly be described as doing anything illegal! She was respected by all, and certainly earned her reputation for doing good, a truly "white" witch.

There was a similar white witch last century in Stallbridge, by the name of Mother Clinton. She lived close by the path that led to the bakehouse - a convenient place for people to call at, while waiting for their cakes, bread or meat to be cooked. As well as earning a reputation for telling the future, and for the curing of illnesses, Mother Clinton was also well-known for being able to reverse the effects of the "evil eye" cast by a black witch living nearby.

It is difficult to draw a dividing line between calling such women as Mother Herne and Mother Clinton true witches, or just women very wise in folk-lore and remedies, perhaps handed down from mother to daughter for many generations in one family. Similar folk remedies were commonly used in private houses, but such cook/housekeepers or even the lady of the house were not accused of witchcraft, even though their remedies came originally from the same source. [It is perhaps to be regretted that the advent of the National Health Service, plus the overwhelming use of drugs and medicines since the middle of the 20th Century, has eliminated so many of these folk remedies that use natural products. Take a walk in the Dorset countryside and there are all these medicines growing for free in the hedgerows.] These old remedies must have worked, or else the white witches like Mothers Herne and Clinton would never have kept their reputations for so many years. Our two most efficient painkillers today certainly must have originated from folk remedies - morphine from poppies and aspirin from willow bark.

When "witches" are mentioned, it is usually the "black witch" that people have in mind: an elderly woman dressed in flowing black robes and tall conical hat, flying on a broomstick with her black cat or other "familiar" (usually a toad or hare), casting spells far and wide, and "overlooking" anyone who offended her.

The origin of witchcraft as evil is very much tied up with the coming of Christianity to this country. Witches were part of the "old religion", the pagan worship of other gods, and it co-existed with Christianity for over a thousand years until the Church took an active - and extremely intolerant - part in trying to eliminate it. In 1484 Pope Innocent III denounced witchcraft as heresy, and before another eighty years had passed (in 1563) witchcraft in this country had become a criminal offence punishable by death - fire, hanging or drowning. The persecution of witches continued until 1750, by which time more than 5,000 witches had died, over 4,000 in Scotland. How many of these were in Dorset was not recorded.

There is clear evidence that a woman by the name of Deanes Gimmerton was put on trial at Dorchester on 1 June 1687. The outcome of the trial appears not to be known, but on the basis of the evidence given, she was almost certainly found guilty. It was stated that in the previous April Deanes Gimmerton had prepared a pipe of tobacco for Nathaniel Scorth. This eighteen-year-old lad was taken ill after smoking it, becoming weaker and weaker until on 23 May he had such a violent fit that six people were required to hold him down. This was the first of many fits, each time accompanied by visions of Deanes Gimmerton. Then Nathaniel was found to have several brass pins and an iron nail in various parts of his body, whose attempted removal made him worse.

His father, Richard Scorth, attributed all his son's afflictions to that pipe of tobacco prepared by Deanes Gimmerton, and had thus brought the charge of witchcraft against her. Further evidence was given at the trial by a Mary Tillman that her eighteen-year-old daughter had been similarly afflicted with fits and visions of Gimmerton during a slow decline lasting three years, until she had finally died. She too attributed the cause of her daughter's illness to being overlooked by Deanes Gimmerton. After all that evidence it is unlikely that Deanes Gimmerton would have been found innocent!

Fifty years before Deanes Gimmerton made her appearance in Court, there are surviving records of the committal proceedings in a case of witchcraft heard before magistrates at the Petty Sessions in Wareham.[18]

This woman's name was Mary Shepheard (or Shephard), and like her predecessor there is little chance that she was found "not guilty" although the trial records haven't survived.

" the examination of Jane Coward, alias Winching, of Wareham, taken upon oath the 28th of March [1638].

"Who says that about midsummer last past, one Mary Shepheard of Wareham, did pull at one of this Witnesses stockings, and within two hours after this, witness was taken ill in all her limbs, that she could not stir either hand or foot. Wherupon this witness conceived that the aforesaid Mary Shepheard had done that hurt, and forthwith cried out upon the said Mary Shepheard (though the said Mary Shepheard was not present), where upon this witness' mother went to Mary Shepheard's house to persuade her to come down to the Witness. But the said Mary Shepheard would not, whereupon this Witnesses mother went unto the Mayor of the town, who commanded the said Mary Shepheard to go to this witness, which at length the said Mary Shepheard accordingly did. She wrung the Witnesses hand, and presently the Witness recovered. Further, this Witness said that about 24th July following, this witness was taken in like manner the second time.

(Syned) Jane Coward
Wareham, spinster.

To appear and give evidence at the next Assizes against Mary Shepheard"

"The examination of Ann Trew single woman of Wareham, taken upon oath as aforesaid.

Who sayth that on the 16th of March last past, she saw Mary Shephard come into the house of John Gillingham, and likewise saw Edward Gillingham come down barefooted very well, without any lameness or sickness at all, and presently after the said Mary Shephard had pulled on a legging upon the legge of the said Edward Gillingham he fell instantly both lame and sick. Further this Witness asked the said Edward Gillingham (on the time of his sickness) what Mary Shephard did unto him, who answered she did put her hand upon his thigh.

(Signed) Ann Trew.
Wareham, spinster.

To appear and give evidence at the next Assizes against Mary Shephard."

So what do you think? It seems impossible that the mere touch from a woman could induce paralysis in one person and lameness in another. And yet that is exactly what two witnesses swore on oath had happened. Could it merely have been psychological auto-suggestion, or was it witchcraft?

Sarah Smith of Sherborne was another Dorset woman who appeared in Court in a case involving her role as a witch. But this was in 1837 when witchcraft was no longer a criminal offence - it had been abolished in the 18th Century. Sarah Smith lived in Cold Harbour, a very poor part of Sherborne, and had probably lived there for all her eighty years. One day she was in her garden digging potatoes when her neighbour, Tamar Humphreys, ran into the garden and scratched her many times with a stocking-needle, saying "Oh, Sal Smith, what's thee done to my child? You're a witch and I'll have the blood of thee." [Remember it was mentioned earlier that this drawing of blood was believed to be a way of removing the evil eye.]

The case came to trial, but the charge was not against Sarah Smith for being a witch, but against her neighbour for having attacked her. It was claimed that Tamar Humphreys, whose daughter had become crippled with rheumatism, was convinced that it was due to the evil eye cast over her daughter by Sarah Smith. The Court decided otherwise; it found Humphreys guilty of a disgraceful assault on an inoffensive old woman, and fined her one pound with eleven shillings and sixpence costs.

Two other Dorset women, Jenny Andrews of Broadwindsor and an unnamed female from Church Knole, were both said to have performed the same act of bewitching - casting their evil eye over horses to stop them from moving. Jenny Andrews lived in an isolated cottage on the now disused road to Broadwindsor that goes over the top of Horn Tunnel at Beaminster. A carrier was passing her cottage one day with a load of coal, and when she asked him for a sack he refused, saying that it was all spoken for. Jenny is said to have cast her evil eye over the horse which then refused all efforts on its owner's part to move on. Jenny Andrews got her coal and the carrier's horse immediately resumed its normal progress.

The other similar story is of the "witch" of Church Knole on her way to market who, when refused a lift on a cart going the same way, cast her evil spell over the horse which then remained rooted to the spot. The poor carter and his elderly mother had to carry all their goods the remaining distance to the market. The horse remained motionless all day but recovered completely when the "witch", returning from market later in the day, reversed the spell.

One wonders how many of these tales were "tall" stories told in the bar of a village inn late in the evening, with each successive speaker trying to cap the previous story! But undoubtedly a belief in witchcraft persisted down the centuries, and many innocent women must have been unjustly accused, punished, or done to death on quite unfounded suspicions, as the two following examples well illustrate.

235

Joanna Guppie was born in the village of Stoke Abbott towards the end of the 16th Century, but moved to South Perrott after her marriage, living in a small cottage (no longer there) opposite the Coach and Horses. As was later revealed, Joanna was very wise in the use of folk-remedies - for animals as well as humans - and had hence acquired a local reputation for being a "white witch".

The local Manor belonged to the Gibb(e)s family, at that time living in the village at Mohun Castle, subsequently destroyed in the Civil War. A young member of the family, Judith, became ill with a disease variously described as "a swelling in her body" and "tympani". When she failed to respond to any treatment over the next three years, the physicians decided that she must have been "overlooked" by a witch, and suspicion fell on Joanna.

On 29 June 1604, Judith Guppie was returning to her home in the village along the lane that ran along the side of the river, just opposite her home. Several members of the Gibbs family were lying in wait: they pulled her from her horse and rolled her in nearby brambles in order to draw blood from her - believed to be the "cure" for the "evil eye".

Subsequently there was legal action over the matter. Not as might be expected over the claim that Joanna was a witch: instead the matter in dispute was the severity of the attack! The papers of the case stated that "this said Joane Guppie in the place where she dwelleth, is suspected to be a witch and is known to have used sorcerie, inchantments, or charmes", but the villagers rallied to Joanna's support and gave a very different interpretation, as is shown by this testimonial:

"To all Christian people to whom this present certificate shall come, wee the parishioners of South Perrott in the County of Dorset where Johane Guppie, the wiefe of Thomas Guppie, nowe dwelleth and of Stoke Abbott where the said Johane was born and of other parishes neere there aboutes whose names are hereunder written send greetings in Our Lord God. Know yee that wee the said parishioners and inhabitants of the said place and thereabouts doe by theeis presentes signifie affirm and declare that the said Johane Guppie during all the time of her abode and dwellings in South Perrott aforesaid and before her coming theer hath did and doth behave herself in all things well and honestlye and never did to our knowledge or as we have ever heard eyther hurte or damage to anye person or persons whatsoever by waye of witchcraft nor was ever accompted reckoned or known to be a woman that ever could use anye such thinge or to be a woman of the sorte condition or qualitie but contrariwise she hath donne good manye thinges as in drenchinge of cattell and such like exercises and alwayes hath lyved of good name and fame without anye spott or touch of enchantment sorcerye of witchcraft. All which wee the parties hereunder named and menconed shall and wilbe alwayes readye to affirm and maynteyne whersoever and when wee shalbe called thereunto."

Then follows the signatures of more than twenty people. Presumably this testimonial was used in Court to help defend Joanna Guppie against the accusation of witchcraft. Although the outcome of the case is not known, on the basis of this testimonial there couldn't have been any verdict other than "not guilty". How she must have treasured this testimonial from her neighbours, and been so grateful to them. But did she go on "drenching their cattell" and treating "dyvers peoples wounds" after this, or had she learned a bitter lesson?

Perhaps the most fascinating of the Dorset women accused of witchcraft is the story of Susan Woodrowe of Toner's (Turner's) Puddle. This is quite an extraordinary story, for we learn of it not from a report of the trial, but from a diary kept at the time by her employer.[17] We can therefore see the complete story unfolding: the recording of the various misfortunes as they happened, and the first inkling that they might be due to Susan; then the suspicions gradually building up, as in retrospect more and more disasters are heaped on the shoulders of poor Susan, until finally the author is convinced that everything that has gone wrong is due to Susan's witchcraft. Fortunately for Susan Woodrowe, these events occurred in 1804 when witchcraft was no longer a criminal offence.

What is also very interesting is that the diary was kept by a clergyman - her employer - and his behaviour is quite remarkable. Surprisingly, he didn't appear to have considered using his Christian faith to counteract the "evil" woman who had entered his home. But let the diary unfold events as they happened.

Susan's employer was a William Ettrick, who had been appointed rector at Affpuddle and Toner's Puddle in 1786, eighteen years before the events recorded. Early in 1804 he decided that he had had enough of working in the garden and decided to employ a local woman, Susan Woodrowe, whom he had heard was very good at gardening. We learn nothing of Susan - her age, or whether she was widowed, etc. - except that she had a son who was obviously more than an infant. She had previously been working for a Mr Saunders (he reappears later) where she had been earning 6d a day: she was employed by Ettrick at 1s-0d, a point that niggled her new employer when he found out, but suggests that Susan had her wits about her if she could negotiate a doubling in her rate of pay. She started work at the Rectory on 23 February 1804, and Ettrick appeared to be well satisfied with her work and gave her every encouragement.

On 6 June, Susan returned to work after being "long time hindered by sickness" (pains in the left side of her chest), and was set to dig a large area of garden ready to plant the potatoes that had been long delayed by her

237

illness. There are various other mentions of the tasks performed in the garden by Susan over the next few weeks, until on 22 July she acted in a different capacity - that of midwife at the birth of the Ettricks' fourth son. From a subsequent entry in the diary, it appears that she was the first to handle the baby after it was born.

The diary continues with further mentions of the jobs performed by Susan; harvesting peas and other vegetables, making vinegar and caring for the bees. But during all these months the attention of Susan's employer and his family was taken up by the illness of the child born in July. Right from the start he had been a very sickly baby, crying almost continuously, and subject to what appeared to be fit-like attacks and convulsions: these occurred most days at bed-time and necessitated someone always being with him, especially during the long night hours when he had to be nursed in someone's arms.

It was Susan's behaviour in connection with this child's illness that first aroused the minister's suspicions that she might be the cause of the problem. It had been observed that when Susan arrived for work in the mornings she occasionally asked how they had fared during the night, but had never once expressed the slightest sympathy for the child.

On 3 October, over seven months after Susan had started working at the Rectory, Ettrick first wrote down that he suspected her of using witchcraft on him and his family. From then on, every misfortune was blamed on Susan. Additionally, he began going back over the various disasters that had occurred since Susan began working for him, and every one was now attributed to "the evil witch", although he had given perfectly reasonable explanations at the time they were dutifully recorded. Their dog had died - it was Susan's doing. Potatoes stored by her went bad. Grass planted by her failed to germinate. So had parsnips and cabbages. The raspberries failed to crop. The bees started dying. Vinegar made by her failed to turn sour. Poor Susan! All these things had gone wrong and in every case it was Susan's fault!

Whether or not Ettrick's mind had become distorted through lack of sleep and worry over his son, he now appeared to become completely unreasonable in his writings. He now "found" the original reason for Susan casting her "evil eye" over his family. It was in retaliation for Ettrick's horse having strayed into her garden through a broken fence, and eating much of the precious grass needed for her own animals. When this occurred is not stated, but it was probably about the time Susan started working for him the previous February, for the first misfortune he attributes to her was four days later. On that day his apparently healthy two-year-old horse fell sick, which at the time he had attributed to its having been left standing for long periods in very cold weather. Ettrick's usual remedy didn't work, but that of the farrier did. The horse went lame after cutting its foot on the same day in June as Susan returned to work after her illness: again it didn't respond to treatment first by Ettrick, and then by the farrier. Indeed, the farrier's treatment - well-described at the time, and quite

238

horrific[22] - itself caused complications; when Ettrick called in a younger farrier, he laughed at the previous farrier's old-fashioned treatment, calling it "a poisonous remedy". In spite of treatment which seems positively barbaric today, the horse grew weaker and finally died on 16 September. It was two weeks later that Susan was first referred to as a witch by Mr Ettrick in his diary, and amongst other things he retrospectively attributed to Susan were these illnesses of his horse, the failure to respond to treatment and its subsequent death - even though his diary recorded perfectly reasonable explanations at the time.

Ettrick now remembered that very soon after Susan started working for him at the Rectory, she came across him grooming his horse's mane and tail. She asked him for a few of the hairs, saying that her son had been collecting horses' hair to sell to the saddler but hadn't got quite enough to make up a full pound weight. Ettrick offered her a lot more, but she would only take the few hairs. In retrospect he now assumed that she had wanted the hairs to make an evil spell against the horse - the one who had broken into her garden and eaten the grass.

He then recollected that when his horse was ill, Susan told him about how the horse of her former employer (Saunders) had also fallen ill while she was working there, and didn't respond to treatment. Saunders had also lost five calves out of his eight - a very unusual occurrence. Ettrick now "realised" that all these animals had fallen sick or died due to Susan's witchcraft.

It was on 3 October that Ettrick had first put into words in his diary that he suspected Susan of using witchcraft against him. He had just purchased two pigs and added that he intends "to kill the fat one D.V., if he be not cut off by the witchcraft of our neighbour". (His previous pig had died only two weeks earlier, and like everything else, its death was now attributed to Susan.) On the following 11 March - after Susan had left his employ - this pig was killed, and in the diary is the comment that the pig turned out better than expected considering Susan had the care of it. He then adds that Susan had not dared to do anything against the pig as he had uttered threats in her presence as to what should happen to the (unspecified) witch who had killed his last one.

But it was Ettrick's baby son that dominated his thoughts. There was no other explanation as far as he was concerned but that it was Susan's evil-doing. He had additional "proof" of Susan's guilt on 3 November. Susan had been absent for several weeks, and he took advantage of this to use a counter-spell on his son, a 'phylactory'. He doesn't say how or from whom he obtained it - possibly a white witch - but it consisted of a paper inscribed with appropriate signs. As soon as this was tied around his son's body, the baby fell into a deep and peaceful sleep, a circumstance not known before in all its four months of life. This continued for the next two weeks while Susan was absent from the house, but gradually proved ineffective after her return. [It is fascinating that he used a pagan counter-spell rather than the power of his Christian faith!]

By 1 December Rev. Ettrick had made up his mind that the family misfortunes would not end until Susan Woodrowe no longer worked for them, but for reasons which he does not explain, he didn't give her notice until 4 January, He wrote in his diary on that date:

> "Gave Susan Woodrowe a sharp and final discharge from ever being employed by me anymore. Her lying and uncommon impudence were easily compensated by her good qualities as a woman of all work, in which, however, her hollowness and deceit too much obstructed the benefits expected therefore. But we have now traced home to her in a manner that sets all doubts at defiance, all the miseries and misfortunes that had befallen so thick and heavy upon us and on our affairs ever since her engagement last February."

Ettrick appears not to have said a word to Susan about his reason for dismissing her, and also banning her from the house totally. This must certainly have puzzled Susan. Three days later she was at the Post Office at Bere where there were two letters for Mr Ettrick. Susan brought them to his house, but he would not accept them from her hands in case it brought him more misfortune. Instead he threatened to go to the Justice of the Peace and obtain a warrant against her if she did not go away. She eventually went, but only after repeatedly asking him what she had done, to which she had no answer.

And so Susan passes out of the picture. What became of her and whether misfortune followed her is not known. Was she really a witch responsible for all the troubles that beset the Ettrick household while she was in their employ? Or was she just a simple countrywoman who happened to work at a house when more things than usual went wrong? If any of us stop and think about what has gone wrong at various times in our lives, then we can almost certainly choose one year that was our particular *annus horribilis,* when everything seemed to go wrong. If we couldn't blame these happenings on the Council or the Government then we would just attribute them to the normal state of affairs, perhaps even encouraged by negligence on our part (our car breaking down when it was overdue for a service, for example). But perhaps there are still some who might say that it was all due to the "evil eye" of a neighbour!

A final anecdote to show that witchcraft is not a thing of the past in Dorset. Last winter a friend of the author was driving home past Pilsdon in the early hours of the morning when he saw a large number of parked cars ahead of him. Thinking there had been an accident, he slowed to see if he could help. He then observed a large group of women climbing the hillside. He suddenly realised that it was the eve of the Winter Solstice (shortest day): he put his foot down on the accelerator and shot off to the safety of his home!

GHOSTLY WOMEN OF DORSET

Some friends of the author's were opening their home to the public for the first time. Amongst other things, they were asked if there were any ghost stories associated with their house. They replied in the negative, but then sheepishly added that since people always expected a few ghosts in old houses, they had invented some for the occasion! I wonder if they were following in the footsteps of many other owners of homes open to the public, for few people actually claim to have seen a ghost for themselves - it is usually someone they know, or have heard about. A vicar at Halstock had heard so many tales of the ghost of St Judith (see Chapter 2) that he deliberately and repeatedly went in search of it for himself - and completely failed to see it.

In 1919 another Dorset vicar, Rev. H.P. Bryan of Askerswell wrote on the subject of ghostly happenings in a letter to *The London Times*. The events had occurred in Askerswell towards the end of the previous century, and led to large crowds walking the four miles from Bridport to view the regular evening occurrences. This was no apparition that attracted them though, but a house that was having things flung around inside it - pieces of rock - and occasionally they came flying out of the window to the great delight of the onlookers. Night after night these manifestations appeared until they suddenly stopped. This coincided with the departure of a young maid from this Askerswell house, saying that she could stand the events no longer. The girl in question was only in her new situation for a day or so when the house where she was living caught fire, and she perished with it. There was no subsequent recurrence of these ghostly events in Askerswell.

Athelhampton has a ghost of a lady in grey that it is claimed has been seen by many of the staff.[18] She was first seen late one afternoon when a member of staff was making her rounds after the house had closed to the public for the day. When she entered the Tudor Room she saw an elderly lady in grey sitting in one of the chairs. Thinking that she was a visitor who had not realised the time, she told her that the house was now closed. Without saying a word, the little old lady rose and walked across the room - and disappeared through the wooden panelling. An identical "lady" has subsequently been seen by other members of staff, always in the Tudor Room, and never frightening or disturbing to anyone who "encounters" her. This is in great contrast to the other Athelhampton ghosts - duellists, a hooded monk in black, a cooper hammering at barrels in the cellar and, not surprisingly, the Athelhampton monkeys.

Perhaps the best authenticated published story of a ghost appears in *A Guide to Dorset Ghosts* by Rodney Legg[18] where it was recounted to the author by a Miss Palmer who had heard it from her father, born just after these ghostly events occurred in his parents' home, at the turn of this century. And it has an interesting ending.

The first manifestations appeared on a Sunday morning just after Mr and Mrs Palmer had returned from Church to the home they had recently bought in Blandford. Mrs Palmer went upstairs to remove her bonnet and shawl, and saw a little old lady in a black crinoline dress standing by the side of the bed. In spite of realising that this was a ghostly vision before her who appeared to be harmless, Mrs Palmer nevertheless panicked and ran downstairs to her husband - who needless to say didn't believe her story.

A short while later, an aunt made an unexpected visit and had to share a bed with one of the Palmer children for the first night. Waking during the night she felt the bedclothes slipping off; thinking it was caused by the child, she merely pulled them up. A little later she was woken once again for the same reason, but this time she saw a little old lady in a crinoline dress pulling at the bedclothes. She had not heard of the previous visitation of this ghost, but realising that there was something wrong, she was about to scream for help when she fainted. After several more manifestations of the same crinolined lady, the Palmer family decided to vacate the house.

But that wasn't the end of this ghost story by a long way. The ghost that had so frightened members of the Palmer family was to re-appear to the next occupant of the house, who reacted in a completely different manner, apparently to his great benefit. Whether or not he knew of the history of the ghostly lady's appearances, he seemed to have no qualms about living there - or perhaps it was that he was so in need of somewhere to live that he didn't mind about her. He was an unemployed baker who had been forced to enter the workhouse. With great benevolence the authorities had purchased the house formerly occupied by the Palmers, and decided to re-establish this man in his former trade as a baker - his name is not recorded. He prospered, far more than would have seemed possible in such a short time. He bought a second oven. Then he bought a horse and cart for his deliveries. In later life when he was a prosperous old man he eventually revealed the secret of how he had made good so quickly - it was thanks to the ghostly lady in the crinoline dress.

He claimed that soon after he went to live in the house, he frequently saw the ghost, but instead of being frightened of her, he had paid her great attention. He claimed that he had discerned that she was anxiously searching for something. The baker followed her example and found a hidden treasure. With this he was able to put his business on a firm footing by the purchase of the second oven and the horse and cart. From then on his business had prospered and the ghost was never seen again.

One ghost that the author finds particularly intriguing is a lady who was seen "dead" although very much alive at the time. Shortly afterwards she committed suicide in a manner that resembled the ghostly apparition. There is a conundrum about the actions of one person concerned in this story who could possibly have dramatically altered the course of events. The story is as follows. In about 1630 the Circuit Judge was visiting Dorchester for the Assizes and had been invited to dine at the home of the Sheriff of Dorset, Sir Thomas Trenchard at his home at Wolverton, just north of Dorchester. As the Judge was about to sit down to dinner he was horrified to see a ghostly apparition standing behind Lady Trenchard: it was *her* ghost that he could see, holding her own severed head.

Without a word to anyone of what he had seen, the Judge immediately ordered his carriage and set out to return to Dorchester. On the way he was telling his assistant what he had seen, when they were overtaken by a messenger from Wolverton with the news that Lady Trenchard had committed suicide immediately after their departure.

One can speculate as to whether Lady Trenchard committed suicide *because* of the abrupt departure of the Judge. Did she see him looking at her (and her ghost) in such an horrific way that might have been the final straw in tipping her over some mental balance, and made her commit suicide? If then, the Judge had carried on with the meal, hiding what he had seen, would Lady Trenchard have gone ahead and taken her life? In other words, if they had carried on with the meal during the time that the gruesome event occurred, would - or could - it still have happened?

Two other ghostly appearances in Dorset are also well-documented; both with a female religious connection. The ghost of a nun has made many appearances walking along the lane between Hinton Martel and Horton, where for many years stood a nunnery that has long since disappeared (see Chapter 2). The last recorded sighting was early this century by a rector's wife - hardly the type of witness one could doubt! The other religious ghost is not that of a female, but of a man who is believed to be anxiously searching for a female, the last of the Abbesses of Shaftesbury (see Chapter 2). He is said to be the monk who was entrusted with burying the gold and other valuables of the Abbey immediately prior to its surrender at the Dissolution. According to legend he died before he could find the Abbess to impart the exact details of where he had buried them - he is said to have had a stroke and died immediately. Those who have seen the ghost claim that he is fore-shortened, only being seen from the knees upward. By coincidence - or not - the level of the ground along the path where he is usually seen used to be a foot or so lower than it is today. Will he ever find the ghost of the Abbess?

10
POSTSCRIPT

In the Introduction I mentioned how the usual response from my friends when they heard that I planned to write a book on the women of Dorset was "But there aren't any famous women in Dorset!". I trust that having read this far the reader will agree that while there may not be many famous women of Dorset, there are certainly quite a few who ought to be! Additionally, there are many more whose stories have been told who might not rank as famous, but nevertheless have tales worth relating.

When I started, I had three general guidelines from the publisher. Firstly, don't write a book on Dorset that could equally be written about men. Secondly, try to steer a middle course between a heavy-going academic book and a frivolous one. Thirdly, give the source material wherever possible, so that a reader wishing to follow up any stories will know what has already been used. I have tried to keep within those guidelines, but admit to having stretched them now and again. Thus leading armies into battle is certainly a male prerogative, but discovering *three* "Boadiceas" in this area were stories that could not be left untold! Wherever possible I have tried to draw attention to the differences incurred by the person in question being female - owning property, for example, or the contrast in inheritance laws, or taking legal action.

For innumerable years I have been a collector of "useless information" and have frequently drawn on this accumulated knowledge to add a few words of explanation concerning various points. I hope that this has enhanced the reader's interest. Wherever appropriate I have included pedigrees in order to give the female's family background prior to her marriage, as well as that of her husband and children. It is so often forgotten that her side of the family may have great influence in her married life, particularly if she is an heiress, with the potential of bringing great wealth to an impecunious husband.

There are over two hundred and fifty women of Dorset described in varying degrees of detail in this book, and another four hundred and seventy-seven of the 14th Century known only by their Christian names. While this appears to be a notable number of women of Dorset, it pales into insignificance when one considers the innumerable thousands - or even millions - of females who have lived in, or been associated with, this

County. There are many more stories that have had to be left out - the second-richest woman in the country (after the Queen) who lives in Dorset and is the only one to own a herd of swans, the young newly-married from Tollard Royal who was killed by lightning while on her honeymoon in the Alps, the woman who appeared on a Tudor Muster Roll of 1542 among the (male) soldiers, the two wives of Thomas Hardy and his (mis)treatment of them, the charming letter from a servant-woman in London to William Barnes telling of her pleasure in reading his poems about her native Dorset, the writers Mary Mitford, Jane Austen, Fanny Burney and Celia Fiennes, the eleven-year-old girl who fell three hundred feet down the cliffs at Lulworth and survived. The list goes on and on, in fact well on the way to providing enough material for another book on the "Women of Dorset"!

APPENDIX

ELFRIDA AND THE MURDER OF EDWARD THE MARTYR

As mentioned in Chapter 5, Alan Miller[2] has investigated the historical origins of the story of Elfrida's involvement in the murder of her step-son, Edward the Martyr, at Corfe Castle in 978 AD. None of the seven contemporary accounts in the *Anglo-Saxon Chronicles* makes mention of Elfrida in connection with this event, merely recording her name ten years earlier in 965 when she became the second wife of King Edgar. All versions of the *Chronicle* only give the date of Edward's death as 18 March 978, the place as Corfes Gate, and state that he was buried without ceremony at Wareham.

A1. 1008 - Vita Sancti Oswald (Life of St Oswald).
The author of this manuscript is unknown but is believed to have been a monk at Romsey, Hampshire, who wrote it about thirty years after the murder, in 1008. It is the first detailed account and tells how it was towards evening when Edward rode towards Corfe Castle. He was surrounded by armed retainers, one of whom "took hold of his right hand as if he wished to salute him, another caught him roughly by the left hand at the same time wounding him. But the king as much as he could cried out in a loud voice 'Why are you breaking my right arm?' and suddenly fell from his horse and died". As pointed out by Miller, there is no mention of the date or where it happened or the complicity of the Queen in the murder.

A2. 1070-1080 - Passio Eadwardii Regis et Martyris (The Passion and Miracles of Edward the Martyr).
This manuscript is believed to have been written between 1070 and 1080, approximately one hundred years after the death of Edward. Its author was probably Goscelin, a professional writer of the biographies of saints, and since Edward's shrine at Shaftesbury was acquiring a reputation for miracles, it was probably written for that Abbey. It is this manuscript that first mentions Elfrida as playing a part in her step-son's death. After praising King Edward it continues:

"Concerning the goodness of this holy man the devil was envious and so was his stepmother, the wicked queen, who was full of treachery for she thought day and night if she could do anything so that Saint Edward would be killed and her son made king because he was the oldest after him and the king's son also. The wicked woman keenly thought how this might be done. To some who were there she made known her wicked thought so that they would help her with some guile to do the evil deed. One day the king was hunting with his knights by chance in a fair wood in Dorset that was beside Wareham. . . . . . As Saint Edward went hunting a great desire came to him to see his young brother. Immediately he thought to do this because he was quite near, as was his stepmother, in a town that was called Corfe that was but three miles away. . . . . . When his stepmother, the wicked queen saw him coming all alone she thought to do with him as she had decided. She immediately called the wicked men who were in her scheme and discussed by what villainy to do this wicked deed. When this holy man had come near, the Queen went towards him with a fair company and great honour, and began to offer him much love. The reception that she gave him no man can tell. And she swore that he should alight and remain with her all day.

'Truly, my Lady,' said the king 'this may not be. But let me speak with my brother for I long to see him, because before I have seen him I will not be happy indeed.'

'Sire' said this wicked queen 'when it may not be otherwise, first I shall drink to you and afterwards you will see him.'

The servant was prepared and brought him drink at once. Amongst all the others were there one villain came and welcomed him with a pleasant demeanour and made great joy, and gave him the kiss of Judas and therewith slew him. For as he bent towards him, he was completely ready, he drew a knife through his stomach and tore all his guts to pieces. It was a long and very narrow knife as can still be seen as it has been in the church at Caversham ever since. [No other writer mentions this.] The holy man sat upright and saw his mortal wound. He only rode a little distance before he fell to the ground and released his sweet life there. His soul went to heaven. When this holy man was martyred they who had killed him considered what they could do with his holy body. They found a secret place and therein they cast the body most vilely and secretly, and they buried him very quickly."

A3. 1120-1140 - Gesta Regum Anglorum (The History of the Kings of England).

Fifty years later - one and a half centuries after the event - the following version was written by William of Malmesbury. It is noticeable that most of the present-day accounts tend to favour this version!

"[Edward] was returning home tired with the chase, and gasping with thirst from the exercise while his companions were following the dogs in different directions as it happened, when hearing that they [Elfrida and Ethelred] dwelt in the neighbouring mansion, the youth proceeded thither at full speed, unattended and unsuspecting as he judged of others by his own feelings. On his arrival, alluring him to her with female blandishments, she made him fix his attention upon herself, and after saluting him with a kiss, while he was eagerly drinking from the cup that was presented, the dagger of an attendant pierced him through. Dreadfully wounded, with all his remaining strength he spurred his horse in order to join his companions, when one foot slipping he was dragged by the other through the winding paths while the streaming blood gave evidence of his death to his followers. Moreover they then commanded him to be ingloriously interred at Wareham, grudging him even holy ground when dead, as they envied him his royal dignity while living."

It is also from the pen of this author that we first hear of two events that are widely accepted as fact in the present-day, even though they apparently originated one and a half centuries after the event. They concern Elfrida's attempt to visit the site of Edward's first burial at Wareham (nowadays transposed to her attempting to join the second funeral procession from Wareham to Shaftesbury), and her beating of her son with candles. Malmesbury describes them thus:

"[At the burial site] the lame walked, there the dumb resumed his faculty of speech, there every malady gave way to health. The fame of this pervading all England proclaimed the merits of the martyr. The murderess, excited by it, attempted a progress thither, and was already urging forward the horse she had mounted, when she perceived the manifest anger of God, for the same animal which she had heretofore constantly ridden, and which was used to outstrip the very wind in speed, now by the command of God stood motionless. The attendants, both with whips and clamour urged him forward that he might carry his noble mistress with his usual readiness. Their labour was in vain, they changed the horse, and the same circumstances recurred. Her obdurate heart, though late, perceived the meaning of the miracles, wherefore, while she herself was not permitted to do so, she suffered to be performed by another. For that Elferius whom I before blamed for destroying the monasteries, repented his rashness and being deeply distressed in mind, took up the corpse from its unworthy burial place and paid it just and distinguished funeral honours at Shaftesbury. He did not however escape punishment, for within a year afterwards he was eaten of the vermin we call lice. Elfrida declining from her regal pride became extremely penitent, so that at Werewell [Whorwell] for many years clothed her pampered body in hair-cloth, slept at night upon the ground without a pillow, and mortified her flesh with every kind of penance."

The other story from the pen of Malmesburg concerning Ethelred runs:

"I have read it that when he was ten years of age, hearing it noised abroad that his brother was killed, he so irritated his furious mother by his weeping that not having a whip at hand she beat the little innocent with some candles she had snatched up, nor did she desist till herself bedewed him, nearly lifeless, with her tears. On this account he dreaded candles for the rest of his life, to such a degree that he would never suffer the light of them to be brought into his presence."

A4. 1130-1140 - Version of Florence of Worcester.

At much the same time as William of Malmesbury was writing his detailed anecdotal version, another monk at Worcester was writing a minimal story.

"Edward, King of England, was foully murdered at Corvesgate, at the instigation of his step-mother Queen Elfrida, and was buried without royal pomp. His brother Ethelred, the illustrious etheling, a youth of graceful manners, handsome countenance, and fine person, was on the Sunday after Easter crowned and consecrated king by Archbishops Dunstan and Oswald, and ten bishops at Kingston."

A5. 1140 - Version of Henry of Huntingdon.

"When the holy King Edward had reigned for five years he was slain by the treachery of his own faithless kin, in the evening at Corfe's Gate, revealing towards him in death the enmity they had shown towards him while living, they buried him at Wareham without the honour befitting a king, so that as they had extinguished the life of the king so they extinguished his name. It is said, on the other hand, that his stepmother, namely the mother of King Ethelred, while she was presenting to him a cup, stabbed him with a small knife."[2]

A6. 1140 - Lestorie des Engleis (History of the English).

More or less contemporary with the previous three scribes, a Norman member of a nobleman's household wrote what we can only regard as a whimsical - and certainly untruthful - account. His name was Geoffrey Gaimar.

"One day the king was dining in Wiltshire and had with him a dwarf of his, Wolstanet, who had many entertaining tricks. After dinner the king ordered the dwarf to perform but he refused and the king grew so angry that he fled and took horse to Elfrida's house which lay a league distant and was near Somerset [sic]. The king in anger followed him, could not find him and called at Elfrida's house. The queen came out and begged him to dismount and rest assuring him that the dwarf had not been there. The king refused but agreed to accept a drink from her hands if she would pledge him first. So the butler filled a horn and she drank half the wine and then gave it to the king. When he returned the cup to her he should have kissed her but at that moment someone stabbed him to the heart with a sharp knife, as he fell he uttered a great cry at which his horse started up and galloped off towards Cirencester [sic]. The queen had his body buried and covered over with reeds on a lonely moor far away. When the king's followers came to the house to search for him, she hid from them. That night a bright ray of light shone down from heaven upon the body of the martyr as it lay on the moor. Many wondered what it could mean until a wise priest, the parson of Donhead, had the truth revealed to him by the holy Spirit and told the people to seek for the martyr's body. Early in the morning the news spread and all the lame and blind came to where King Edward lay murdered and were made whole. He was carried to Shaftesbury. St Dunstan, Archbishop of Canterbury, when he was dying, absolved Elfrida of her crime, and she did penance at Wherwell, serving God well there until her death."

A7. 1200 - Courtier's Trifles

The last of these early versions of the story of Elfrida was written by Walter Map, a member of the retinue of King Henry II, in about the year 1200. Now even the site of Edward's death has been moved!

"The mother of the younger son, envying Edward the kingdom, first gave him poison and when this failed of its effects, had him slain at Shaftesbury by the soldiers of her company."

BIBLIOGRAPHY AND NOTES

DORSET

a   Bayley, A.R. *The Great Civil War in Dorset.* (1910).
b   Bickley, Francis. *Where Dorset Meets Devon.* (1911).
c   Britton, John & Edward Wedlake Brayley. *The Beauties of England and Wales;* Volume IV, Devon and Dorset. (1803).
d   Darton, F.J. Harvey. *The Marches of Wessex.* (1923).
e   Foster, J.J. *Wessex Worthies .* (1920).
f   Gardiner, Dorothy. *Companion into Dorset.* (1949).
g   Herbert, Jane. *We Wander in Wessex.* (1923).
h   Hutchins, John. *History and Antiquities of the County of Dorset,* (2nd & 4th Editions).
i   Hyams, John. *Dorset.* (1970).
j   Lloyd, Rachel. *Dorset Elizabethans at Home and Abroad.* (1967).
k   Ordnance Survey. *Dorset.* Landranger Guidebook. (1987).
l   Oswald, Arthur. *Country Houses of Dorset.* 1st & 2nd editions, (1935, 1959).
m   Trenchard family papers, in possession of author.
n   Treves, Frederick. *Highways and Byways of Dorset.* (1906).

GENERAL HISTORY

(These were the principal reference books used, although numerous others were consulted in order to verify particular facts.)

o   Carpenter, Clive. *The Guinness Book of Kings, Rulers & Statesmen.* (1978).
p   Green, John Richard. *A Short History of the English People* (4 volumes), (1902).
q   Jenner, Heather. *Royal Wives.* (1967).
r   McWhirter, Norris, (General Editor). *Guinness Book of Answers.* (1980).
s   Richardson, John. *The Local Historian's Encyclopaedia.* (1989).
t   Anon. *Romance of the Nation.* Amalgamated Press. (1935).
u   Strickland, Agnes. *Lives of the Queens of England.* (1891).
v   Thompson, Arthur Bailey. *The Victoria History of England.* (1865).
w   Waller, John Francis, (Editor). *The Imperial Dictionary of Universal Biography,* (3 volumes), (1863).
x   Williams, Henry Smith, (Editor, for Encyclopaedia Britannica). *The Historians History of the World,* (27 volumes). (1926).

1 D.C.R.O. Feet of Fines.
2 Best, Rosemary. *Poorstock in Wessex.* (1980).
3 Herring, Christine. Abbotsbury - and its famous battle. *Dorset Life* (1975), vol 9; 10.
4 Bell, Mrs Arthur. *Harbour to Harbour: the story of Christchurch, Bournemouth and Poole from the earliest times to the present day.* (1916).
5 Paris, Matthew. *Historia Anglorum.* Cited by Mrs Arthur Bell (above).
6 Davis, G.R.C. *Magna Carta.* (1977). Booklet published for the British Library.
7 *Notes on the History of Canford.* Published for the DNH&AS.
8 Heath, Sydney. *The Story of Ford Abbey.* (1911).
9 Thompson, Gladys Scott. *Family Background.* (1949).
10 Bond, Thomas. On the Barony of the Wife of Hugh Fitz Grip. DNH&AS, 14, 114-8.
11 Wansborough, Richeldis. *The Tale of Milton Abbey.* (1974).
12 Original material at D.C.R.O.* Reference: D616/LI.
13 Alcock, N.W. *Old Title Deeds.* (1986).
14 Weinstock, M.B. *Somerset & Dorset Notes and Queries,* 447, p224 (1980).
15 The original Magna Carta was signed by King John in 1215, the year before his death. On Henry III's accession it was hastily re-issued in a substantially revised form and re-edited to meet the changed conditions of the new reign. A further re-issue, with amendments, occurred the following year, and the final revision was in 1225. It was the last one that has been confirmed by subsequent Kings, and it was a copy of this that was held by Ela.
16 Hadwidia's husband was usually known as "Hugh of Wareham". His father's name had been Grip (or Grippon) and hence he was also referred to as "Hugh Fitzgrip". "Fitz" derives from the Norman/Old French word *Fits* meaning "son of". There are a few present-day examples of the descent of such surnames, e.g. Fitzgerald, but in later centuries the designation was usually restricted to the illegitimate children of princes and kings.
17 In fact John Tregonwell Junior wasn't far wrong in his belief that the Martins might try and usurp his inheritance, for after his grandmother's death in 1584, her son Nicholas Martin and his wife Ann (née Wadham) remained living in Milton Abbey. It was only after the death of Nicholas Martin in 1597 that his widow finally vacated the house and returned to Athelhampton. By this time the grandson John Tregonwell had died (1549-1586) and his fourteen year old son (John, 1572-1650) eventually came into the rightful inheritance of the Tregonwells, thirty-two years after the death of the first Sir John Tregonwell of Milton Abbey.[11]
18 Such lotteries were nothing new. The first recorded one in England was held at the instigation of Queen Elizabeth I in 1569 to help defray the costs of repairing harbours, and they continued to provide a useful source of government revenue - the first Westminster Bridge was built on the proceeds of a series of lotteries starting in 1736. State lotteries were finally banned in 1826, although private lotteries had been abolished earlier in 1709. Now, in 1994, they are to recommence.

CHAPTER 2 Religious Women of Dorset

1 Fletcher, J.M.J. Some Saxon Saints of Dorset. DNH&AS. 32, 199-205 (1911).
2 Chambers, W & R. (editors). *Book of Days* (2 volumes), (1878).
3 Anderson, Bonnie S., & Judith P. Zinsser. *A History of their Own: Women in Europe from Prehistory to the Present* (2 volumes),   (1988).
4 Brown, Mary. *Dorset Customs, Curiosities and Folk Lore.* (1990).
5 Gasquet, Francis A. *Monastic Constitutional History* (1896). Quoted by Percy Dearmer in *Highways and Byways in Normandy,* (1904).
6 Warren, F.C. *Tarrant Valley: the Tarrent Villages.* (1933, revised 1945).
7 Long, Edward T. Religious Houses of Dorset. DNH&AS, 53, 16-50, (1932).
8 Information from exhibition at Stape Hill Abbey.
9 Catholic Record Society, 43, (1949) & 56, (1964).

10 Translation of *Ancren Riwles* by Camden Society.(Cited by reference [d]).
11 Stuart, Dorothy M. *The Girl through the Ages*. (1933).
12 Fosbroke, Thomas D. *British Monachism*. (1843).
13 Lemmey, Pamela. *A History of Halstock*. (1986).
14 Waters, Christine. *Who was St Wita?* (1980).
15. Walcot, Michael. *Stars for all Eternity*. (1992).
16 Fletcher, Walter. The Lady Margaret, Countess of Richmond, and her Connections with Wimborne Minster. DNH&AS 62, 50-53 (1940).
17 Fleming, Kaye Le. Notes on the Royal Peculiar of Wimborne Minster. DNH&AS, 28, 219-24 (1940).
18 Rival, Paul. *The Six Wives of Henry VIII*. (1971).
19 Macalpine, Joan. *The Shadow of the Tower*. (1972).
20 Anon. *Iwerne Minster; Church and Village Story*. At D.C.M. (no date).
21 The original Latin was:
Arbiter omnipotens, solus qui cuncta creavit,
In regno patria semper qui humine fulget,
Qua jugiter flagrans sic regnat gloria Christi,
Inlesem servet semper te jure perenni.
22 Margaret St John's father, Oliver St John, was half-brother to Margaret Beaufort, mother of the Lancastrian King Henry VII, whose story is told later. Margaret Beaufort's mother, Margaret Beauchamp, had married twice, firstly to Oliver St John by whom she had at least two sons: the eldest was a staunch Yorkist; the youngest, Oliver, was the father of Margaret St John. Margaret Beauchamp then married the Duke of Somerset by whom she had the one daughter, Margaret Beaufort, a descendant of King Edward III in the Lancastrian line.
23 F.C. Warren in his two booklets on the villages of the Tarrant valley[6], suggests that Ralph Kahaines (or Cahagnes) who came over with the Conqueror married Alice, daughter and heiress of Gilbert Maminot, the Bishop of Lisieux in Normandy. The latter was both personal physician and astrologer to William the Conqueror, and after the Conquest he was rewarded with the lands that later became Tarrant Keyneston, as shown in the Domesday Book. Ralph de Kahaines came into possession of them by marriage with the Bishop's daughter. Their son was called William; their grandson Ralph (mentioned in deeds of 1167/8) - probable founder of the nunnery - and their great-grandson was called William (mentioned in deeds of 1186/7).
24 This should not be confused with *The Silent Woman* at Wareham Forest. This latter name is said to commemorate a former landlady of the Inn who was a notorious gossip. When the Inn was to be used by a ruthless band of smugglers, it is said that they cut out her tongue to prevent her gossiping about their affairs in case it came to the ears of the Excise men. As she was illiterate, she couldn't communicate with them by writing - a truly "silent woman".
25 The first of these two principal rival contenders is Gwen Teirborn (her Celtic name), who is also known to the Bretons as Blanche. 'Wita', 'Gwen' and 'Blanche' each means "white" in Saxon, Celtic and Breton respectively, and she is also known as Candida which is the Latinised form of Wita. The other contender was Witta, a male companion of St Boniface - see earlier.

CHAPTER 3 Crimes and Women of Dorset

1 Chamberlayne, Edward. *Angliæ Notitia, or the Present State of England*. (1669).
2 French, Geoffrey. *Stoke Abbott*, (1974).
3 Kemp, John. *The Book of Weymouth and Portland*, (no date).
4 Chadwick, John C. *Wessex Peculiar: a Search for the Peculiar*. (1986).
5 Tullett, Tom. *Murder Squad*, (1981).
6 Gaute, J.H.H. & Robin Odell. *The Murderer's Who's Who*, (1979).
7 Anon. *Dorset County Chronicle*, (13 January 1938, 14 August 1856).
8 Milne, Taylor. *A History of Broadwindsor*, (circa 1934).
9 Legg, Rodney. *A Guide to Dorset Ghosts*. (1969).

10 Anon. *Dorset County Chronicle*. (14 April, 15 May 1887).

11 "The King's Evil" was a scrofulous disease of the neck - probably tuberculosis. In the time of Edward the Confessor a person afflicted with this disease accidentally touched the King and was said to have been immediately cured. From this incident is believed to have grown the tradition that the touch of the Sovereign could cure the disease. It probably did in many cases (for psychological reasons), and as a consequence, many hundreds of people arrived to form a long queue to touch the Sovereign whenever he visited an area.

CHAPTER 4. Working Women of Dorset

1 Kelly, Alison. *Mrs Coade's Stone,* (1990).

2 D.C.M. (Various articles in Box File: Coade Biography).

3 D.C.R.O. Lyme Regis Borough Archives. Reference DC/LR 7-11.

4 Edmonds, J.M. The Fossil Collection of the Misses Philpot. DNH&AS 98,43-9, (1976).

5 Miller, Alan J. *Stories from Dorset History.* (1987).

6 Phillips, Patricia. *The Scientific Lady.*,(1990).

7 Lang, W.D. DNH&AS, 60, 142-164, (1938).

8 Lang, W.D. DNH&AS, 71,184-188, (1949).

9 Guest, Revel & Angel V. John. *Lady Charlotte: A Biography of the 19th Century* . (1989).

10 Dewar, H.S.L. *Portland Arrowroot or Starch: a vanished Dorset industry.* (Unpublished article at D.C.M.)

11 Gerard, John. *Gerard's Herbal.* (1636).

11 Atkins, N.J. *Somerset & Dorset Notes & Queries,* 30, 453, (1979).

12 Perry, Robert. *Bygone Blandford Industries.* From unknown newspaper, 1950's.

13 The author grew up in Shrewsbury within sight of what is probably the tallest of Mrs Coade's masterpieces, but with no knowledge of its history. It is a column, 112 feet high, and surmounted by a statue of Lord Hill, one of Wellington's commanders.

14 Although titanium is widely used today to produce a hard, white acid-resistant porcelain, its use at that time was very unusual. It is a metallic element whose properties were only discovered in 1791, and its use for strengthening steel, etc., was many years in the future. Its use in Coade Stone was therefore probably accidental, and was almost certainly due to its being an impurity in the local clay used for its manufacture.

15 The clay was fired in a kiln, and then ground into a fine powder before being added to fresh clay and fired again at a higher temperature than is usual for earthenware.

16 Henry de la Beche was born in London in 1796 but came to live first in Ottery St Mary, then Charmouth and finally in Lyme, where he developed a boyhood delight in geology. After a brief period at Royal Military College he decided that there wasn't going to be much future in his destined army career post - Waterloo. Returning to Lyme at this point, he developed the strong friendship with Mary Anning that was to last their lifetimes. He also decided to make a career of his hobby: a wise choice as it turned out, for he went to the very top of his profession - see later.

17 Ivor Guest, later the first Lord Wimborne, became very popular both at Canford and Dowlais. He certainly made an impact when he had his coming-of-age party at Canford, when there was a celebration lunch on the lawns in front of the house for over 1,000 estate workers and tenants. This was followed in the evening by a Grand Ball for family and friends. It was certainly the talk of the neighbourhood for many years to come.

18 At that time the Royal Society of Arts still had its original title of "A Society Instituted at London for the Encouragement of Arts and Commerce". For convenience it is referred to by its present-day name.

CHAPTER 5. Dorset Women of the Dark Ages

1 Murphy, Elinor. Some Questions around the Anglo-Saxon origins of Shaftesbury.

Unpublished manuscript (at D.C.M.) submitted for Mansell-Pleydell Prize Essay Competition, (1990).

2   Miller, Alan J. *Stories from Dorset History*. (1987).
3   Vesey-Fitzgerald, Brian. *Hampshire and the Isle of Wight*. (1949).
4   Anon. *The Will of King Alfred*. (1828). Reprinted from the Oxford Edition of 1788, with a preface and additional notes.
5   There are several different ways of spelling Anglo-Saxon names: alternatives are therefore also given in brackets.

CHAPTER 6. Royalty and Dorset Women

1   D.C.M. Letter concerning discovery of Scottish penny. (1981).
2   D.C.M. Close Rolls, (as cited by Treves).
3   J.B. *Somerset & Dorset Notes & Queries*. 2, 233-4. (1891).
4   Anon. *Bridport & West Bay*. Ward Lock. (circa 1934).
5   Frampton, Mary. *Journal*. (1885).
6   Philip was accompanied to Windsor by a young nephew of the Trenchards, John Russell of nearby Berwick in Swyre. He had been used by his "country-bumpkin" uncle to help entertain the royal visitors, consequent on his travels on the Continent. This first visit of Russell to Court was so successful, that he stayed there and eventually became the first Earl of Bedford, (next century it became a Dukedom). Russell's initial lifestyle at Court was funded from the sale of properties fought over in the law-courts by one of his female Dorset ancestors, Alice Russell - see Chapter 1.

CHAPTER 7. Dorset Women and the Civil War

1   Bond, Dennis. *A Private Chronology of Denis Bond of Lytton in the Isle of Purbeck* made 1630-40. (D.C.M.)
2   Bankes, Viola. *A Dorset Heritage: the Story of Kingston Lacy*. (1953).
3   Aspinall-Oglander. *Nunwell Symphony*. (1945).
4   White, T. Hedley. *Dr Thomas Sydenham (1524-1689)*. *Dorset Worthies*. (Published by D.C.M.), (1984).
5   Payne, Joseph F. *Thomas Sydenham* (1900).
6   Jennings, Abraham. The Flight of King Charles through West Dorset, September 22,23 and 24, 1651, as related in *Miraculum Basilikon:* extracted from one of the two imperfect copies in the British Museum. Edited with notes by A.M. Bradley. (1909).

CHAPTER 8. Dorset Women and Marriage

1   Dearmer, Percy. *Highways and Byways in Normandy*. (1904).
2   Anon. *Iwerne Minster: A Church and Village Story*. At D.C.M. (No date).
3   Anon. *Bridport & West Bay*. Ward Lock, (circa 1934).
4   Wanklin, Cyril. *Lyme Leaflets*. 68-71, (1944).
5   Carré, Mrs. *Notes on Lytchett Minster*. Unpublished scrap-book at D.C.M. (1927).
6   Redding, Cyril. ´*Memoirs*. (Quoted in reference [c]).
7   Bankes, George, N., (Editor). *The Autobiography of Sergeant William Lawrence*. (1886).
8   Anon. *Biographical Anecdotes of the Reverend John Hutchins*. (1785).
9   Hussey, Christopher. *Story of Ely House*.(1953).
10   Rowse, A.L. *Ralegh and the Throckmortons*. (1962).
11   Routh, C.R.N. *Who's Who in Tudor England*. (1990).
12   Cohen, Julia & Andrew Alderson. Article in *Sunday Times* 23 March 1993.
13   Wallace, Marjorie. *The First Vaccinator*. (1981).
14   Christie, Mr. *Fragments of Autobiography*. Cited by reference[c] as being the original description published of Henry Hastings, but previously published in *The Connoisseur* no 81, and also the *Gentleman's Magazine* vol 24 (1754).
15   Anon. *Notes on the History of Canford*. Published for the DNH&AS, (1930).

16 Newspaper articles by Diana McLellan in *Sunday Express,* 13 December 1992, & Michael Goss in *Sunday Times Magazine,* 7 March 1993.

17 Epton, Nina. *Love and the English.* (1960).

18 Brown, Mary. *Dorset Customs, Curiosities & Country Lore.* (1990).

19 Pentin, Rev. Canon Herbert. *Dorset Year Book.* (1948-9).

20 Norsworthy, Laura. *The Lady of Bleeding Heart Yard.* (1935).

21 When hunting lands belonged to the King they were referred to as "Forests", and he was the only one who had any hunting rights there. If the King gave any of these lands to one of his noblemen, they were referred to as a "Chase", and the hunting rights were extended to the lucky recipient. Thus with Cranborne Chase, Enfield Chase, etc.

22 It was only a very short time afterwards that a reverse family journey led to a better conclusion. Catherine's cousin Matthew Prior had been born in Wareham in 1664, the son of the same uncle to whom Catherine had been sent. Shortly after Catherine's elopement, this uncle died, leaving Matthew an orphan: he made the reverse journey to go and live with his Uncle Arthur in London (Catherine's father). Matthew was fortunate to catch the eye of of the Marquis of Dorset who helped to further his education and fortune. Subsequently he became the well known poet, Matthew Prior.

23 A mark was not a true English coin as such, but was a value used in accountancy, book-keeping, etc. One mark had an equivalent value in weight of any metal, originally valued at 128 silver pennies.

24 Nicholas Throckmorton, youngest brother of Bess Raleigh, assumed the surname Carew when he was adopted by, and became the heir of, his maternal uncle Sir Francis Carew of Beddington (now Croydon) Surrey.

25 The word "vaccination" originates from this connection with cowpox. *Vacca* is the Latin word for "cow".

26 It is interesting that the OED gives the principal meanings as"buxom" as "tractable, gracious, obliging, kindly" and secondary meanings of "blithe, bright, lively, gay (archaic 1590)" and "full of health, vigour and good temper, plump and comely, jolly (chiefly of women, 1589)". Nowadays it is usually only interpreted as "plump and comely".

CHAPTER 9. A Miscellany of Dorset Women

1 D.C.R.O. Unpublished notes. Reference PE/WYK:IN 5/5.

2 Anderson, Bonnie S.& Judith P. Zinsser. *A History of their Own: Women in Europe from Prehistory to the Present.* (2 volumes), (1988).

3 Bettey, J.H. Revolts over the Enclosure of the Royal Forest of Gillingham, 1624-30. DNH&AS 97, 21-24 (1975).

4 Mills, A.D. The Christian Names of Women in Fourteenth Century Dorset. DNH&AS 88, 203-206, (1966).

5 Rudd, Chris. The Rustic Mystic of Burton Bradstock. *Dorset Year Book.* (1985).

6 Anon. *The Guardian* . (18 September 1990).

7 Anon. *The Countryman.* 80, no 2, (1975).

8 Anonymous newspaper article. Old Tales of Dorset: soldiers of Dorchester and Weymouth. (Plus the author's imagination).

9 Anon. *Dorset Evening Echo,* (12 April 1983).

10 Pugh, H. Cooper, (London's Saddest Poet). *Songs from Beaminster,* (1931).

11 D.C.R.O. *Inquisitions taken before William Filliter, Coroner for Dorset 1751-1771.* Reference D/FIL/X9.

12 Atthill, Robin. *The Curious Past.* (1955).

13 Anon. Lady of Lydlinch, heart at West Parley Church. *DNH&AS* 19, p66.

14 Knott, Olive. *Witches of Dorset.,* (1974).

15 Meredith, Rev. R.F. Letter by; quoted in Knott, above.

16 Daw, Emmy, (of South Perrott). Personal information. (August 1993). Plus copy of testimonial in D.C.M.

17 Hole, Christine. *Witchcraft at Toner's (Turner's) Puddle in the Nineteenth Century.* Article for Dorset Record Society "from transcript by Lt. Col. Drew which he made from the original MS loaned to him by an unknown and so far untraced owner". (1964).

256

18   Legg, Rodney. *A Guide to Dorset Ghosts*, (1969).
19   Udal, J.S. Witchcraft in Dorset. DNH&AS. 5, 35-36 (1885).
20   Mansel-Pleydell, J.C. On Sorcery and Witchcraft. DNH&AS. 5, 1-15. (1885).
21   These heart burials became very popular with Crusaders who died in foreign lands. While their body was buried close to where they died, their preserved hearts were brought home for burial in their own Church (an example is at Mappowder). This tradition still held into last century when the heart of the poet Shelley who had died in Italy was buried with his wife at Bournemouth.
22   The horse was first bled and then given what Ettrick called a hotch-potch ointment, which later blistered the horse's throat so that he couldn't eat, and he also developed lung problems. The following day the farrier gave him a drench, a purge and put a "rowel" into his chest (this was a circular piece of leather with a hole in the middle, inserted between the skin and flesh of the chest, in order to drain off fluid, pus, etc). The horse was also given some more of the ointment, in spite of the complications it had caused the previous day.

Abbreviations

D.C.M.   Dorset County Museum, Dorchester
D.C.R.O. Dorset County Records Office, Dorchester
DNH&AS   Dorset Natural History and Archaeological Society (Dorset County Museum)

INDEX